Nancy L. Carter
1965

THE NATURE OF METAPHYSICAL THINKING

By Dorothy Emmet

*

FUNCTION, PURPOSE AND POWERS

THE NATURE OF METAPHYSICAL THINKING

BY

DOROTHY EMMET

PROFESSOR OF PHILOSOPHY IN THE UNIVERSITY OF MANCHESTER
AUTHOR OF "WHITEHEAD'S PHILOSOPHY OF ORGANISM"

LONDON
MACMILLAN & CO LTD
NEW YORK · ST MARTIN'S PRESS
1961

—

First Edition February 1945
Reprinted 1946, 1949, 1953, 1957, 1961

MACMILLAN AND COMPANY LIMITED
London Bombay Calcutta Madras Melbourne

THE MACMILLAN COMPANY OF CANADA LIMITED
Toronto

ST MARTIN'S PRESS INC
New York

"The procedure of rationalism is the discussion of analogy. The limitation of rationalism is the inescapable diversity."
WHITEHEAD.

"Man is an analogist and studies relations in all objects."
EMERSON.

PRINTED IN GREAT BRITAIN

PREFACE

I AM very conscious of the incomplete character of this study. That is partly due to my own deficiencies; perhaps it is also partly due to the present state of the subject. We are, I believe, at the end of a period of metaphysical thinking; and the proper method and scope of a new constructive movement of metaphysics, in relation to logic, science and religion, has yet to be determined. In the meantime, though few of us may be able to embark upon systematic metaphysics in the grand style, we are perhaps justified in making the venture of writing, and so inviting criticism, if we can see a line of thought concerning method which may prove capable of further development. To make the venture may be the more necessary in present circumstances, when we have few opportunities of face-to-face discussion.

The general view which I am putting forward in this book is that metaphysics starts from the articulation of relationships, which are judged to be constitutive of an experience or experiences in a significant way. (I have tried to show what might be meant by "significance" here by considering the notion of "Importance".) A conceptual expression of such a relationship is then extended analogically as a co-ordinating idea, in terms of which further ranges of experience may be interpreted; or it is used in making a judgment concerning the nature of "reality". I am convinced that metaphysics is in *some* sense an analogical way of thinking; and that we should not leave it exclusively to the Thomists to explore its possibilities in this respect. But I can well believe that the indications I have given of the kinds of judgment and evaluations which may underlie the selection of metaphysical analogies, and still more what I have said about their scope, limits and justification, may need supplementing and perhaps correcting. I have given some indications in Chapter IX as to how this method might be applied in interpreting some of the great philosophers of the past. To work it out in detail would call for a longer and independent study.

I have considered metaphysical thinking not only in relation to sensory knowledge and to scientific theories, but also in relation to religion and theology. This is partly because I believe these to be inherently relevant; but also because the question of the nature of theology, particularly in its relation to philosophy and to history, seems to be in for a drastic overhaul at present. In considering sensory experience, I have been concerned to observe how the interest in symbolic forms begins to play a part even at this elementary level. But I recognize that there are further problems of sensory knowledge, and in particular the nature of perceptual " apprehension ", with regard to which I cannot claim to have reached a position which satisfies me.

If this enquiry serves no other useful purpose, it may at least help to make a few of us more critically aware of the lavish way in which certain words are used in extended senses, without due regard being paid to their analogical character when so used. Among those in fashion at present, I would only mention " evolution ", " field ", " dynamic ", " dimension " " demand ", " pattern ". I suspect that I am in danger of being hoist with my own petard for the wide use I have made of the word " responsive ". I can only hope that I have made sufficiently clear when I am using it in its physiological sense, to mean the selective reactions of an organism, and when I am using it in an extended sense, to mean a modification of activity as the result of a consciously directed judgment concerning the nature of a relationship.

Some parts of Chapters VIII and IX were originally drafted in a paper published in the *Proceedings of the Aristotelian Society*, N.S. vol. xli, under the title " The Use of Analogy in Metaphysics ". These sections have, however, been largely recast in incorporating them in this fuller discussion.

I am indebted to Professor Kemp Smith, Dr. A. C. Ewing and my colleague Professor A. D. Ritchie, who have read the MS. and made valuable suggestions. None of these should be implicated in a share of my heresies. But without their friendly criticisms, the heresies would have been still more heretical, and the confusions still worse confounded, than they may be at present. In dedicating this book to Professor Whitehead I have sought to express my regard for a teacher to whose inspiration I owe more than I can easily estimate, however much I may have found myself differing from him at times in the course of this discussion.

DOROTHY EMMET

THE UNIVERSITY, MANCHESTER
February 18th, 1944

TO

A. N. WHITEHEAD

CONTENTS

CHAPTER X

CHAPTER I

THE PROBLEM OF METAPHYSICS

A READER who has tried to follow even cursorily the discussions which are going on in contemporary philosophical literature must be conscious that something strange is happening to metaphysics. If he turns to contemporary theological discussions, he must be aware that something strange is also happening to metaphysical theology. Both have fallen on evil days. A new order, it seems, is being proclaimed, in which " the ex-Queen of the sciences " (as I have heard metaphysical theology called) is being sent into exile, like the Bourbons and Hapsburgs, and other crowned heads who have outlived their day. Her constitutional advisers, the systems of secular metaphysics, are being overtaken by the same fate.

Meanwhile the non-specialist reader, if he is aware at all of the currents and cross-currents of these somewhat technical debates, is apt to lose patience. What, he may ask, does all this discussion of verification and of the meaning of terms amount to? It is a harmless pursuit maybe, played with a certain virtuosity by those who like that sort of thing, but singularly unproductive of what the non-specialist has always looked for from the philosophers — the articulation of ideas in terms of which he can interpret his experience.

The layman's suspicions may not be altogether groundless; though his attacks, if he forsakes his usual politeness sufficiently to make them, are sometimes delivered with more rhetoric than clarity, and assume too pretentious a view of what philosophy can be expected to achieve in the way of giving an " explanation " of the world. But behind the dissatisfaction of the layman and the analytic debates of the specialist, it is impossible not to sense a real crisis in philosophical, and particularly in metaphysical thought.

The nature of metaphysical method and the sense, if any, in which metaphysics can be called knowledge, is an open question as it has been at no time since Kant wrote his Critique. A spate of books and symposia, variations on the theme " What is Philosophy? ", are symptomatic. In the ages in which philosophers have been sure of themselves, they have not been self-consciously obsessed with the problem of method. If, like Descartes, they have started from the question of method, this has not obsessed them as a problem, but they have seen a way of determining their method which pointed to a positive line of advance. They have then gone ahead and constructed some new spiritual alternative, some positive way of interpreting the nature of things. There are few to-day who make this venture; in the full sense perhaps only Whitehead and Alexander, and these belong to the passing generation.

In this book I shall try to do no more than add a fumbling attempt to examine the nature of metaphysical thinking. Yet I believe this pre-occupation with the problem of method is a necessary task of our time. We need a new Kant rather than a new Hegel; someone who can determine the distinctive nature of metaphysical thinking in relation to the new types of scientific concepts, as Kant did in relation to those of Newtonian physics; and in relation to whatever may be most significant in the art, literature and religious thought of our time.

" It was suggested by Hamann that Kant would have done better to have written a Critique of Language than a Critique of Reason. It has been suggested by others that this is precisely what he did. Much can be said for this interpretation. For one way of stating the Kantian problem is this. Our language, made to deal with the material world, the world of phenomena, has constantly been extended for discourse about the noumenal. Kant asked the question whether knowledge in this sphere is possible. He might just as well have asked whether discourse about such objects is meaningful or intelligible. Kant's questions are now being asked in this form." So writes Professor

Urban in a recent book.[1] We may put the problem in this way. Our minds seem impelled to seek or to create significance in their world as a whole in terms of concepts originally formed to express relations within experience. But, we ask, what warrant have we to suppose that the world views which result are more than the products of the mind's own impulse towards the creation of forms in which the imagination can rest, and a feeling of significance can be enjoyed? (This impulse, I shall suggest, is fundamental to all the mind's activities.) May not such world views, whether metaphysical or theological, prove in the end to be simply word patterns, drawn by developing the implications of ideas, such as the idea of " Being ", the idea of " Perfection ", the idea of the " Good "; ideas which have indeed the power of evoking emotional response, but which are none the less merely ideas, and do not say anything about reality transcending appearance?

Our concern will therefore be to study concepts drawn from particular relations within experience in so far as they claim to throw light on metaphysical questions about " reality "; and thereby to examine the nature of metaphysical thinking and its methods. For we need to recognize that metaphysics is concerned not only with some pretentious or ambitious system or theory of the universe, but, as the logical positivists have rightly seen, wherever questions of truth about " reality " are raised at all; so that to expunge everything " metaphysical " from philosophical thinking would call for a drastic revision of its traditional scope.

We shall also be concerned with the nature of theology, and its relation to metaphysics, since theology also claims to be a way of saying something significant about " reality ". We shall ask whether the antitheses which are sometimes drawn between philosophy and faith, metaphysics and theology, are based on a searching enough view of what metaphysical philosophy is. There may be, and perhaps are, real " either-ors ", what von Hügel calls " costing

[1] *Language and Reality*, p. 15 (London, 1939).

choices ", dialectical oppositions which we cannot resolve into higher syntheses, between these ways of thought; but this cannot be assumed until we have examined their characteristic methods.

Religious thinking may well have other concerns besides the epistemological question of the relation of our ideas to reality beyond ourselves. But here, if anywhere, this question cannot be avoided, since religion loses its nerve when it ceases to believe that it expresses in some way truth about our relation to a reality beyond ourselves which ultimately concerns us. It is more possible for other forms of thought and expression, such as art and science, to go on doing their specific work without raising metaphysical questions. Religion, when its implications are thought out, must raise them in an acute way. But our concern is with religious thinking only in so far as this is part of the general epistemological question of the relation of thought to " reality ". We shall have to examine the conceptions of " transcendent " and " empirical ", and shall have to ask what is meant by the " data " of experience and see whether such data should be interpreted in purely phenomenalist terms, that is to say, in terms of co-ordinations of sense impressions. Or is even our sense experience constituted by relations to what is other than itself, although we may need to concede that we can only apprehend what is " other " through the perspective of our own experience?

" Experience " is an unsatisfactory, vague and general word, but we must use it, or some synonym, to express our amalgam of as yet unanalysed feelings and intuitions and the sense of the impact of things on us. The analysis of the primary " experience " from which conscious awareness starts is no easy task, just because we cannot think away all our forms of interpretation and catch ourselves with some pellet of raw experience. To be aware at all is to have begun relating and distinguishing, and so to have begun to use some rudimentary schema of interpretation, even if this be only the dichotomy of the world into edible and non-edible, or, with Bradley's dog, into smelly and non-smelly. Hence the strength of the idealist contention, that we should start from experience as *ideas* in a vague and confused form, and then show how the movement of thought articulates these into greater clarity and coherence. We shall need to examine this contention in some detail and ask whether it gives a plausible account of what we mean by the " empirical " in perceptual knowledge. At this stage I would only point out that if the idealists are right, the problem of the meaning of the " transcendent " and its relation to the " empirical " does not properly arise. For " transcendent " and " empirical " merely become words which mark stages in the development of an idea, the latter standing for the fragmentary experience from which we start, the former for the potential experience necessary to bring this partial experience to completion. The metaphysical problem then resolves itself into the problem of the idealist logic; and into the examination of the claim that " reality " is contained (or expressed?) in the self-development of an idea to systematic completion according to the principles of this logic.

In contradistinction to such epistemological idealism, the view we shall try to develop is that metaphysics is an analogical way of thinking. That is to say, it takes concepts drawn from some form of experience or some relation within experience, and extends them either so as to say something about the nature of " reality ", or so as to suggest a possible mode of co-ordinating other experiences of different types from that from which the concept was originally derived. We shall look at the considerations which lie behind the judgments of significance or importance which lead to the selection of particular concepts as providing key ideas capable of extended use. We shall have to ask with what justification concepts may be drawn from some particular type of experience and extended analogically to say something about " reality ", " God ", " the external world " or " the world as a whole ". Are such analogies not in the end products of the form-creating activity of mind, constructing pictures of the world (whether we call these pictures metaphysical or theological) seen through the medium of a particular kind of experience? And if we have to concede a substantial truth in this, have we any warrant to suppose that such theories can be more than expressions of particular ways of feeling about the world which, because of some maybe personal or traditional associations, have seemed to people significant?

But first let us clarify the sense in which we are suggesting that metaphysical theories are analogical. An analogy in its original root meaning is a proportion, and primarily a mathematical ratio,[1] *e.g.* 2 : 4 : : 4 : x. In such a ratio, given knowledge of three terms, and the nature of the proportionate relation, the value of the fourth term can be determined. Thus analogy is here the repetition of the same fundamental pattern in two different contexts. 2 : 4 and 4 : 8 exhibit the same relational pattern. Mathematical thinking has developed from the discovery that identities of pattern can be abstracted from different contexts, *e.g.* the number of a group of days abstracted from the days, and of a group of fishes from the fishes, and the analogous function which the number performs in each context can be considered by itself.

In the logic of induction, analogy means argument from parallel cases. We argue from some resemblance either of relation or of properties that resemblance of further relations or of properties is probable. The argument thus points to a hypothesis to be further tested. A famous example is Darwin's hypothesis of Natural Selection, which was suggested by analogy by considering the development of certain varieties of plants and animals as a result of selective breeding. Analogy may also be used to bring out a relation by exhibiting it in a different context, which may be either more familiar, or one in which the significance of the relation may be seen without prejudice: parables are instances of analogies of this kind. Such an analogy is contained in a Rabbinic parable illustrating the relation

[1] Cf. the use of ἀναλογία in Book V of the Elements of Euclid (in Heath's edition of the *Elements*, vol. ii).

between soul and body and the responsibility of the whole person, comprised of soul and body, for his sin. "R. Ismael said that the matter resembled a king who had a garden with fine early figs. He put two keepers in it, one was blind, and one was lame, and he bade them to look well after the figs. After a time the lame man said to the blind man, 'I see some fine figs in the garden.' The blind man said, 'Bring me to them and we will eat.' The lame man said, 'I cannot walk.' The blind man said, 'I cannot see.' Then the lame man got on the shoulders of the blind man and they went and ate the figs. After a time the king came to the garden, and he asked, 'Where are the figs?' The blind man said, 'Can I see?' The lame man said, 'Can I walk?' But the king was clever; he set the lame man on the shoulders of the blind man, and made them walk a little, and he said, 'Even so have you managed and you have eaten the figs.'"[1]

Whether such analogies can be *arguments* as well as *illustrations* of something known or partly known on other grounds depends on whether the relation illustrated is sufficiently alike in both cases for it to be possible to draw further conclusions from the one case to the other. An example of a doubtful argument from analogy of this type is that brought forward by Hume in support of his contention that virtue and vice are not attributes of an act or agent, but describe feelings which an act may arouse in a spectator. "To put the affair, therefore, to this trial, let us choose any inanimate object, such as an oak or elm; and let us suppose, that by dropping of its seed, it produces a sapling below it, which, springing up by degrees, at last overtops and destroys the parent tree: I ask if in this instance there be wanting any relation, which is discoverable in parricide or ingratitude? Is not the one tree the cause of the other's existence; and the latter the cause of the destruction of the former, in the same manner as when a child murders his parent? 'Tis not sufficient to

[1] *Lev.* R., Wayikra IV, 5. In Montefiore and Loewe, *A Rabbinic Anthology*, p. 312 (London, 1938).

reply, that a choice or will is wanting. For in the case of parricide, a will does not give rise to any *different* relations, but is only the cause from which the action is derived; and consequently produces the *same* relations, that in the oak or elm arise from some other principles."[1] The force of this argument turns on whether the relation is only the similar relation of physical parenthood; or whether in the case of the human father and child additional elements of a psychological or spiritual kind enter in and make a relevant difference to the relationship.

A metaphysical analogy is clearly not an argument based on mathematical proportion, nor is it an inductive argument from parallel cases of a homogeneous type. It is more likely to resemble an illustrative analogy, but it will probably turn out to be an illustrative analogy of a very special kind. There seem to be at least five senses in which it might be said that metaphysical theories are analogies.

1. There is first what I shall call the "deductive" sense. The term "metaphysical analogy" may suggest that we can start from some knowledge of the pattern of the universe, and can deduce the patterns of empirical things or events within the universe from this. This is the principle behind many ancient and mediaeval allegorizings, bestiaries, number mysticisms and the like. An example is Irenaeus' argument as to why the number of canonical Gospels must be four. The argument is based on a tradition widespread in antiquity (and probably of Pythagorean origin) that the basic pattern of the world was four-square. "As there are four corners of the world in which we live, and four winds throughout the world, and as the Church is sown over the whole world and the breath of its life, consequently the world must have four pillars inspiring it with incorruptibility and reviving man. Thus it follows that the Logos, the architect of the world, who is enthroned on the Cherubim and supports the world,

[1] *Treatise of Human Nature*: Of Morals, Part I, Sect. 1 (edition by Selby-Bigge, Oxford, 1896, p. 467). (I owe the reference to Mr. Joseph's *Introduction to Logic*, 2nd ed. p. 534.)

when He became manifest among men gave us the Gospel in four forms. . . . For indeed the Cherubim had four faces, and their faces are images of the dispensation of the Son of God. . . . For the Living Creatures are quadriform, and the Gospel also is quadriform." [1]

Dante argues for the political unity of the world under the Emperor by saying that man is the child of heaven, and that therefore his proper form of political organization can be deduced from the order of heaven, "Wherefore the human race is best disposed when it follows the track of heaven in so far as its proper nature allows. And since the whole heaven in all its parts, motions and movers is regulated by a single motion (to wit of the *primum mobile*) and a single motor, God, it follows that the human race is then best disposed when it is ruled in its motors and motions by a single prince as single motor, and by a single law as single motion. Wherefore it appears necessary to the well-being of the world that there should be a monarchy or single princedom which is called empire." [2]

Metaphysical analogies of this type depend on the belief that there is a predominant pattern of being. Their use depends on two questionable assumptions; first that we know the basic pattern of the macrocosm, and secondly, that it is repeated in the sub-patterns of microcosmic events.

2. The second way in which metaphysics might be called analogical could be by claiming that there is an analogy between concepts derived from experience and the "reality" to which these are referred. Such a view would start from something like a phenomenalist view of experience. That is to say, it would analyse experience in terms of sensations and ideas derived therefrom, and, saying that we can only be aware of appearances—signs within phenomenal experience,—would define the "transcendent" as standing beyond and outside experience. If it does not then go all the way with the positivist conclusion that assertions about "noumenal reality" behind phenomena are meaningless, it might suggest that the intrinsic nature of the

[1] Irenaeus, *Adv. Haer.* 3, xi, 8.

[2] *De Monarchia*, I, ix.

transcendent reals (*e.g.* physical objects) should be conceived *by analogy* with the constructions built out of phenomenal experiences. But this is to suggest something like a representative theory of ideas. It would only hold if it were possible to maintain that the relation between the conception of a thing and the thing itself could be that of some kind of copy, or at least of structural identity. We shall have to examine this theory later, and shall see reason to question whether the relation between our sensations and whatever non-phenomenal objects they may be connected with can be that of repetition of structure, and *a fortiori* whether the relation of signs to that which they signify can be so conceived. But although there are philosophical objections to be brought against a "representative" theory of ideas, it is probably the theory most generally and popularly assumed, once people give up the naïvely realist conception that our ideas give us direct knowledge of things just as they are in themselves. It is perhaps equally natural to assume that our ideas are somehow duplicates of things, copying their essential characters. If this were true, the idea might be described as the analogue of a thing, reproducing its properties, and perhaps particularly its structural relations, in a different medium. We can sometimes point to such a structural relation between something we experience, *e.g.* the perceived lines on a map, and something else we can experience, *e.g.* the measured roads on a landscape, so that the former could be referred to the latter as an analogical symbol. But can we jump from phenomenal experiences and ideas to the nature of *transcendent objects*, except by assuming the "representational" character of the former? If the transcendent is defined as that which is entirely "beyond" or "outside" our experience, we have no grounds for assuming that the latter can even give us analogical knowledge of its nature. For this would mean that we could compare a phenomenon with something which is not a phenomenon, which is obviously impossible since it is only in so far as anything enters experience that we are aware of it to do the comparing. So, if " metaphysical analogies " are of this nature, we can only say that they are attempts to *imagine* the noumenal by analogy with the phenomenal. Such analogies as we construct from intra-experiential ideas would then be " projections " of these ideas upon what is intrinsically unknowable. Hence it could be argued that to speak of physical objects as " causes ", or of God as " Father ", is merely to make an analogical projection of ideas drawn from familiar intra-experiential relations without any ground for the analogy. The conclusion we must draw is that, if we start from an analysis of experience which exhibits a complete break between the " phenomenal " and the " noumenal ", no significant analogies can be drawn from the former to the latter. Such pseudo-analogies would only be projections of a phenomenal relationship on to a transcendent real which was strictly unknowable. We may call them " projective analogies ".

It might be suggested that metaphysical analogies are, in fact, pseudo-analogies of this kind. It will be difficult to contravert this, unless we can find some sense in which there can be some direct, non-analogical relation to the " transcendent " which our analogies may then serve to illustrate and express. Hence it will be necessary for us to examine the phenomenalist view of the nature of experience and see whether any such relation is precluded.

3. Certain metaphysical theories have claimed to be *probable hypotheses* about the nature of the world as a whole, for instance the teleological argument as stated by Paley. The discovery of a watch points to a watchmaker as its designer; the signs of intelligent order in the world point to a designing mind behind it. Arguments of this type presuppose that we can draw analogies between the nature of the world as a whole and some class of phenomena within it. Though speciously like inductive analogical arguments from parallel cases, they are not so in fact. For the world as a whole cannot be an object of experience, hence the hypothesis is unverifiable; and, as Hume and Kant pointed out, the analogy is drawn in terms of certain selected

phenomena. There are some phenomena in the world which look like the result of intelligent contrivance, others which do not. So the question must be asked, why this particular type of relation is selected. Hence we might have a teleological view of the world, interpreted in terms of the experience of purposive action; or a mechanomorphic view of the world, interpreted in terms of the structure of a machine. Those who hold such views are not generally conscious of their analogical character; they are prepared to present an interpretation of the nature of the world as a whole in terms of some intra-mundane or intra-experiential relationship and use the conception univocally. The possibility of doing this successfully would depend on there being in fact some unitary character in the world, whereas there may be real breaks and diversities which cannot be brought under the same categories, so that the univocal use of terms derived from one kind of experience may be misleading when applied to the whole.[1]

On these counts, such metaphysical theories are not best described as " probable hypotheses " concerning the world as a whole. For the procedure of applying to the world as a whole concepts drawn from some relation within the world can only be undertaken, if at all, with every recognition of the analogical character of such concepts, not pressing them so far as to distort real and relevant diversities. And this is slurred over by the term " probable hypothesis ". Moreover, the term suggests that some method of verification should be possible in a sense appropriate to the inductive study of parallel cases.

4. From metaphysical analogies as " probable hypotheses " we should therefore distinguish " co-ordinating

[1] I would not foreclose the possibility that there may be a unitary categorical character or relation within the world which could be formulated univocally. We should then have a non-analogical metaphysics. But *de facto* attempts to formulate such a character or relationship are made by analogical extensions of certain selected characters or relationships. Moreover, if the metaphysical nature of the world should be that of the relation of finite existents to an *absolute* existent, the absolute existent would be *sui generis* and *in principle* could only be described analogically.

analogies ". These would be attempts to co-ordinate different kinds of experience in terms of an analogical extension of a key idea derived from one type. I shall suggest that some of the great metaphysical systems of the past have been analogical in this sense. They start out from an idea drawn from some form of intellectual or spiritual experience which for some reason is judged to be especially significant or important, and then extend this idea so as to achieve some wider co-ordination in terms of it.

5. A metaphysical analogy might express a relation to an object in part experienced and in part not experienced, describing it in concepts drawn from intra-experiential relations. In this case it would be necessary to understand " transcendent " not as meaning " beyond " or " outside " any possible experience (spatial metaphors which may for that reason be misleading, since it is not clear that the relation between our minds and what is other than our minds is a spatial one). We should need to understand the word " transcendent " as standing for that which is " other " than our minds — " being " or " existence " apart from our interpretations. But this would not preclude our interpretations from arising within some situation in which we are related to that which is " other " than our minds. Then we should have to see whether analogies might not be drawn between our various relationships to other being; and whether through these analogies anything might be said about distinctions in the character of being itself. Such analogies must of necessity be indirect attempts to say something about being through our judgments concerning the relationships in which we find ourselves. We must ask to what extent our experience can be held to be constituted by relations to what is other than ourselves, and whether a study and comparison of such relationships in different types of experience might enable us to say anything analogically about the nature of that to which we are related. Such a conception of metaphysical analogies would be difficult to sustain. To defend it, it would be necessary to show that there must be relationships in which we

stand to that which is other than our ideas, and that the nature of that other or others could be suggested indirectly by drawing analogies between the feelings and the judgments evoked in such relationships, in order to suggest possible characterizations in that which evokes them. This would be a peculiar type of analogy, but it is not obviously a pseudo-analogy, such as would be an analogy between phenomenal and noumenal when the latter is regarded as standing completely outside experience. Hence "God is Light" would be an analogical expression drawn from the discovery that an experience described as religious is an intellectual and spiritual experience analogous to the sensory experience evoked by physical light. So God would be thought of as the source of such intellectual and spiritual "illumination". I shall call analogies of this kind, drawn from elements within experience to the nature of that in relation to which the experience is constituted, "existential analogies" or "analogies of being".

But before we can proceed, some defence of the use of the word "being" is called for. If we would use it, we must make both our defence and our apology. Our apology is due to the Thomist writers, since the term "Analogy of Being" might be said to have become the special property of their great tradition. I have tried in Chapter VIII to indicate my debt to and my divergences from the Thomist philosophy of the *Analogia Entis*; the divergences are mainly due to epistemological differences of a fairly far-reaching kind. A Thomist will, no doubt, detect signs of metaphysical relativism in my view. If so, I accept the rebuke, and ask that my use of the plural "*analogies*" be taken to indicate that I acknowledge this, and am trying to develop a view of the analogical element in kinds of metaphysical thinking outside the frontiers of the *philosophia perennis*.

I must also defend the use of the word "*being*". I am using it to refer to "that which exists".[1] But the path

[1] The attempt of certain philosophers, notably the critical realists, to distinguish "being" and "existence" by saying that "being" includes

of existential propositions has been fraught with pitfalls ever since Kant's attack on the Ontological Argument showed that whatever is meant by "existence", it is not a logical predicate. Russell's well-known analysis of the logical use of the existential "is" makes it apply properly to descriptions and mean that values can be assigned to propositional functions. So "Men exist" means that the propositional function "x is a man" is sometimes true.[1]

Russell's method of substituting a statement about the truth value of propositional functions is of service in so far as we are concerned to distinguish logic from epistemology and metaphysics. But if we do not confine ourselves to logic as a study of relations between propositions, but go on to raise epistemological and metaphysical questions, we can still ask, when confronted by Russell's analysis, "Why should the propositional function 'x is a man' sometimes be true?" And the answer might be that it would be possible to point to an instance — "*This* is a man" — and it would not be true unless "this" *is* a man. That is to say, what makes a true proposition true is something other than another proposition to which reference may be made. Russell himself does not seem to be concerned to deny that "existence" is significant in some such sense, when he is concerned with epistemology as well as with logic. So in *The Analysis of Mind*[2] he says "the feeling of reality" belongs primarily to whatever can have effects on us, without our voluntary co-operation, and the content of the feeling of reality is best expressed by the words "the existence of this". This description obviously needs further expansion. A nightmare can have effects on us without our voluntary co-operation, and it can of course be said that the nightmare *qua* nightmare "exists", though

subsisting possibilities, such as universals, and even subsisting impossibilities, such as round squares and hallucinations, does not seem to me convincing. I agree with Professor Laird's observations on this point in *Mind*, N.S. vol. li, No. 203.

[1] *Introduction to Mathematical Philosophy*, pp. 164 *sq.* (London, 1919).

[2] P. 186. Cf. also *Introduction to Mathematical Philosophy*, pp. 169-170.

it might be said also that it was " unreal ". The nightmare exists in the sense that it is the case that we are dreaming, and having certain beliefs, but it is " unreal " in that our belief that we are being entertained by Hitler dressed as Julius Caesar refers to what is not the case. The distinction between " reality " and " existence ", if such can be drawn, seems to consist in the way the word " reality " is used in an evaluative sense with reference to some interpretation. So the real is the genuine, the authentic, as opposed to the spurious, or the misleading (" That is not a real door ", or " a real pound note "). Hence " reality " has come to have emotional associations which make it something of a " blessed word " (we remember Eddington's remark about " Reality! Loud cheers! "). In this discussion we shall use " reality " as meaning that which is needed over and above other propositions in order to make true categorical propositions true, and in this sense it will be synonymous with our use of " existence " or " being ".[1] I take it to be implied in the notion of truth that to say a proposition is true is to refer it to something other than itself. The difficulty in stating the truth relationship satisfactorily (a difficulty to which we shall return) need not at this stage deter us from saying that to call a proposi-

[1] The statement that reality may be defined as that which makes true categorical propositions true might be challenged by those who maintain that propositions are true with reference to the context of a " universe of discourse ". So " Othello killed Desdemona in jealousy " is said to be true *in Shakespeare's play*, and we need not hold that Othello was a " real " man, or " existed ". But the existential reference is to the play as Shakespeare in fact constructed it, as a story in which Othello killed Desdemona in jealousy. In another sense we should say that the proposition was not " true " but " fictitious ".

Hypothetical propositions are true within a defined system of relations; hence it may be said that " if p, then q " can be true without postulating the " existence " of p. But if hypothetical propositions are to be said to be true in any sense other than as statements of possible formal connections, it will be with reference to some categorical proposition which states that the nature of reality is such that the relation is sustained. " If it rains, the grass will be wet " depends on a categorical proposition that the nature of physical conditions is such that. . . . And this categorical basis of the hypothetical proposition will only be true if reality *is* such. Mathematical propositions are either hypothetical; if you assume the axioms and definition true is to refer it in some sense to something beyond itself. The possibility of this something being only other propositions will be considered later on in our criticism of the coherence theory. We shall find reason to question the adequacy of this; and so shall be brought to hold that what makes true propositions true cannot in the end be merely other propositions. Hence we shall hold that there must be in some sense " matter of fact " beyond propositions, and we shall enquire whether this can be exhaustively described in phenomenalist terms. Our warrant will be largely, to use Russell's description, " a feeling of reality aroused primarily by whatever can have effects on us without our voluntary co-operation ". We shall, however, need to distinguish the " feeling of reality ", which gives impetus to our interpretation, from that which is not " feeling of reality ", but, by being what it is, makes our feelings trustworthy or non-trustworthy. " That which is what it is " apart from our interpretations is, we suggested above, the meaning we should give to the word " transcendent ". Yet we shall maintain that we have no direct apprehension of the intrinsic properties of " that which is " in itself. We have only indirect apprehensions, arising out of relations in which we stand to it.

But first it is necessary to see whether we can look on our ideas of " reality " as constituted by indirect, symbolic interpretations of certain types of relationship. To do this we shall need to examine realism in so far as this asserts that there can be direct apprehension of the intrinsic nature of being other than our minds; idealism in so far as it claims that the nature of being can be understood univocally through developing the categories of thought; and

tions, then the statements follow as their necessary implications; or, if they are said to be true in so far as they are applied, there is implicit reference to a categorical proposition, and so to " existence " (*e.g.* the nature of space within this defined field is such that the angles of a triangle equal two right angles). But pure mathematical propositions would be hypotheticals; if you take Euclidean axioms, it is true that the angles of a triangle equal two right angles; if you take Riemannian axioms, then it is not true that they equal two right angles.

phenomenalism in so far as this constructs experience out of sensory states and does not see any special significance in describing these as *responsive* states. We shall start our enquiry at the level of sense perception. This may seem somewhat technical and perhaps tedious; and I ask indulgence during the next two chapters from any readers whose interests may not lie in considering the elementary foundations of knowledge. But it is only if we can establish the legitimacy of our method of interpretation at this elementary level that it may be possible to see whether it is capable of further development.

Our view will attempt to combine the types of analogical thinking described under (4) and (5) — the co-ordinating and the existential analogies. The first three types, the deductive, the projective and the hypothetical, we hold to rest on mistaken views of the nature of metaphysical thinking.

CHAPTER II

REALISM, IDEALISM AND PHENOMENALISM

We may define "experience" provisionally as the sum-total of appearances, feelings, impulses, together with the thinking which seeks to find or create some sort of significant order in these. This suggests a distinction between *data* to be ordered and thought as ordering activity. What are the data? The usual answer is that they are sensations. But "sensation" may be used in two ways. (*a*) It may be used to mean "sensa", or sense data, as contents of awareness (*e.g.* colours, sounds, smells). This can be called the phenomenological meaning. (*b*) It may be used to mean processes of sensing. This can be called the physiological meaning. We shall see that the precise relation between "sensations" in these two meanings is not easy to determine; but at this point we are only concerned to distinguish them.

When we are considering sensations as rudimentary data in experience, the phenomenological meaning (*a*) has the obvious advantage. For experience would seem to be built up on "sensa" as contents of awareness; while "sensations" in the physiological meaning, if by these are meant cerebro-neural events, are interpretations made by physiologists as a result of the phenomenological sense data which they obtain in their dissecting rooms when examining other people's brains. So Professor Price in his book *Perception* deals entirely with our awareness of phenomenological sense data, and is not concerned with "sensations" as physiological conditions. (He remarks significantly at the end of his book that he has nowhere mentioned "stimuli".) "Sensa" in the phenomenological meaning are elementary contents of awareness of colours, sounds, pressure, etc. As contents of awareness, they are within our experience; and even if we hold that they are connected in some way yet to be determined with events in an external world, yet we have no warrant for supposing that they are either direct awareness of external objects or representative copies of those objects.

The former view, namely that "sensa" are states of direct awareness of the surfaces of external material objects (the view commonly called "naïve realism"), is one of the philosophical theories which I should say can be shown to be as certainly wrong as anything in philosophy can be. For if we say that by awareness of sensa we mean immediate awareness of the surfaces of material objects, the physiological account of sensation at once presents a difficulty. According to this account, a number of steps intervene between the stimulating of the receptor organ and the neural events in the brain (which are the furthest point to which the physiologist can trace the sensory impulse). Is the sensum modified by this process, of which we are, it may be granted, quite unconscious? If it is not modified, we must say that the physiological organism is merely the instrument through which the perceiver is able to be directly aware of the surfaces of external objects, and does not itself affect the nature of what is perceived. But then the fact that sensa can also be obtained under drugs or in dreams presents a difficulty, since it certainly seems that in these cases the state of the physiological organism is affecting the nature of what is perceived.

Moreover, the physiological events are presumably continuous and form a system with the world of physical objects. The naïve realist might say that he can accept the physiological theory and at the same time hold that in perception we are immediately aware of the surface of external objects if he could maintain a thorough mind-body dualism. In this case the *physiological* account of sensation describes neural events within the brain; while the epistemological account tells us that the mind is directly aware of the surfaces of external objects and these two orders of events, though possibly parallel, are quite distinct. But if the naïve realist goes on to hold that the external objects which we perceive are "material" objects in a common space with our bodies and brains, then these ought to be causally interconnected in the same system as our bodies and brains. If the external objects, on the other hand, are merely "contents of awareness", then they form a system of ideas distinct from the physiological process and from the physical events of the external world. In that case they are mental events; but then how can they be surfaces of material objects? They could at best only be their mental duplicates. It was these considerations which led to Descartes' theory of "representative ideas". As Professor Kemp Smith, writing of Descartes' view of the psycho-

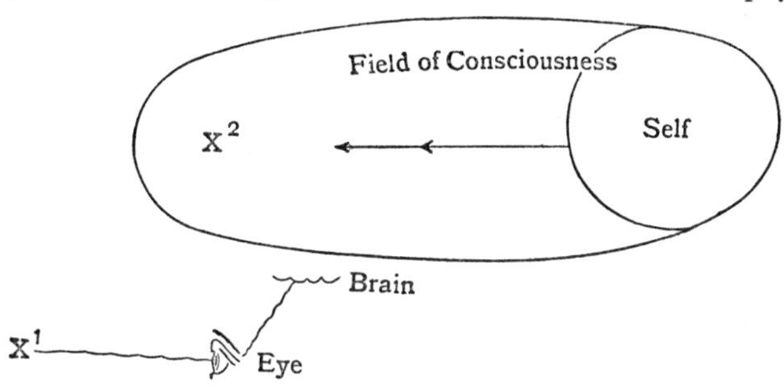

physiology of perception, puts it[1] — "The processes, physical and physiological, above enumerated, must have as their ultimate function the bringing into existence, or at least the occasioning so to exist, of certain entities, viz. those which we are now accustomed to entitle *sensations* of light and colour. These entities, Descartes further argues, differ in quite radical fashion from the antecedents which generate them. For whereas these antecedents are mechanical processes, occurring in public space, the resulting sensations are, he contends, not so describable, and occur in what may be entitled the field of consciousness. . . . In ordinary consciousness the self seems to itself to look out through the eye at X^1; what alone it directly experiences is X^2;

[1] N. Kemp Smith, *Prolegomena to an Idealist Theory of Knowledge*, pp. 18-19 (Macmillan, London, 1924). This passage and the accompanying diagram are reproduced by kind permission of the author and of Macmillan and Co.

and X^2 is a copy, image or representation of X^1, constructed by the self, in the light of past experience, out of the sensations that X^1 arouses by acting on the eye, and through the eye, on the brain. X^1 is invisible. What alone can be seen is X^2; and it is not a material body, but a mental image in the field of consciousness."

The crux is obviously the connection between the brain, and the self-as-conscious-of-X^2. In the diagram they are disconnected. Descartes believed there was a link between brain and mind in the pineal gland. It was bad luck that he did not know that this is merely an obsolete eye. The problem of the relation of mind and brain is one for which we have as yet no satisfactory solution. The strength of Descartes' view lay in his seeing that a psychological idea is not in the least like a physiological stimulus. Its weakness lay in his failing to show how physiological stimuli can occasion psychological ideas which he thought of as *representations* of the causes of the stimuli. We are left with faith in a parallelism between two orders of substances, substance thinking and substance extended. A logical sequence leads to Berkeley, who saw that not only secondary, but also primary, qualities must be described in terms of ideas in the mind; for if we start from the assumptions of naïve realism concerning the relation of our ideas to external material objects, we find that we have no warrant for supposing the existence of an order of material substance outside the range of mind and its ideas.

It seems, then, that if naïve realism be true, it must either say that the physiological account of the process of perception is irrelevant to the nature of what is perceived, or else it must hold some sort of psycho-physical parallelism; but in the latter case it will have to give up its contention that we are directly conscious of external material objects, and will have to say that we are only directly conscious of an order of representative ideas. In this case we should end, as Berkeley saw, in a form of phenomenalism. Rather than draw this conclusion, it might be suggested that instead of the naïve realist view that sensa are surfaces of material objects, they can be held to be psycho-physical events caused by the action on us of external objects.

This is the so-called " causal theory of perception ", generally accepted by common sense, but against which pertinent objections can be raised. The defence generally made for the common-sense belief in physical objects as " causes " of our sensations is that our sensations are fragmentary and intermittent, and that we can only interpret them coherently if we think of them as arising in us through the agency of external objects which have the properties of (relative) permanence which our sensations lack. But there are difficulties in this common-sense view as so stated, viz.:—

(1) The most it entitles us to say is that there must be some sort of ordered plurality in the things we do not sense. It does not take us any further in saying *what* the things we do not sense are; they might be, as Berkeley suggested, the ordered plurality of God's thoughts.[1]

(2) There is the difficulty of postulating causal interaction between things as apparently different as physical and psychical events. This difficulty depends on the assumption that " like causes like ", to which we shall have occasion to refer in another connection.[2]

(3) If " cause " be defined as the total combination of the necessary conditions of a given event, it becomes indistinguishable from the effect, *e.g.* when all the conditions of an explosion are actualized, we have the explosion. But if the cause is a selected condition, on what grounds is it selected when others are also necessary for the production of the effect? And what is meant by " necessary " (a term of modality) as applied to events? [3]

(4) It may be held that the notion of " cause " itself is merely an analogical projection of our experiences of acting and willing, and should be discarded in more exact thought about nature. Here it should be displaced by the notion of " law ", by which is meant a differential equation or

[1] Cf. Price, *Perception*, p. 93 (London, 1932).

[2] See *infra*, p. 183.

[3] Cf. *infra*, p. 172.

equations correlating rates of change. Given an equation expressing the configuration of events at one instant, the configuration at earlier and later instants is theoretically calculable. But no assumption need be made concerning one event or set of events "causing" another.[1]

Professor Collingwood has made an analysis of the notion of cause[2] in which he distinguishes the anthropomorphic sense, in which events are said to "cause" each other on analogy with the ways in which a person manipulates other things, from a meaning of the word cause in which it bears a precise, but non-anthropomorphic, reference to human actions. It is the sense called for in experimental sciences and in practical life, whereby we mean by cause "an event or state of things which it is in our power to produce or prevent, and by producing or preventing which we can produce or prevent that whose cause it is said to be".[3] Other uses of the word can be shown either to be anthropomorphisms or properly reduced to the conception of "law". If we accept this restricted interpretation of "cause", we can say that the charge that it is an idea derived from our own activities must be allowed. It is, however, an idea strictly applicable in the experimental sciences and in practical life, wherever we can say that by producing or preventing one thing, we can produce or prevent something else. In this sense we might say that, while the whole series of extra- and intra-bodily events may form a continuous system, by varying certain extra-bodily events we find we can perceive one object rather than another, and this is what we mean by the "cause" of our perception. But this really only says that certain extra-bodily events are differential conditions of our perceptions. It cannot tell us anything about the intrinsic nature of these events, and whether they are properly described as "material objects".

[1] Cf. Russell, "On the Notion of Cause," *Mysticism and Logic*, ch. ix (London, 1918).

[2] *Essay on Metaphysics*, chs. xxix-xxxiii (Oxford, 1940).

[3] *Op. cit.* p. 296 — cf. his illustrations on p. 299.

Besides these difficulties implicit in the naïve realist view that in perception we are directly aware of the surfaces of material objects, there are further objections of a strictly phenomenological kind. These are the difficulties raised as a result of experience under drugs, or optical illusions, or dreams, in which we may be very vividly aware of sensa, which are not parts of the surfaces of material bodies. The distinction between veridical and "wild" sense data (to use Professor Price's word) would be unmeaning if *all* sense data were simply parts of surfaces of external objects. And if we allow that "illusory" sense data are not parts of the surfaces, of external objects, how do we know that "veridical" sense data are such parts? Any empirical evidence we bring forward will be of the nature of further sense data, so that we are simply left with sense data and criteria drawn from their coherence or incoherence with one another. This, again, is the phenomenalist conclusion.

Moreover, if the direct realist maintains that at some one point our awareness of sensa is identical with awareness of external objects as they are in themselves, we have the problem of the distortions due to perspective. At what point do we see the object as it is in itself? If it be said, at the point of normal standard perception, defined as the point of maximum stereoscopic vision, would the fact that the appearance of an object alters when we examine it more closely under a microscope mean that we are not then seeing it as it is? And if we say that the point of direct awareness of the object as it is in itself is obtained at the point of maximum magnification, can any absolute limit be assigned to this?

Direct realism, then, in so far as it claims that we have an immediate apprehension of the nature of things as they are themselves, can give no satisfactory explanation of error, illusions and the changing perspectives of our sensa. Idealism, on the other hand, starts from the fact that our primary awareness is already an ordering and interpretative activity. Idealists recognize the impossibility of going beyond experience and stating in any intelligible fashion the relation between an experience and anything other than an experience. But idealists believe they can trace some necessary systematic character within experience itself which makes sense of experience. We should start from experience as a vague and confused world of ideas. The sense data, as events in psychical experience, are the most elementary form of idea; and they convey " meaning " which can be articulated into ideas of greater complexity and significance.

We may here recall the psychologist Wundt's definition of sensations as " those constituents in our thought which cannot be analysed into simpler elements ". If we accept this, sensations are ideas of a rudimentary kind. They are " ideas " because, to be aware at all, we have already had to employ some conceptual interpretation of recognition, comparison, discrimination; or, as idealists tell us, universals. This would seem to commit idealists to holding that animals, who undoubtedly enjoy sensuous and perceptual awareness, also make use of " implicit universals ". Here Bradley at least had the courage of his convictions. We remember his dog, who dichotomizes the world into the smelly and the non-smelly, using as criterion " what is smells, and what does not smell is nothing ".[1]

So from the beginning in perception we have mental processes of selection, abstraction, interpretation at work, bringing the initial vagueness into some more or less sharp focus. A " fact " for idealism is not something objective which we apprehend outside our experience; it is an interpretation of a part of experience which other coherent interpretations of experience oblige us to believe. We start, therefore, not from a datum outside thought (of which we could know nothing), but from a confused judgment which is clarified as it gains greater scope and coherence. (The metaphysical question, therefore, for idealism is identical with the logical; the development of ideas into greater coherence and comprehensiveness according to certain inherent principles of thought.) The strength of the idealist logic lies in showing what can be achieved in the

[1] *Logic*, vol. i, pp. 31, 36-38 (2nd edition, Oxford, 1922).

systematic organization of experience, when reason moves under the guidance of the ideals of coherence and comprehensiveness. Idealists can also make out a strong case for a view of different forms of experience — science, history, art, religion, morality, philosophy — as "ideal worlds" built up and sustained through a tradition of thought following faithfully the principles of its own procedure.[1]

Idealism, then, finds the clue to "objectivity" not in going outside thought and experience, but in exhibiting experience as the necessary articulation of an idea. The "data" given as sensations, are described as "implicit" grounds of belief, which a more developed judgment makes explicit. The argument proceeds as follows: Perceptual judgments are based on sensations. Sensations are not to be identified with physical stimuli nor physical reactions from stimuli, nor are they representations of these, nor of physical objects. They are events within mental experience.[2] So Bosanquet says that in principle no line can be drawn between the given and its extension.[3] Hence the distinction between perceiving and conceiving begins when we select and attend to connections which were already "thought" in sensory awareness, though they were not "thought about". The distinction, therefore, between perceptual data (sensa) and conceptual data (ideas and propositions) is not one of kind, but of degrees of definiteness. Both are "grounds" of inference. But the former have not yet been articulated into reasons, or intelligible necessities. "Empirical" grounds would mean, then, I take it, those grounds for belief which have

[1] Cf. *e.g.* Oakeshott, *Experience and its Modes* (Cambridge, 1933).

[2] Cf. Mitchell, *Structure and Growth of the Mind*, p. 157 (London, 1907). "Avoiding the error that our experience of things is a copy or impression of them we also avoid the error that we learn part of things by sensation and supply part from our minds. If we say that our minds give form or connection to things, we have also to say that they give them their sensory qualities; and if we say things take form in our minds, we must also say that they take sensory qualities."

[3] *Logic*[2] I, p. 72. Quoted by Blanshard, *The Nature of Thought*, vol. i, p. 118 (London, 1939).

not yet been fully articulated as intelligible necessities; but there is no reason in principle why with greater clarification "empirical" grounds should not be articulated into intelligible necessities, and shown to be implicated in a system of ideas. "Empirical" therefore means here an "implicit" ground for inference. The corollary of this would be that when the ground can be brought out to full and specific attention, it becomes an explicit proposition. The perceptual data are only "data" in the sense of being implicit grounds of inference, and this apparently means that when made explicit, they are seen to be propositions from which other propositions may be validly derived in a system of implications.

But if "empirical" simply means an "implicit ground of inference", the distinction between data and inferences based upon them reduces itself to one of different stages in the judging process. There is nothing about empirical "data" which is *in principle* different from inferences drawn from them. They are simply the propositions from which we happen to start; and when the total system of propositions has been elaborated into a system of mutual implications, presumably the question which were "data" propositions will merely be of interest as a question concerning the biography of the individual thinker. Here Russell has some pertinent remarks; in *An Inquiry into Meaning and Truth*[1] he writes: "There are some schools of philosophy — notably the Hegelians and the instrumentalists — which deny the distinction between data and inferences altogether. They maintain that in all our knowledge there is an inferential element, that knowledge is an organic whole, and that the test of truth is coherence rather than conformity with 'fact'. I do not deny an element of truth in this view, but I think that, if taken as the whole truth, it renders the part played by perception in knowledge inexplicable. It is surely obvious that every perceptive experience, if I choose to notice it, affords me either new knowledge which I could not previously have

[1] Pp. 123-124 (London, 1940).

inferred, or at least, as in the case of eclipses, greater certainty than I could have previously obtained by means of inference. To this the instrumentalist replies that any statement of the new knowledge obtained from perception is always an interpretation based upon accepted theories, and may need subsequent correction if these theories turn out to be unsuitable. If I say for example, ' Look, there is an eclipse of the moon ', I use my knowledge of astronomy to interpret what I see. No words exist, according to the instrumentalist, which do not embody theories or hypotheses, and the crude fact of perception is therefore for ever ineffable.

" I think that this view underestimates the powers of analysis. It is undeniable that our every-day interpretations of perceptive experiences, and even all our every-day words, embody theories. But it is not impossible to whittle away the element of interpretation, or to invent an artificial language involving a minimum of theory. By these methods we can approach asymptotically to a pure datum. That there must be a pure datum is, I think, a logically irrefutable consequence of the fact that perception gives rise to new knowledge."

Russell defines a datum as a piece of knowledge not deduced from previous theories; or a proposition for which the evidence is not wholly derived from other propositions. We need not assume that the actual data which we can obtain are ever completely certain, nor yet that a proposition which is a datum cannot be also a consequence of other accepted propositions. " This latter case occurs whenever we see a predicted eclipse. But when a proposition concerning a particular matter of fact is inferred, there must always be among the premisses other matters of fact from which some general law is obtained by induction. It is therefore impossible that all our knowledge of matters of fact should be inferred."

I am not sure how far by whittling away we can approach to a " pure datum " devoid of interpretation. I prefer to rest the argument on the point that by a datum we mean a piece of knowledge not deduced or inferred from previous propositions. This is to challenge the idealist contention that knowledge is the development of an idea according to the character inherent in thought itself. It is to raise the question whether a meaning must be ascribed to "empirical data", not derivable from the demands of thought itself. Is there a real distinction in kind to be drawn between judgments based on sense perception and judgments based on inference from other judgments? Some propositions are verified by reference not to other propositions, but to judgments based on perception. But if perceptual judgments are only "implicit" judgments not yet fully articulated, why do we give them the peculiar weight we do in certain kinds of "verification"? The idealist view says that what we call "knowledge" is in fact only a multitude of hypotheses each of which supports and is supported by a number of others. "If any one of them is true, a number of others will be strengthened thereby; if one is false, a number of others will be weakened. And what we call the improvement of knowledge consists in tightening up this network of hypotheses." This is the most we can hope for. The coherence view says that "the word 'truth' only *means* supportedness, *i.e.* that by '*p* is true' we only mean '*p* is supported by *q*, *r*, *s*, and other judgments, and they are supported by it'".[1] This view makes all probability *relational*, *i.e.* *q* is probable means *q* is supported by other judgments. But may there be, as Price suggests, another kind of probability, the *intrinsic* probability of empirical judgments of perception, introspection and memory? These are still judgments, but they are of a distinct kind, since their probability does not *only* depend on their being supported by other judgments. It may of course be increased by this. These judgments are not only corrigible, but *corrigent*, *i.e.* we give them particular weight in correcting other judgments.[2]

[1] Cf. Price, Inaugural Lecture on *Truth and Corrigibility*, pp. 20-21 (Oxford, 1926).
[2] This distinction is amplified by Price in *Perception*, pp. 182 *sq*.

Let us consider in what sense we can say that there is some element distinctively other than the conceptual involved in a judgment of perception, so that this element may afford evidence of a distinct kind — distinct, that is to say, from the evidence afforded by the fact that a judgment is brought into coherent relation with other judgments. In other words, is there a distinctive element, a " given " in sense perception which (*pace* Bosanquet) is in principle different from the extension of this " given " element in interpretative thought?

We may be able to get at this by considering the difference between percipient and conceptual activity. It will not do simply to point out the dependence of percipient activity on bodily conditions, the physiological sense organs and cerebro-neural system, because (1) we have seen that it is a question whether perception in the phenomenological meaning of awareness of contents can be identified with physiological functioning; and if we merely say that conscious perception and physiological functioning are closely bound up together in some way as yet to be defined, we can say the same of conceptual thought. Or, to put it the other way round, perceptual behaviourism presents some of the same difficulties as conceptual behaviourism; and *some* of the same difficulties are presented by the idea of disembodied conception as by disembodied perception. (2) If we are trying to see whether there is anything involved in perception besides the comparing, developing and connecting of mental experiences, we cannot assume knowledge of the body, of brains, nerves and sense organs, as anything other than interpretations of particular groups of sense data. (Perhaps at this stage of the argument this is the weightier objection.)

It will therefore not do simply to say that percipient activity depends on the functioning of the bodily organs, assuming their existence in some other sense than that of interpretations of sense data. But even if we call the body and its organs a group of sense data, they are sense data which play a peculiar rôle. For variations in all our other sense data seem to be a function of variations in these particular data. Bergson has put this well in the first chapter of his *Matter and Memory*.[1] "Here is a system of images which I term my perception of the universe, and which may be entirely altered by a very slight change in a certain privileged image — *my body*. This image occupies the centre; by it all the others are conditioned; at each of its movements everything changes, as though by a turn of a kaleidoscope." But in our conceptual interpretations this variability of all other images in accordance with slight variations in the position and state of the image called my body is corrected — the "privileged" position is counteracted; and all images alike are interpreted as belonging to a system of nature in which no one of them occupies this focal position. "Here, on the other hand, are the same images but referred each one to itself; influencing each other, no doubt, but in such a manner that the effect is always in proportion to the cause; this is what I term *the universe*. The question is: how can these two systems co-exist, and why are the same images relatively invariable in the universe and infinitely variable in perception?"

The difference between these two sets of images answers to a difference between conceptual and perceptual activity. In the former case the data are related according to judgments of rational connection, and developed in a systematic order. In the case of perception the data are intermittent, and the patterns in which they are related seem partially (at least in so far as perspective and proportion are concerned) to depend directly on changes in the percipient activity. On the other hand they cannot be summoned by deliberate effort to the same extent as thoughts can be; in other words, they are both less and more dependent on our voluntary activity than are our sequences of thought. I can think of St. Paul's Cathedral when I like. I cannot perceive it while I am in Manchester. If I go to London and walk up Ludgate Hill, I can put myself into a position in which I can perceive it. Also I can make myself perceive

[1] P. 12 (English translation, London, 1911).

it now larger, now smaller, now in one perspective, now in another, according to the ways in which I dispose myself. But if I am standing somewhere near the City, facing St. Paul's, particularly in present circumstances where it stands up amid a level waste, I cannot help seeing it, unless I deliberately shut my eyes or turn in the other direction. The conclusion we are tempted to draw is that in perception we are engaged in an interaction between our percipient activity and other forces or objects. But this takes us further than we are yet ready to go.

We can, however, say at this point that in perception the processes by which we connect and judge are dependent on forms of activity which are not themselves processes of judging and inferring. We can say this, without prejudging the question of what we mean by our body, when we speak of " disposing our body in a certain way " in order to perceive. It will be sufficient for our present purpose if we can say that this is a process recognizably distinct from the processes of judgment and inference.

Moreover, our given sense data are fragmentary and intermittent; and when we try to distinguish between which of them are veridical and which of them are illusory, we set about seeing how far they can be interpreted as coherent — for instance how far present sense data enable us to predict others, which we find can be obtained so as to corroborate the former data. (" Is that a real door, or or a dummy painted on the wall? If it is a real door, I shall be able to grasp the handle and turn it.") We have to express this in terms of coherence of present with future obtainable sense data, not of comparison of present sense data with fact, since a " fact " *as we know it* can only be a construction out of present and obtainable sense data. But in order to assure ourselves that our sense data are veridical, *i.e.* constructible into a coherent set with any other obtainable data, we have to set ourselves to obtain the anticipated data. We have to walk round and look at the " thing " from different angles, compare visual data with those of touch, etc. And even when we simply wait for a recurrence of a similar datum, we are by waiting deliberately setting ourselves to obtain it. For instance, if I am walking in the mountains and hear a sound, I may say "Listen, was that someone shouting?" and even if I do not walk in the direction of the sound but wait where I am in a state of expectancy and anticipation to see if the sound is repeated, I am still trying to obtain corroborative data through adopting a particular experimental attitude. Now adopting a particular experimental attitude is not a process of judging or of inference; it is a way in which we seek to obtain data for judgment and inference which we cannot obtain simply by reflection on or expansion of the logical implications of the data we already have. So, even if I apply the criterion of coherence, I am not simply finding whether certain propositions are coherent with other propositions. I have to set about obtaining the propositions, and to do so I exercise "percipient" activity. Now this percipient activity is distinguishable from inference, in that through it we derive new propositions by action, and these are not, as in inference, related to our former propositions by logical entailment. My hearing a second shout in the mountains is not logically entailed by my hearing the first shout. But by disposing myself in a certain way I am able to obtain the data on which I pass to the new proposition "There is that shout again". In such experimental cases we may say perception demands voluntary activity; but it does not necessarily do so when we are not concerned with whether our perceptions are veridical, *e.g.* we can open our eyes and look at the room we are in at present, and our perceptual experience involves no voluntary activity, except in so far as we can choose to look from right to left, or from window to door, or from door to window, and so on. (And we can of course decide to shut our eyes.)

Here I may comment on a contention of Professor Price's.[1] He writes: "In defining subjective succession" (*i.e.* of sense data) "we have made no mention whatever

[1] *Perception*, pp. 268-269.

either of the *will* or the *body* of the observer. Some philosophers seem to hold that a subjective succession is to be defined as one which is preceded by a voluntary change in the position or state of the observer's sense organs, and an objective succession is one not necessarily so preceded. This will not do at all. When I am carried round a house in a closed vehicle and can only see through a small hole, I sense a series of visual sense data of the house which is certainly a subjective succession ; for nobody thinks that the front door objectively precedes the back door or the kitchen window. But there is no *voluntary* change in the position or state of my eyes. I am not driving the vehicle; and perhaps even the driver himself cannot control it, so that even his sense data are not consequent upon an act of will."

I do not dispute Professor Price's contention that we cannot define the difference between a subjective and objective succession by saying the former is dependent on the will of the observer; under hallucinations we may entertain subjective successions entirely apart from our wills. But in the passage just quoted Professor Price says, " *nobody thinks* that the front door objectively precedes the back door or the kitchen window ". In other words, he has selected an example where the subjectivity or objectivity of the succession is not looked on as a question to be determined. But suppose we consider examples when *we want to know* whether the succession is objective or not. Suppose I am sitting in a train at a station and have a succession of sense data which give me the impression that my train is moving and the train opposite me at rest. I see my carriage passing the engine, tender and carriages of the other train successively. But I may then wonder whether in fact the other train is not moving and I am at rest. I can only tell by deliberately looking at something I judge to be at rest, *e.g.* the station building. If I am moving past the other train, I shall also be moving out of the station — or in phenomenalist language, I shall have to be able to co-ordinate the succession of data I call the engine, tender and carriages of the other train with a succession of data I call the refreshment room, booking office and goods yard. But if I find that I get a succession of data which I can call engine, tender, carriages of the other train, while in the background I simply get a continuing constellation of data which I call the outside of the refreshment room, I then conclude that my train is at rest, and that the other train is moving. That is to say, where the subjectivity, or, as in this case, the correct interpretation of a succession, is in question, we do voluntarily set ourselves if possible to obtain further sense data, which we may compare with the original set in order to decide the question.[1] Now this means we must be conscious of setting ourselves to carry out percipient activity. This can, I think, be stated without saying that we are conscious of changes in our bodily organs. Professor Price continues (p. 269): " If we leave out the will, and define a subjective succession as one preceded by a change in the state of the observer's sense organs, whether voluntary or not, we are not much better off. . . . If we are capable of knowing that our eye or brain is suffering a physical change, we are *already* capable of knowing that other material things are or are not suffering them. Our knowledge of our sense organs and brains and their changes is in no way logically prior to our knowledge of other objects."

This is perfectly true; there is, that is, nothing to be said for what I venture to call " physiological solipsism ", but I should say that we are introspectively conscious of the exercise of percipient activity, sometimes voluntarily and sometimes involuntarily, and when we are exercised in distinguishing veridical from illusory successions of images, we cannot avoid reference to the will of the observer. And this percipient activity is a factor distinct from inference. I say " percipient activity " and not " physiological

[1] We may take Price's criterion of " constructibility ", and say veridical sense data are those we can arrange in perspective series with reference to some nuclear datum (say that obtained at the point of maximum stereoscopic vision), whereas hallucinatory data are not so constructible. But the word " constructible " surely has reference to a possible act of constructing — *i.e.* we set ourselves to see whether the data can form a perspective series.

functioning of our sense organs", since our sense organs, in so far as they are objects of perception, are (as Price says) themselves successions of kinaesthetic sense data. And, of course, we are not directly aware at all of a great many of the physiological events (the processes in the nerves and brain) which are said to condition perception, but only know about them because of what physiologists tell us. But without raising the question of the sense organs, I suggest that we are introspectively aware of carrying out percipient activity, especially in the cases in which we set ourselves to obtain sense data, and are aware of the data we obtain as varying with slight variations in the percipient activity (as Bergson pointed out). Through this consciousness of a process, other than the process of inference (however much it may involve an inferential element), we are aware of a distinction in kind between perception and thought.[1]

Phenomenalism is not open in the same way as idealism to the criticism of being unable to give any satisfactory account of the difference between perception and thought. Phenomenalism is a name used to cover the views of a number of different philosophers, from those of Kant to those of certain of the logical empiricists. In some of these, and notably in the case of Kant, phenomenalism, as a view about the nature of physical objects, only represents one part of the philosophy, and is supplemented by other parts, such as, in Kant's case, a view of the nature of moral experience. In others, phenomenalism comprises the whole of what can significantly be said in terms of those philosophies. But all forms of phenomenalism hold in common that propositions about material objects can be translated into propositions about immediately experienced sense contents and their relations to each other. Such a view, as

[1] Cf. Whitehead, *Concept of Nature*, p. 3 (Cambridge, 1926): "Sense-perception has in it an element which is not thought. It is a difficult psychological question whether sense-perception involves thought; and if it does involve thought, what is the kind of thought which it necessarily involves. . . . But . . . the fact of sense-perception has a factor which is not thought. I call this factor 'sense-awareness'."

we have seen, has the advantage over forms of naïve realism of starting from a clear recognition that in so far as any sense object is a content of our awareness at all, it must be as phenomenal fact, from which the interpretation that it is associated with a " material object " can only be an inferential construction. And, as against idealism, phenomenalism is able to maintain a distinction of kind between perceptual appearances and thought as ordering and interpreting them, though it may be difficult to say just why, on phenomenalist grounds, there should be this distinction in kind. For the distinctive character of perception calls, as we have seen, for explanation with reference to some form of *action*. Sense data must be *constructible* into series, and we must be able so to dispose ourselves as to be able to obtain further sense data. Phenomenalist theories have to make use of the notion of " possible " sense data (as in Mill's description of an object as a " permanent possibility of sensation "). For instance, if I go through the door, I should be able to get possible data which I could call " its other side ". But phenomenalists cannot presumably hold a kind of critical realist view of " possible sense data " as entities subsisting apart from what is actually sensed, since they are pre-eminently concerned to eliminate all entities " beyond " what is sensed. The term " possible sense data " must therefore mean data obtainable as the result of some action. Moreover, verification may not merely be a matter of entertaining or even of comparing private sense data. It is often a matter of obtaining corroboration of our sense data through communication with other observers. " Do you see what I see? " may be a pertinent question in other situations besides those in which it is popularly supposed to be asked. Even if we say " comparing reports of other observers ", as a less question-begging term than " communication with other minds ", even this calls for the possibility of understanding the meaning of language. And the meaning of language grows up in a social tradition of intercourse. Moreover, verification in any exact sense depends on the use of instruments, and so sets the observer in relation to the work of the makers of these instruments. Hence verification depends on the possibilities of constructive activity and of intersubjective intercourse.

In the young days of Logical Positivism, phenomenalism was reduced to a method of correlating private sense data, and so ended in solipsism combined with a behaviourist account of the " experiences " of other people. But if phenomenalism be simply a theory concerning what we mean by " physical objects ", it is not debarred from accepting the possibility of constructive activity and intersubjective intercourse. It is only debarred from saying that we can talk significantly about what lies beyond any possible experience. But I believe that, if we take seriously the contention that interpretation and verification arise within a situation demanding constructive activity and intersubjective intercourse, we shall find that it is impossible to set a complete barrier between the " phenomenal " and the " transcendent ". " Constructive activity " calls for some reference to purposive activity, and so for some kind of unitary character in a subject beyond the state of the present moment. (This may in the end imply some view of the substantial unity of a self. Or it may not; fortunately it is not material to our argument to decide this.)[1] Intersubjective intercourse calls for the possibility of communication by means of symbols, that is to say, signs used purposively to convey information which a recipient does not already possess.[2] Hence verification calls for interrelated activities. These are partly voluntary activities of the subject, partly activities impinging on him and which he interprets. If we find that we must go as far as this, and say that interpretation arises within some situation of interrelatedness, it is no great step to go further and say that the differential conditions of such elements

[1] A penetrating defence of the possible meaning of substantial unity in terms of the unity of intentional action is given by A. M. Farrer in *The Finite and the Infinite*, Part II (London, 1943).

[2] Cf. Price, " Our Evidence for the Existence of Other Minds ", *Philosophy* (October, 1938).

in experience as are not due to our own activity or to inter-subjective communication may be due to our relation to some external world containing other types of existence, besides our own purposive activities and the purposive activities of other subjects, and which we can describe as "physical objects", provided that we recognize that physical objects *as we know them*, including the "objects of physics", are phenomenal interpretations, and we do not assume any view as to their intrinsic nature.

The difficulties in a view of experience as a transformation arising within a situation in which we are dynamically related to events beyond ourselves will become apparent in the next chapters. In defending some such position, we shall go most of the way in accepting a phenomenalist account of the contents of experience. But we shall differ from pure phenomenalism in stressing the *responsive* character of experience, and by "responsive" will be meant that experience will be described as arising out of situations in which the subject is related to activities other than his own interpretative activity. We shall look for a meaning of "transcendent" in terms of the implication of elements *other* than itself in a subject's activity, and not in terms of some unknowable "noumenal reality" behind the veil of phenomena.

CHAPTER III

THE CHARACTER OF PERCEPTUAL EXPERIENCE

Our discussion hitherto has been concerned to point to the distinction between perceptual awareness and conceptual processes of inference; it has not assumed any view as to the status of sensa, apart from their rôle as contents of awareness, nor as to their relation to events transcending the percipient. We have, however, said that the distinction between conception and perception suggests that the latter arises within some situation of interrelated events or processes. The experience of percipient awareness within such a situation is of two types — the experience of involuntary process which would ordinarily be described as sensitive reaction to stimulus, and the experience of voluntary process, as when we set ourselves to obtain further sense data in order to interpret those we already have. These two types might be called the lower and upper limits of percipient activity. How far down the scale of nature the lower limit extends is a question which we cannot yet answer; "sensitivity" is a word used (perhaps analogically?) for what appears to be purely chemical reaction, as when we say a photographic film is sensitive to light. But at some stage "sensitivity" meaning chemical reaction is accompanied by sensitivity meaning affective response. At this stage we can begin to speak of sensation. Here we must recall the ambiguity in the word "sensation" noticed at the beginning of the last chapter. It may mean a content of awareness (the phenomenological meaning) or it may mean a process of sensing accompanied by feeling tone (the physiological meaning). It may be said that as soon as it is possible to be aware of sensations in the latter meaning of the word they have already become phenomenological sensations, *i.e.* contents of awareness; in fact this looks like a tautology. We may therefore distinguish physiological cerebro-neural events from sensations *qua* feeling tone. But I think that a distinction can also be drawn between the immediate feeling of a process, *e.g.* a feeling of discomfort, and the interpretation of the contents of that feeling by selective attention, so that, *e.g.*, I say " I have got toothache ". The *feeling* of discomfort is not of course to be identified with the physiological process; *qua* feeling, it is psychical. But the feeling of uneasiness is a datum for the interpretative judgment, " I have toothache ".

We may call these two modes of sensation the adverbial and the accusative mode. The adverbial mode is an integral feeling, qualifying a state of experience. The accusative mode is a differentiation of contents of awareness. There is reason to suppose that the latter is the more highly sophisticated, calling for developed powers of discrimination. Sight, which is the most highly developed of the senses in the ordinary person, is nearly always considered simply in its accusative aspect, as awareness of contents. But it is possible to be aware of seeing in the adverbial mode, as when we experience jarring discomfort in looking at a flickering light. Apart from this primitive adverbial mode, there seems to be an integral adverbial aspect on a higher level, realized in aesthetic seeing, when we are concerned not only with differentiating contents but with enjoying the integral feeling conveyed by the composition as a whole. Hearing, on the other hand, is less frequently differentiated into contents, except where some practical interest leads a person to discriminate and identify particular sounds. But it almost always conveys emotional tone, generally of the more primitive kind, as in the feeling of discomfort accompanying the hearing of a pneumatic drill. The ordinary untrained person listening to an orchestra will experience a generalized emotional feeling of pleasure or excitement or hypnotic restfulness. The person with a trained ear will experience an integral emotional tone, and will also differentiate contents; he will be aware of what the 'cellos are doing, and what the wood-wind, and recognize themes as taken up by the different parts. Smell and taste are still less highly developed in the ordinary person; the ordinary person experiences integral feelings of pleasantness and unpleasantness and can make crude discriminations of contents; but it is only the person of special aptitude who is able to discriminate the finer shades of difference in smells and tastes and identify their contents with exact precision. The sensitive power of discriminating contents by means of touch enjoyed by blind persons shows how much this sense is undeveloped in the normal person who relies on sight for the purpose. In animals such as dogs it would seem that the contents of the senses of smell and hearing are more differentiated than those of sight. This indicates that the primary mode of experience is the "adverbial" mode, an integral state of feeling with a certain affective tone; whereas discrimination of contents (*e.g.* "I am seeing a green patch") is not the primitive experience but the result of a differentiation produced by practical, aesthetic or theoretic interests which themselves may lead to a further and "higher" adverbial sensory experience.

I shall suggest that the impulse to achieve forms through which experience may be clarified is at the root of mentality. But the process of selective simplification does not begin here; it is also a function of organic activity with its selective responses. In achieving the simplifications which are found in sense perception, the body plays a part, whatever view of the physical body we may take; we might, as in the passage I quoted above from Bergson,[1] look on it as a particular kind of "image" among other "images" (though I should not myself favour this way of speaking). Even so, it would be an "image" which occupies a peculiar position as a centre from which perspectives are developed. The inescapable impression of what Whitehead has called the "withness of the body" has led him and others to make the organic categories the key categories, and to try to develop a theory of sense perception in which the "sensa" are derived by abstraction from physiological

[1] See *supra*, p. 32.

functionings defined in terms of " feelings ". This takes account of what I have called the " adverbial " mode, an integral state of bodily feeling, as the primary phase, and seeks to derive from this the " accusative " mode of apprehension in terms of differentiated contents.

But if a theory of *knowledge* is to be developed from such a source, it will be confronted by two outstanding difficulties. First, a response is not necessarily at all like that to which response is made; in what way do physiological responses give theoretic knowledge about the environment, as distinct from practical information as to how the organism should adjust itself? Secondly, can we derive *psychological* sensations from physiological responses, or must we also recognize that some radical transformation takes place at the psychical level? Whitehead has attempted to answer these questions by a view of the sensa as derived by the selective activity of emphasis and elimination from the total complex of physical feelings. They are thus said primarily to be experienced as derived from and qualifying physical feelings, and are then referred symbolically as qualifying regions of the contemporary world.[1] The primary mode of perception to Whitehead is thus what we have described as " adverbial ", a feeling with a certain affective tone, from which the sensa are abstracted as contents in what we have called the " accusative " mode. But in the first instance they are elements in the subject's feeling state. " This notion of the sensa as qualifications of affective tone is a paradox for philosophy, though it is fairly obvious to common sense. A red-irritation is prevalent among nerve-racked people and among bulls. The affective tone of perception in a green woodland in spring can only

[1] I am aware that this summary statement of Whitehead's view must sound dogmatic, and, in view of his very individual use of terms such as " physical " and " feeling ", may even be misleading. But to try to give a longer explication of it here would mean a technical and perhaps distracting intermission. In case, however, any reader should wish to consult an interpretation of his doctrine of " prehensions ", in so far as this bears on his theory of perceptual experience, I have attempted to give a fuller account in an Appendix. (See p. 228.)

be defined by the delicate shades of the green. It is a strong aesthetic emotion with the qualification of green in spring-time. The intellect fastens on smell as a datum; the animal experiences it as a qualification of his subjective feelings. Our developed consciousness fastens on the sensum as datum: our basic animal experience entertains it as a type of subjective feeling. The experience starts as that smelly feeling, and is developed by mentality into the feeling of that smell." [1]

This certainly sounds like a paradox for more than for philosophy, especially when we remember that for Whitehead the feelings referred to are the "subjective forms" of physiological and neural events. We are reminded of Bradley's difficulty in believing that "when I smell a smell I am aware of the stinking state of my own nervous system".[2] Marvell's description of his state of mind as a "green thought in a green shade" may, however, be an instance of what Whitehead is seeking to convey. Marvell's state of mind would illustrate what Whitehead means by a "reversion to a primitive stage", in which we become aware of the integral feelings from which our more sophisticated perceptions are abstractions; such a state, he rightly says, is the root of much poetic experience. But we may question whether it is legitimate to describe this state of feeling as qualified by the sensum. The sensum is a differentiated content, apprehended in the "accusative" mode. The integral state of feeling, the "adverbial" mode, can be described only metaphorically, surely, in terms of the sensum. Otherwise when I say "I perceive green", I should really say "I have a feeling of becoming greened". Now we may imagine what a feeling of becoming green means on a Channel crossing, as a metaphorical description of an emotional state; but this is not the same as making a colour, when we look at a green field, a qualification of emotional tone. If when we look at a green field we are really feeling greenly, how are we feeling when we look

[1] *Adventures of Ideas*, p. 315 (Cambridge, 1933).
[2] Quoted by Price, *Perception*, p. 127.

at the variegated mass of colour in a herbaceous border in June? If our feeling state were qualified by all the different colour sensa we were perceiving, our emotions might be analogous to what are alleged to have been those of the chameleon when he sat on a tartan. Instead, we are conscious of an "adverbial" emotional tone of elation, whereas the contents of our awareness can be differentiated into a large number of distinct sensa of which we can be conscious simultaneously. Whitehead might of course reply that in accordance with his "Category of Transmutation" the feeling of elation could be a generalized derivative from the feelings of the differentiated sensa of which we are aware in looking at the border. But we may still question whether the emotional tone can ever be described literally as qualified by the sensa which are differentiated contents of awareness; if "transmutation" takes place, it is not the sensa, but a feeling derived from their entertainment which characterizes the emotional tone.

Professor Price [1] has criticized the theory that sense data may be adverbs of feelings. He does not mention Whitehead's view, but his remarks are pertinent to it. "It is true", he says,[2] "that we speak of *feeling* hot and of feeling bodily pains, and even of feeling pressures of various kinds: indeed all tactual, kinaesthetic and koenaesthetic sense data are said to be felt. But we speak in this way because we take these sense data to qualify various parts of our own body, and we ordinarily consider our bodies as somehow parts of ourselves; so that a bodily process is regarded as a process *in ourselves*. On the other hand it is possible, though difficult, to regard one's own body as just one object among others; this we do by suspending as far as possible the practical or outwardly directed attitudes of ordinary life. In so far as we succeed in this, tactual sense data and even bodily pains simply confront us as objects of acquaintance like visual or auditory data; we are intuitively aware of them, but we should no longer say that we feel

[1] In *Perception*, pp. 120 *sq*.

[2] *Ibid.* p. 122.

them. On these grounds it seems impossible to hold that we *feel* red or loud or striped as we feel hungry or afraid." The only question I want to ask here is whether, if we can achieve the degree of detachment from our bodies which enables us to be aware of pains as objects of acquaintance rather than as states of feeling, the same would not be possible in the case of hunger and fear. If the distinction between pains as koenaesthetic sense data and feelings as affective states is held to consist in the possibility of localizing pains as qualifying some part of the body, whereas hunger and fear are modes of our whole affective state, I doubt whether this distinction will stand. An ache in my stomach may pervade my whole affective state, while focussed, as it were, in my stomach; but so, too, when I am feeling hungry, the feeling pervades my whole affective state, while focussed, as it were, in my stomach. Similarly when I feel afraid, the feeling may be focussed in certain visceral sensations. We cannot therefore say that the distinction lies between those feelings which we can regard objectively as sense data qualifying parts of our bodies, and feelings not so connected with parts of our bodies.[1]

But nevertheless, the distinction between sense data as differentiated contents (accusatives) of awareness, and feelings as modes (adverbs) of awareness does appear to be valid. Now Whitehead tries to show that veridical information about the world beyond the percipient may be conveyed through the former as derivative from the latter. This, he holds, can only happen if there is at least a partial identity of structure between (*a*) the sense data, (*b*) the physiological events, and (*c*) the events beyond the percipient, so that the sense data can function as symbols first of

[1] Professor Price's presidential address to the Aristotelian Society (1943–1944) on "Touch and Organic Sensation" came into my hands after this had gone to press. Professor Price here recognizes that the sense datum analysis does not fit organic sensations. These, or at least their sub-class muscular sensations, are best described as feelings of encounter, or of bilateral dynamic transactions. This is entirely congenial to what I have tried to say in what follows; and I am grateful to Professor Price for having clearly stated in this paper the difference between the two types of sensation.

the physiological events (of which the "adverbial" feelings are said to be "subjective forms"), and through these of the events of the contemporary world.[1] But, apart from the question whether the sensa are properly to be described as "symbols", is the essential property of a symbol to repeat the structure of that which it symbolizes, transposed of course into a different medium? This raises a question of immense importance, bearing directly on the nature and validity of what I shall later be describing as modes of analogical thinking. Meanwhile, let us consider the postulate that there should be some identity of structure between conscious sensations and (*a*) their physiological correlates, and (*b*) events in the external field. The plausibility of this theory — "isomorphism" as it is sometimes called — consists in its being the simplest hypothesis to adopt; and it also seems to follow from the strong probability that there must be some very intimate connection between physiological and neural events in our sense organs and brain and our conscious sensations. Colour sensations may be a function of rates of electric discharges from the optic nerves (though this is an unsolved puzzle); auditory sensations are with more assurance correlated with periods of vibration in the mechanism of the inner ear. But though colour and sound sensations may be correlated with these neural events, do they necessarily reproduce their pattern?

The *Gestalt* psychologists, like Whitehead, have questioned the primacy of sense data as basic atomic elements of experience; and, from a consideration of the physiological background of a perceptive activity as a whole, they seek to give an account of "sense data" in terms of the structure of a total state of interrelated dynamic and functional processes. Since Whitehead's treatment is highly individual and full of neologisms, it may be better to consider this particular question in the more familiar context of the *Gestalt* theory.

There would seem to be two different sides to *Gestalt*

[1] I have tried to indicate in the Appendix how Whitehead relates sense data to other events *via* events physiologically conditioned.

theory, which may not necessarily stand and fall together.

1. The description of the part played by form or pattern in our perception of objects.
2. The hypothesis of "isomorphism" between such perceived forms and cerebro-neural processes.

The latter is the theory developed by Köhler, but I do not think all *Gestalt* theorists, and notably Koffka, would subscribe to it. Köhler starts by putting forward a theory as to the spatial distribution of nervous stimuli in certain areas of the brain.[1] In visual perception, images (light spots) are projected by waves on the retina of the eye, as are photographic images on the sensitive film of a camera. Then nerve impulses from the various points on the retina travel along the fibres of the optic nerve and then along more central paths until they arrive at the striate areas of the cerebral cortex. There discharges of nervous energy take place which seem, as far as physiological knowledge goes, to be the final phase of visual perception. The puzzle for a philosophical account of perception is to give some plausible account of how discharges of electrical energy in the brain can be translated into sensations of shapes and colours giving us knowledge of an external world. Certainly the physiological events in the brain are not "representative" of such objects in any literal sense; but here Köhler suggests that the link by which physiological events in the brain can give us some veridical knowledge of the external world is to be found through some kind of structural identity. The processes in the cortex may be no less well distributed than are the spots on the retina, and develop as an orderly pattern. Moreover, the spatial properties of this pattern may be to some extent akin to those which the pattern of images exhibits on the retina. We should thus have an "isomorphism", or likeness of pattern, between (*a*) the spatial distribution of events in the external world, (*b*) light waves coming from

[1] Cf. *The Place of Value in a World of Facts*, pp. 132 *sq.* (New York, 1938).

the external world to the eye, (*c*) distribution of spots on the retina, (*d*) distribution of events in the striate area. The act of perception would then be the reaction of the perceiving subject, which " reaction " has a certain structure as a whole determined by the physiological disposition of neural events in the brain, a disposition which in its turn reproduces the form or pattern of the object perceived.

Here isomorphism joins forces with an essential part of *Gestalt* theory, namely, that this reaction must be considered not as a composite result of associated local stimuli, but as a whole. The processes in the nervous apparatus are not to be considered as single excitations which are circumscribed as local stimuli, but as dynamic processes operating in a " field " which must be taken as having certain properties as a whole as a distribution system. The phrase " sensory dynamics " continually recurs in Köhler's writings. How far is it intended as an " analogical " term, taken from electro-magnetics, or how far is it meant literally? And if the latter, what exactly does it mean? Petermann [1] says that the physical manifestations of a distribution system are the quite specific interrelationship of actions determined by the laws of action of the material and the topography. As applied to perceptual *Gestalten*, the term " dynamics " simply appears to mean the interaction of processes in a total neural response. The question is whether a conscious sensation can be defined in this way; or, in other words, whether we can say that phenomenal *Gestalten* are of this nature. Köhler's hypothesis is that the relation between objects as we experience them and the physiological properties underlying perception is one of " isomorphism " in their systematic properties. So " all experienced order in space is a true representation of a corresponding order in the underlying dynamical context of physiological processes ". This hypothesis has of course the attraction of being the simplest one to adopt. But it is by no means established; in fact there is a certain amount of evidence of cerebro-neural physiology to indicate

[1] *Gestalt Theory*, pp. 68 *sq.* (English translation, London, 1932).

that it cannot be true. Sherrington cites several considerations which can be urged against it; for example, the "singleness" of binocular vision. "Congruent images from corresponding retinal points give one single image to the mind, a single mental image. This has often been taken as evidence of central conjunction of the nervous mechanism of the two retinal points. Thus, as meaning a single nerve-fibre which forks into a branch for each optic path, or twin fibres from one and the same cell in the brain, or central confluence of the two nervous reactions right and left to 'a common physiological centre' or point."[1] But in fact this is not so. "There is no evidence that the nervous paths from two corresponding retinal points R and L reach a common mechanism in the brain." "That the conjoined reports are not misread indicates their conjunction is mental, not physical. It is not, therefore, a physiological conjunction in space, but a temporal conjunction in 'mental' space. It is not spatial conjunction of cerebral mechanism which combines them."[2] Moreover, mental experience attends to one thing at a time. "We might imagine this principle pursued to culmination in final supreme convergence on one ultimate pontifical nerve-cell, a cell the climax of the whole system, of integration. Such would be a spatial climax to a system of centralization. It would secure integration by receiving all and dispensing all as the unitary arbiter of a totalitarian State. But convergence toward the brain offers in fact nothing of that kind. The brain region which we may call 'mental' is not a concentration into one cell but an enormous expansion into millions of cells."[3]

Gestalt theory gives a convincing account of our tendency to perceive objects as segregated groups. But this group organization is not given in the original sensory stimuli on the retina, which just gives a mosaic of local stimuli. Nor is it given by "habits" of association of stimuli unrelated except by contiguity. But Köhler is not content to say that

[1] *Man on his Nature*, p. 272 (Cambridge, 1940).
[2] *Ibid.* p. 273.
[3] *Op. cit.* p. 277.

the root tendency of mental activity is to find pattern. He tries to find a theory in terms of physiological response. He speaks of "the idea of dynamical self-distribution with functional coherence and structure of process"; "the stability of organization of an actual whole".[1] "A process-in-extension, coherent functionally and self-maintaining dynamically, is supposed to contain those dynamical relations between segregated objects which in experience appear as positions of objects in mutual relation and order." I take this to mean that a distribution system of neural energy having a certain stability and equilibrium determines a total reaction to the external stimuli so that we see objects patterned in a certain way. What is the evidence for "isomorphism" which ensures that this "structural reaction" maintains the structure of the external situation? Or have we here an assumption which is a ghost (in terms of electro-dynamic analogies) of the old "copy" theory of correspondence? And what is the evidence for this, beyond the assumption of a one to one correspondence between the elements of a sensation and its physiological conditions, and the further assumption of one to one correspondence with a structure external to the organism? Petermann [2] compares this view of perceptual structure with the epistemology of Democritos, in which a stream of εἴδωλα (images), coming from objects, impress themselves on the sense organs. This is perhaps hardly fair, although some of the less judicious statements about "isomorphism" might suggest it. I suggest that Köhler has succumbed to the attractiveness of the notion of "identity of pattern" as supplying the links between physiological reaction, sensation and external object. To question this is not necessarily to question the insistence of the *Gestalt* theorists that we must start from the whole situation of organic inter-relatedness of the percipient embodied event to the environment, and that this relation is "felt" as having certain stresses and strains interpreted as giving information about the environing world. But these stresses and strains are

[1] *Place of Value*, p. 204. [2] *Gestalt Theory*, p. 304.

felt in the total relation of organism-responding-to-environment; they may not be reproduced with one to one correspondence in the physiological events in the brain of the percipient and in the external structures perceived. Still less need mental sensations be a reproduction of these structures with one to one correspondence.

But this means we have to bring in the notion of "interpretative" mental activity, which Köhler's physiological realism had sought to avoid. Köhler's view would seem to lead to our seeing the conceptual patterns of thoughts as *Gestalten* of the same order as the structural reactions of the neural processes. He writes:[1] "The principle of evolution postulates that certain processes of which the organism is capable have the structural characteristics of mental operations. If there are any such processes they must obviously be the neural correlates of these operations. Thus mental operations and their neural counterparts must structurally resemble each other. In other words, the principle of psychophysical isomorphism follows from the principle of evolution. Isomorphism represents indeed the only way in which mental life can be dynamically interpreted, in which it can become a subject matter of physics." How are we to understand the "principle of evolution" here? Does it mean that all processes must be describable in terms of the laws of physics? But in a mental operation a pattern is developed in terms of relations and correlates between symbols. Does "isomorphism" ask me to believe that when I formulate an equation $2x = 4 \therefore x = 2$, the variable x is correlated with an indefiniteness in the distribution of forces in the cerebral field, which indefiniteness then passes into an equilibrium having the same structure as that of the force correlative to 2? And what is the neural pattern equivalent to an infinite convergent series, *e.g.* $1 + \frac{1}{2} + \frac{1}{4} + \frac{1}{8} + \ldots = 2$?

It is true that Köhler is guarded when it comes to applying the principle of isomorphism to "higher" mental operations, though he has hopes that it may be so developed.

[1] *Place of Value*, p. 396.

But even in the *perceptual* situations which he describes, it is open to question whether phenomenal and physical structures can be explained as " isomorphic ". We perceive a segregated whole in the field before us because of a " *Gestalt* disposition " physiologically conditioned. But does this dispose of the problem of " meaning "? We may respond to certain formal properties in the object before us because they form a pattern for which we have some sort of physiological *rapport*. But what about cases where perception of pattern depends on some apprehension of the meaning of the content? *E.g.* I see a *book* lying on the table. Is *Gestalt* theory trying to get to a stage of vision and design when we see formal patterns of shapes and colours without intuiting content? If so, it would be in line with certain movements in modern art. But may I not pick out a " book " from its background not only because of its structural properties, but because I am interested in books, and so notice the book and ignore, *e.g.*, the colour of the wall-paper? Does the theory allow enough for the element of *interest* as selective, leading to a mental attitude which partly determines the particular forms seen? Moreover, in the examples given by the *Gestalt* writers, where it is possible to see two or more figures in the same presented picture, we can switch our attention and see first one figure and then the other by a deliberate effort of choice. The switch appears to be discontinuous and to be voluntary. There are only a limited number of figures in which we can see the presented material, but *which* we see seems to be guided by interest and choice.[1]

These considerations suggest that the important contribution of *Gestalt* theory to an understanding of the nature of symbolism lies not in the doubtful theory of isomorphism, but in showing how perception is governed by our interest in the development of organized forms. We learn to perceive not just by addition of isolated local stimuli, but by distinguishing patterns in a presented whole. We experi-

[1] Cf. *infra*, p. 203.

ence continuity in the dynamic processes in the environment some of which we come to see as relatively stable patterns, and so as "significant". The interest in pattern obviously develops very early in young children; the experiments of the *Gestalt* psychologists may throw light on whether it can be found also in animals. If so, animals have passed the divide towards intelligence, since the capacity to distinguish and develop *relevant* patterns is distinctive of mental activity.

But the *Gestalt* theory considers patterns as literally spatialized (or temporal successions, as in sound *Gestalten*, *e.g.* melodies). Can it explain symbolism as an "abstract" non-spatial and conventional way of representing structural relations; for instance, the difference between an algebraic equation and a graph, or an alphabetic script and an ideogram? Are we misled by the spatial analogies concealed in so many of the words, *e.g.* pattern, form and εἶδος, by which we try to describe conceptual symbols? The fact that symbols are arranged in relation to other symbols in an order of "before and after" tempts us to think of the relation of implication between them in spatialized terms.

An example of an analogical use of the concept of "logical space" is Wittgenstein's statement of the relation between a proposition and what it symbolizes. Wittgenstein asks what a sentence can have in common with a fact in order that it may symbolize it, and answers that it must exhibit the same form of representation. This form is not what the sentence *says*, but is *exhibited* in the way its elements are combined (hence his famous saying that what cannot be said can be shown). The meaning of this can best be seen in the case of a literally spatial symbol such as a picture or a map. The "sense" of the picture or map is the way in which its elements are combined, and it symbolizes the fact if the elements of the fact are combined in a similar structure. So "The form of representation is the possibility that the things are combined with one another as are the elements of the picture".[1]

[1] *Tractatus Logico-Philosophicus*, 2. 151 (London, 1922).

Ramsey, reviewing Wittgenstein in *Mind* (1923),[1] interprets this as meaning " the things with which the elements of the picture are co-ordinated by the representing relation are of such types that they can be combined in the same way as the elements of the picture ". The elements in the situation or fact symbolized must be able to be combined in the way in which are the elements in the picture. Does this enable the conception to be extended beyond actually spatial projections, *e.g.* maps or mechanical models, to non-spatial expressions such as equations or propositions, in which the position of elements may be transposed (*e.g.* by conversion or obversion or mathematical operations?). Even if it be said that these operations still preserve the logical structure of the original, the transpositions are only possible because there are kinds of symbolism which name, but do not represent, the relations symbolized. But must all symbols to be valid in some way reproduce the structure of that which they symbolize, *i.e.* be " analogies " in the root sense of a proportionate structure exhibited in different terms?

This principle seems fruitful in forms of spatialized symbolic representation or projections, such as maps, Kekulé's benzene ring, graphs, etc. However conventional the mode and abstract the schematism, it exhibits in abstract and conventional terms an important structural identity with the process symbolized; as in (1) a graph of the path of a projectile, and (2) the benzene ring.

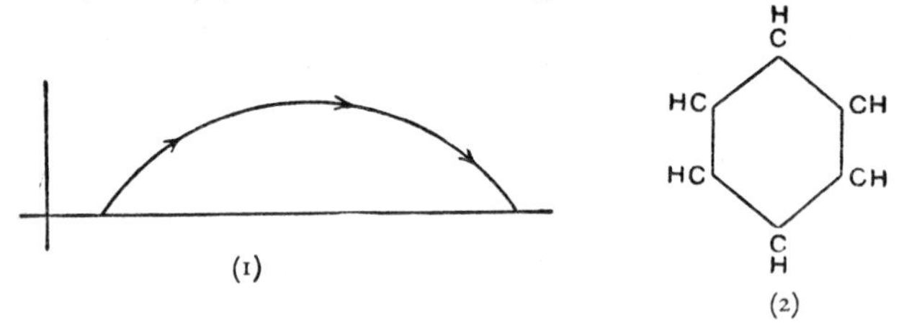

These are *projections* — *i.e.* they exhibit in two-dimensional form a certain systematic correspondence to the structure of that which they symbolize. If there is a distortion of

[1] Reprinted in *Foundations of Mathematics*, pp. 270 *sq.* (London, 1931).

structure, it is a systematic distortion made deliberately and reckoned with in interpreting the projection (as in maps of the world on " Mercator's projection ").

But can the principle of " identity of structure " be applied to non-pictorial symbols (*e.g.* the equation of a curve)? Here we need the notion of conventional signs rather than projections. There is some systematic relation between the signs and the objects signified, but this is not necessarily a relation of *structural representation*, in however conventional a form. The equation of a curve can be translated into the spatialized projection of a graph, but the equation itself is not thus spatialized. The signs must of course be written in some order, but it rests with the conventions of the symbolism to determine whether or no the spatial order is relevant to their interpretation. Thus in a commutative algebra $x \times y$ can be written as xy and is equivalent in value to yx; in a non-commutative algebra this is not so. The position of the symbols affects the value of the equation not in virtue of their spatial position, but in virtue of the rules of syntax, *i.e.* the rules for the operations of the symbols in the notation. In a sign notation, as distinct from a projection, the order can be rearranged provided we observe the syntactical rules which define the relations in which the signs stand to each other.[1] Hence the advantage of equations over spatialized projections; they can be manipulated until we can get them arranged in the form in which we can best deal with them.

So also in language. The order in the sentence in which the words symbolizing relations between objects occur is not essential to symbolizing those relations. The order is accidental to the grammatical rules of the language, which determine what are nominatives, accusatives, etc. In an uninflected language this may be shown by position; in an inflected language it is shown by declension. The signifying of other relations depends largely on the use of prepositional words. So we can say " The dog lies in the

[1] Is this what is meant by " logical space "? If so, it can only be an analogical expression.

manger ": and " In the manger lies the dog ", or even " Lies the dog the manger within "; and mean the same proposition. The logical structure of the proposition is not of course to be identified with the grammatical syntax; and it might be held that a logically perfect language should exhibit the structure of that which it symbolized. So Russell at one time advocated that a logical language should be so constructed that the word order of a sentence should always exhibit the spatio-temporal order of the things being talked about. In this case, in the proposition quoted above, would the symbol for " dog " have to lie inside the symbol for " manger "? If so, this would be to reverse the process of development from pictorial scripts and agglomerative words (holophrases) describing whole situations to alphabetic scripts and words which can be brought into different combinations with one another in different contexts.

So we conclude that some symbols can be interpreted as projections, *i.e.* as simplified representations of structure on a reduced scale in a different medium. But others are better interpreted as signs, naming but not depicting relations between objects. Perhaps part of our difficulty in holding firmly to this distinction is that we continually oscillate between " projection " and " sign " without noticing it. Something is supplied in verbal signs and is at once projected as images; something is given in images and then verbalized. Both may work together in an apprehension of meaning; but I should say that, while it may be possible to think by means of signs without projections, it is not possible to think by means of a projection without introducing an element of conventional sign, *e.g.* words or numbers. Conventional signs must be related to each other in some systematic way, but their spatial order need not be the key to the pattern. It might be possible (and this is probably what Wittgenstein means) to say that symbols, set in relations to each other to which their spatial order was not the essential key, might express a meaning the structure of which yet corresponds in *some* way to the structure of the things to which it refers. But in this case Wittgenstein's phrase "logical space" would be used in an avowedly analogical sense, which needs further elucidation.

It would, of course, be much easier to construct an analogical interpretation of the relation between our ideas and reality if we could be sure that this identity of structure obtained. Both Whitehead and the *Gestalt* writers have made a sustained attempt to show that it should be so. But we have seen reason to question whether, even in the case of sense perception, there can strictly be identity of structural pattern between the phenomenological sensa, the physiological events, and the disposition of forces in the energy field beyond the body. The gap between phenomenological conscious experience and the underlying physiological conditions is a wider one than these theories admit. There is a gap, in which a transmutation occurs, of which no satisfactory account has yet been given, between agitations in the cortex and conscious sensations. The sensation depends on the co-ordination of cerebral events, and on muscular and motor reactions of which we are quite unconscious. But it is certainly not a "representation" of these. Nor is it even probable that there is a structural resemblance between the disposition of physiological events and the elements of the sensation which is projected as a perception of the contemporary field. The most we can say with assurance is that the physiological events and their stimuli provide certain differential conditions, as a result of which we perceive one object rather than another. There should therefore be some systematic relation between perceptions and physical and physiological events, a relation of functional dependence of the former on the latter, but no one to one correspondence of pattern or structure. Thus far, but no further, can we go with "isomorphism"; and, moreover, as soon as sensations are used not for merely practical ends, in helping the organism to direct its responses to its environment, but for *theoretic* ends, in interpreting meanings, some element of conventional, non-"isomorphic" symbolism is brought in.

It will not do to speak of mental activity as "decoding

messages" received along the nerve fibres. For one thing, we are quite unconscious of the terminal neural events in the brain. For another thing, in order that messages may be decoded, it is necessary to have some independent knowledge of a systematic kind which provides a key to the code (*e.g.* the order of the letters of the alphabet). But if all our knowledge of the external world is derived from the impulses conveyed along the nerve fibres to the brain, then there is no independent knowledge to provide the key by which these "messages" may be "decoded" into sensations, so the analogy of "decoding" will clearly not do. Hence it is very inviting to give an account of sense perception in purely phenomenological terms, without referring to physiological conditions. Nevertheless, if we are concerned with the problem of how perceptions can give knowledge of a physical world transcending the percipient, we cannot, as far as I can see, avoid trying to describe our experience of what Whitehead has called the "withness of the body". For the embodied mind, the physical body is the instrument of perception, although to the phenomenalist it is but one system of sense data among others. In one sense, the body is but part of the total energy system called the physical world; in another sense it is the nodal point at which the physical world is organized into a particular perspective by percipient activity. From the latter point of view, it is the point of contact between percipient (mental) activity and the energetic activities of the physical world. Hence there is value in Whitehead's description of such an actuality as a "percipient organism" as "bipolar". On the one hand, it is part of the dynamic system of nature, a field of energetic processes of which the cerebro-neural events are terminals. Through these processes it is in continuity with the events of its environment. On the other hand, the pole of mental activity indicates the possibility of originative response, which becomes first selective emphasis, then abstraction, then symbolic construction. (Whether Whitehead is successful in minimizing the difference made when the mental pole emerges as *consciousness* is another story.) The essential point to bear in mind is that the distinction is drawn not between two different entities, body and mind, but between two modes of activity integrated in one actuality. The one, physical prehension, is a direct *rapport* with other actualities; the other, conceptual prehension, is a selective interpretative activity. Mind is thus not a separate entity " decoding " messages received through the bodily nervous system, but an originative form of activity arising out of these physical activities, and through them in contact with the environing physical world. Hence we are not directly conscious of the physiological neural mechanisms, but they form the instrument through which mental activity is orientated to the environing world. But if mental activity is closely integrated (in some way which cannot as yet be satisfactorily defined) with physical functionings, fine distinctions between contents of awareness should be closely correlated with the delicate adjustments and graduations of physiological-neural activity. The " bipolar " embodied mind as a whole is the percipient actuality, orientated in responsive *rapport* with its environment. Hence the " direct " mode of perception will be what we have called the " adverbial " mode; a responsive state of the organism in *rapport* with, or receiving shocks from its environment. These may be accompanied by an integral feeling tone, an " adverbial " mode of perception which is the result of a *response* to the environment. And where there is response some " transmutation " takes place, as Whitehead would say, so that we have not mere conformity of pattern, but some novel experience created out of *how* the organism responds. But when we come to the level of conscious mental activity, something different in kind is happening. Mental activity I believe to be essentially *symbolizing* activity. That is to say, it seeks to understand a thing by expressing or seeing it simplified in terms of another. The world as grasped in sense perception is a highly simplified and selective perspective. Its function in the first instance is practical, to provide the organism with clues for its orientation to its environment. Mental activity takes these patterns, built out of the practical responses of the organism, and uses them for *theoretical* ends. It first redintegrates them though judgments of meaning into a world of objects. But this world of objects remains a simplified and distorted appearance. Mental activity then treats it as a " projection "[1] in which it can study clues concerning objective relations in the external real world. Such conclusions as it reaches can only be indirect and inferential constructions from the perspectives of sense experience. If we consider sense experiences as symbols, in this particular way, namely as able to be treated for theoretical ends as projections in which real relations are cast, they are symbols behind which we cannot go, in the way of directly intuiting the contents into which they should be translated. Our translation can only be an indirect construction out of the " projective " appearances. This means that the relation of our perceptual experience to nature should be thought of neither in terms of direct apprehension nor of likeness, but as a highly simplified and abstract " projection " which nevertheless bears some relation of systematic concomitant variation to the things projected. These variations are mediated through the physical organism which adjusts its responses in *rapport* with changes in the environment with which it forms a field of interrelated energetic activities. But since the organism is responsive to, and not merely reproductive of, these energetic activities, the actual characters of the environing events are not directly known, but indirectly inferred through the character of its sensory responses. This means that we must admit what Whitehead would call a " bifurcation of nature " at least as between our direct sensory responses to external events, and the indirect inferences as to the characters of those events

[1] I am using " projection " here, as above, not in the sense in which psychologists speak of " projecting " our ideas on the world, but in the sense of a highly simplified symbolic representation in a distorting medium (as in " the world on Mercator's projection ").

which we build up from those responses. Whitehead's attempt to avoid " bifurcation ", and his low estimate of the importance of consciousness, has led him to underestimate the extent to which mental activity is concerned with indirect constructions as well as with emphasis and elimination.

Conscious thought goes beyond perception and attempts to translate a multiplicity of data into some definite form. The responsive activities of the organism provide data which are somehow transmuted into conscious perceptions; perceptions, which are intermittent and fragmentary, provide data which are translated by conscious thought into exact hypothetical constructions. At each level we have a transmutation into a new form of data provided in the underlying level. The transmutation means that data are interpreted in a form which is increasingly more definite, abstract and general. But the conceptual activity which interprets in symbolic form is dependent on data supplied through the underlying mode of activity. These, as we saw in the last chapter, are *data* for inferential activity; they are not merely rudimentary stages of inferential activity. Whitehead's insistence that perception involves the integration of two modes of activity has the great merit of emphasizing this.

But his calling the direct and primitive mode of perception " causal efficacy " is not altogether happy. It suggests that he is simply giving us a form of the so-called " causal theory of perception ", the difficulties of which we noticed in the last chapter.[1] But we saw there that there is a way of taking the theory which need not assert that " material objects " are causes of our mental perceptions but only that certain external events are the differential conditions for our perceiving one thing rather than another. It may be that if we express this by speaking of " cause ", and extend the notion of cause to processes where it cannot be interpreted in terms of possible actions on our part, we are guilty of an " animistic projection ". Indeed if we

[1] Cf. *supra*, p. 23.

confine ourselves to a purely phenomenalist account of perception, any assumption concerning an external world would be an animistic projection, since on this view sense data are subjective states. But the comparison with animism is perhaps instructive. For anthropological critics of animism say that its picture of the primitive philosopher is altogether too sophisticated. He does not start from consciousness of the self and its powers, and then project them on to an external world, but he starts from a sense of the continuity of his functions and activities with those of an environing world; a feeling of *rapport* or of uneasiness. This vague sense of interpenetrating and interrelated powers, making themselves felt, for instance, in the rhythmical periods of nature in the seasons, the weather and of animal and vegetable life, is prior to " personification ", even of oneself as a subject. As conscious thought develops these vague surrounding potencies are endowed with form and thereby " objectified ", and at the same time man comes to a consciousness of himself as a distinct subject over against them. But the primary stage is not one of " self-consciousness ". There is no sharp differentiation between " I ", " you " and " it ", but rather a feeling of a continuity of life assuming various forms.[1] Dr. Marett has called this vague sense of an environing world charged with mysterious powers and activities " pre-animism ". I would suggest that something like this " pre-animistic " stage lies at the basis of all our experience. That is to say, that the framing of the epistemological problem which starts from conscious mental states, and then asks how you can prove the existence of anything beyond them, is a question *mal posée*. If put in this form, there is no escape

[1] Cf. Cassirer, *Philosophie der symbolischen Formen*, vol. iii, p. 84 (Berlin, 1923–1929). " Alles ist mit allem durch unsichtbare Fäden verknüpft; und diese Verknüpfung, diese universelle Sympathie behält selbst einen schwebenden, einen seltsam-unpersönlichen Charakter. ' Es eignet sich, es zeigt sich an, es warnt ' — ohne dass hinter dem allem notwendig ein persönliches Subjekt, ohne dass hinter der Warnung, in klar erkennbarem Umriss, ein Warner stehen müsste. Das Ganze der Wirklichkeit, weit mehr als ein einzelner Teil desselben, bildet vielmehr eben dieses Subjekt."

from phenomenalism, or subjective idealism, since " experience " has been defined in terms of subjective states, and the idea of an object transcending them can only be a pure act of faith or the result of an animistic projection. This holds just as much of the idea of an external object of perception as of the idea of a deity or of other minds.

But if something like a " pre-animistic " stage underlies experience, we do not start from projecting modes of our consciousness, or analogies of our own activities, on to a world beyond us. We start from consciousness of ourselves as arising out of *rapport*, interconnection and participation in processes reaching beyond ourselves. Such feeling is a pre-condition of self-conscious experience. Both Whitehead and Heidegger are trying in their respective ways in their epistemology to go behind the explicit Subject-Object type of thinking and express this basic stage out of which the possibility of thought grows.

Heidegger [1] speaks of " *Sorge* ", " care ", as the basic characteristic of an actual thing (we may recall Whitehead's word " concern "). An actual thing (*Dasein*) is primarily to be described as something which finds itself " thrown " into a world in the midst of others which concern it in varying degrees. Although the final outcome and emphasis of his philosophy is very different from Whitehead's, both Heidegger and Whitehead are starting from an analysis, in terms of organic categories and analogies, of a subject of experience as arising out of a way of feeling its world.

Part of the difficulty of Whitehead's, and no doubt also of Heidegger's, thought (both are egregiously difficult for other reasons) is due to the fact that they are trying to express this basic stage of experience, which, just because it is different from the experiences of explicit conscious awareness, is vague and resists exact expression. They have to try and describe it in organic analogies, since it is primarily concerned with a mode of feeling; and then, in my opinion not altogether successfully, they try to extend the categories drawn from these organic analogies upwards

[1] Cf. *Sein und Zeit* (4. Auflage, Halle, 1935).

and downwards, to the worlds of conscious thought and of the inorganic.

The view we shall develop in the subsequent chapters, where different forms of thought and experience come under consideration, is that knowledge is only possible where there is some actual situation of relatedness together with conscious awareness of relationship. The objection to saying that conceptual activity is dependent on non-conceptual relationships is presumably that this seems to commit us to thinking of material objects as acting on mind and " causing " its perceptions. But the reader will note that we have described the distinction not in terms of two distinct orders of mind and matter, but in terms of two types of activity exercised by a " bipolar " organism; and that we have not spoken of physical objects as causes of perceptions, but described perceptions as arising through an integration of two types of activity in an organism which is related dynamically to its environment. This relatedness provides the direct element, and furnishes " data " as distinct from inferences. " Transcendent " then should be taken to mean that which exists in its own right beyond our categories of thought and explanation; but not necessarily that which is entirely outside our experience in all its modes. For our basic experience may be constituted by a responsive relation to, or even interpenetration with, " transcendent " events and objects. I say " interpenetration ", since, if we can follow Whitehead in his denial of what he calls " simple location ", to speak of an object as " beyond " us in any absolute local sense would be incorrect. If " simple location " be denied, everything which exists is a modification of the conditions of space-time throughout its whole extent. But there may be a central focal region of activity which we call " where the thing is ". (We may think of the analogy of waves spreading out in all directions from a central region of disturbance.) Hence everything which exists could be said in a sense to occupy the whole spatio-temporal continuum, and its structure would accordingly be modified by that of the other occupants. We should thus have a dynamic field of activities modifying each other; each of them is associated with a certain focal centre, which in this case we call the percipient organism.

In the case of sense perception, the ways of responding through the functioning of the bodily organism have become relatively stabilized, and the forms of interpretation derived therefrom are relatively involuntary and uniform (though it is interesting to speculate as to what the world would look like organized according to the interpretative forms of a different kind of consciousness; or if our sense organs were selective receptors responsive to wave-lengths of different frequencies from those to which they are in fact receptive). But when we turn to other types of interpretative activity expressed through symbolic forms, such as art, religion and the creation of metaphysical theories, the scope for the form-creating powers of thought and imagination is far greater, and the ways in which they may be guided by actual relations to what is other than ourselves are more difficult to discern.

CHAPTER IV

REALISM, IDEALISM AND ANALOGY IN THE INTERPRETATION OF SCIENTIFIC THOUGHT

We are now in a position to examine the question of the relation between the empirical and the transcendent and ask in what senses the main forms of human thought — science, religion, history, philosophy — claim to be true of reality beyond our experience. Our examination of the nature of perceptual experience has shown that such experience, when used for theoretic ends, demands both a conceptual activity which orders and interprets in symbolic forms, and also a non-conceptual activity of response to interrelated energetic activities. We have also seen that we can hardly venture to go so far as to assert identity of pattern or structure between the two.

We shall now ask in what sense, if any, the explanatory concepts of physical science may be taken to make assertions which go beyond phenomenal experience, and in particular ask how realistic an interpretation should be put upon the " models " with the help of which scientific explanation seeks to make its world intelligible.

Working science is incurably realist; and the very suggestion that scientific results can be obtained by the " self-development " of ideas is generally repugnant to the practising experimentalist. Yet *theorists* of physical science find themselves hard put to it to give a plausible account of what exactly the " realist " elements in their study are. The first obvious answer is that they are sense impressions; but to say this is to pass the ball at once to the phenomenalists, unless we can show that a purely phenomenalist account of sense perception breaks down.

The speculative idealist conception of scientific thought as a partial aspect, or phase, in the self-development of philosophical ideas has been discredited among working scientists largely thanks to the unfortunate efforts of some of the 19th-century Hegelian *Naturphilosophen*. In so far as this school produced valuable results, it is arguable that this was due to the introduction of empirical material as well as *a priori* principles. It is questionable whether even in Hegel himself we do in fact find a "self-developing system", from a logical idea stated "abstractly" and partially, and then developed by a process of inner necessity. Where Hegel's own work was most fruitful, as in the *Phenomenology*, he was, in fact, starting from the materials supplied by practical life, history and institutions, and showing how these could be interpreted by the use of certain organizing ideas. Where he was least successful was in the *Philosophy of Nature*, where the free use of analogies based on the principle of a necessary movement from Thesis-Antithesis to Synthesis produced some surprising results. A passage on the moon is quoted by Sidgwick:[1] "The moon is the waterless crystal which seeks to complete itself by means of our sea, to quench the thirst of its arid rigidity, and therefore produces ebb and flow". He also made free use of the notion of *Wahlverwandtschaften*, the elective affinities of chemical elements seeking union with their opposites. Meyerson[2] has collected references to a series of such misfortunes in the *Naturphilosophie*, such as Hegel's argument for the necessity of a void in the planetary system between Mars and Jupiter, at the very moment when Piazzi discovered the first minor planet, Ceres.[3]

But there are more powerful accounts of scientific theory in idealist terms, given by Cassirer[4] and Eddington,[5] who understand (as Hegel did not) the rôle played by mathematical thinking. These writers draw their strength

[1] *Philosophy, its Scope and Relations*, p. 89. The passage comes from Hegel, *Werke*, VII. Bd. p. 151 (Duncker u. Humblot, Berlin, 1847).

[2] *Identity and Reality*, English translation, pp. 398-399 (London, 1930).

[3] *De orbitis planetarum* (Jena, 1801).

[4] In *Die Philosophie der symbolischen Formen*.

[5] See especially his *The Nature of the Physical World* (Cambridge, 1928), and *The Philosophy of Physical Science* (Cambridge, 1939).

from their recognition of the difficulty of asserting any realistic correspondence between our forms of thought and objects in themselves. The materials out of which the house of science is built are mathematics and observations based on sense impressions, both of which, it is said, can only be understood in terms of the self-development of symbolic forms.

The first comment which might be made on this is that the conception of the " self-development " of a symbolic form or of an idea calls for elucidation. Does an idea " develop " *itself* except by metaphor, or do *we* develop its implications and see how it can be exemplified in the " matter " of some region of experience? The idealist might answer that what he means by a mind is the medium through which an idea is brought to development; that the more coherently we are thinking, the less do the personal and accidental features of mind intrude, and the more does the logic of the idea itself take command. Nevertheless, unless we attribute some kind of spontaneous life to ideas, I cannot help suspecting that the phrase " self-development " brings in a tacit assumption and ignores the fact that ideas are in fact developed through the mental activity of thinking subjects, so that the question arises as to how the thinking subject obtains the data from which his thought is developed. And we saw in our second chapter that this was through the exercise of a percipient activity, of whose distinctive character idealism does not give a sufficient account.

But the nerve of the idealist position consists in holding (*a*) that reality is the self-development of thought, and (*b*) that therefore everything in principle is permeable by thought, and (*c*) that the goal of thought would be the understanding of an Absolute Idea whose differentiations showed the whole of experience as a single articulated system. Such an idea would be the supreme, perhaps in the end the only true, instance of a " concrete universal ". The notion of the " concrete universal " is the means by which idealism tries to overcome the cleavage between ideas and reality. It is distinguished from the abstract universal, which is a general name given to a class characteristic, *e.g.* red or round, which is said to be exemplified in a number of instances. This latter presupposes that we can find instances of the class, in the description of each of which enters a pellet of identical meaning. This is only possible if things are susceptible of classification in these terms, and the idealist would contend that such classification is always abstract and pragmatic, and ignores individual variation. In the study of "concrete" phenomena, the general terms are not class concepts, but express an idea not exemplified in each instance, but articulated throughout the whole structure of the phenomenon — *e.g.* the Industrial Revolution, the British Commonwealth, Robinson Crusoe, are concrete universals. It might be said that the notion of the abstract generic universal would work at any rate in mathematics, where individual variation is irrelevant; a triangle or square can express the class of all figures possessing a certain common quality. Cassirer, however, whose Neo-Kantianism is a particularly radical form of mathematical idealism, denies this. In fact he makes the doctrine of the concrete universal seem far more plausible in mathematics than its other defenders have succeeded in doing in more "concrete" modes of thought. The traditional doctrine of abstraction holds that generic concepts are arrived at by noticing common properties in objects perceived by sense. But this does not work, he says, for mathematical concepts. These must be interpreted in terms of concrete universals, *i.e.* principles which determine their own variations. "Every mathematical function represents a universal law, which, by virtue of the successive values which the variable can assume, contains within itself all the particular cases for which it holds." So the root idea is that of *function*, the law giving form to the series.[1]

This is plausible in mathematics because here we are

[1] *Substanz-Begriff und Funktionsbegriff*, English translation, *Substance and Function*, p. 21 (Chicago, 1923).

not concerned with empirical elements, but with the development of an idea defining a functional relationship. So Cassirer criticizes the "class" theory of numbers. According to this theory we write under a "number" all the manifolds for which there exists a relation of equivalence, or of one to one co-ordination. A number is therefore defined as the class of all classes equal to a given class. But he argues that the specific meaning of 4 or 7 could never be reached as a result of putting together any number of groups with 4 or 7 members; the individual groups must first be determined as ordered sequences of elements (*i.e.* by the ordinal theory, according to which what a number is depends on its place in the system). What intellectual motive would there be to relate such dissimilar groups as that of the moons in Jupiter with that of the seasons of the year, or the pins in a group of nine-pins with the Muses, unless you had the idea of number first to suggest comparing them? So number is a relational concept, *i.e.* you start from a notion of a relation between symbols in a certain form of serial order; it is not a generic concept, arrived at by abstracting the common element from *e.g.* all classes with 4 members. This relational view has the advantage that according to it negative, irrational and transfinite numbers are not additions to the series of natural numbers, but grow out of the continuous unfolding of the fundamental logical function by which the system is generated; *e.g.* Gauss' negative and imaginary numbers have obviously no correlate in experience. So we have an ordered series defined by a law, and this is in no sense a copy or representation of "things". Hence the puzzle why complex mathematical concepts which possess no possibility of direct sensuous representation are continually used in the constructions of physics and mechanics. Physical concepts, *e.g.* the atom or ether, must disclaim any perceptible or pictorial content. They are intellectual schemata by means of which relations between perceptions can be represented. To call them "conventions" is to recognize that thought does not proceed merely imitatively, but that it has its own spontaneity, which, however, is not unrestrained, but guided by the criterion of the " law " of the systematic concept itself.

Cassirer brings out this essentially *non-representative* character of mathematical symbolism, and claims that in this it is the most highly developed example of what the nature of thought should be in so far as it is *scientific*. In his *Philosophie der symbolischen Formen* he is concerned with the development of the forms of speech, and traces three stages: (1) the Representative stage, when words and signs are looked on as things having power in themselves; a kind of magical duplicate of the things they represent, having the potency of the things themselves. (2) The Analogical stage, in which words are not duplicates of things, but held in some way to be structural models of things. (3) The Symbolic stage, in which there is no natural connection or " model " relation between word and meaning. In mathematics we are able to get rid of the " thing " concept altogether. We are not concerned with the meaning of symbols at all, but with the laws according to which series of relations can be developed. Mathematical thinking is therefore the perfect type of scientific thinking; and in so far as we still use concepts of " thing " and " cause ", we are embodying relics of mythical thinking. We have here a complete development of idealism.[1] We must find the discipline and criteria of our symbols through laws produced by the mind's own spontaneity, and not in some conformity with " things ". For the further we go in scientific thought, the more impossible it becomes to maintain the concept of the " thing " apart from a system of symbols. Hence it is more and more displaced by the concept of " law ". We can never compare the experience

[1] I am here and throughout this discussion understanding by idealism *epistemological* idealism (of which Professor Blanshard's *The Nature of Thought* is a distinguished contemporary representative). There are, of course, forms of ontological idealism, which combine a different epistemology with an assertion of the metaphysical supremacy of " spiritual values ". But these are, to my mind, better considered as forms of spiritual realism.

of things with things themselves apart from experience, but we can replace a narrow aspect of experience by a broader. Each later member of the series is then necessarily connected with the earlier ones in so far as it answers a question latent in them. We have therefore a perpetually self-renewing process with relative stopping points, and these define the concept of objectivity at any time, *i.e.* it is what the state of thought at the time obliges us to believe. We cannot answer the question as to the objectivity of experience in general, but only discriminate between ways in which we are and are not obliged to think in the different bits and stages.

This recalls the view set forward by Collingwood in his *Essay on Metaphysics*; indeed one might look on that book as a complete calling of the bluff of idealist metaphysics, if " metaphysics " is used in the sense of a system of ideas claiming ontological truth. Instead, " metaphysics " becomes the discovery of " absolute presuppositions ", that is to say, the final assumptions presupposed by scientific thought at any time. We cannot ask whether these presuppositions are true or false; we can only discover whether they are in fact presupposed. If they are presupposed, they are not answers to questions (relative presuppositions), but the basic assumptions which enable scientific thought at any time to ask the relevant questions (*e.g.* in Newtonian science some events have causes, in Kantian all events have causes, in modern physics no events have causes). We can't ask which of these statements is *true*; we can only see that at each stage of civilized scientific thought certain absolute presuppositions are made, and they enable thought at that stage to ask its questions and get on with its job. I have called this a calling of the bluff of idealist " metaphysics " if metaphysics is concerned with the theory of thought and reality. Idealism describes the movement of a system of thought; and Hegelian idealists assume the real *is* the self-realization of an absolute idea in the movement of the system of thought. The presupposition was laid down by Parmenides: " *to be is to be thought* ". From

Parmenides to Hegel we have a succession of development; in *principle*, though not in actual execution, Hegel's Logic says the final word on this way of thinking. But both Cassirer and Collingwood might be described as radical idealists, who see that in fact all we are left with is the developing system of thought itself. We cannot have a metaphysics which asks whether ideas expressed in this system are true " of reality ". There is no relation between the system of thought and a reality outside it. Our criterion of objectivity must be found within the system itself; and this criterion is not that of truth and falsehood (if truth and falsehood have to do with a relation of ideas to some reality which is not ideas), but of whether certain assumptions are necessarily made at certain stages in order to make possible the development of the dialectical process of the system of thought itself. The criterion is therefore set by the internal requirements of the process. " Each later member of the series is then necessarily connected with the earlier ones, in so far as it answers a question latent in them." [1] And, we may add, in so far as it gives rise to further questions which give the process its incentive to go forward to the next stage (as with a fruitful piece of research). This means that the criterion which disciplines the process is internal to the process itself — a coherence theory, interpreted dynamically, in terms of the requirements of a developing system; not statically, as the fitting together of elements in an already existing pattern (like a jig-saw puzzle). " Truth " here must mean that answer to a question which the evidence at our disposal obliges us to give. The strength of this coherence theory is, as we have seen, that it recognizes that in thought we cannot get outside the boundaries of experience, and compare ideas with things in themselves, or " real " physical objects in themselves. We can only be aware of anything in so far as we know it through the interpretative forms of our experience. So, as Cassirer says, why not throw over the " thing " concept as a piece of myth thinking, and be left

[1] Cassirer, *Substance and Function*, p. 278.

with the interpretative and symbolic forms, and the laws of their development? This is particularly tempting when we recognize that we have no warrant for supposing any relation of representation or likeness between our symbolic forms and things in themselves. To think that there should be such a relation is, Cassirer holds, to show that one is still thinking in the primitive mode of myth-consciousness.

I have said that idealism is based on the assumption that there is nothing in principle not permeable by the categories of thought, as thought is developed to greater clarity and comprehensiveness. In these radical forms of idealism, metaphysics is concerned with nothing outside the categories of thought, in the sense that what we are always trying to do is to bring a vague or confused bit of experience (informed by vague and confused thinking) into greater clarity and coherent relationship with other experience.[1] Truth then must be sought in the coherence of an idea with other ideas, whereby it becomes a more developed systematic idea. As a *test* of truth, it is hard to controvert this, because (1) we can never know things in themselves apart from interpretative ideas, and therefore we can only compare one experience-informed-by-idea with another experience-informed-by-idea; (2) even if there be things in themselves, if the relation of idea to thing is not that of copy or representation, in what sense can an idea be said to " correspond " with a thing? [2]

[1] Cf. B. Blanshard, *The Nature of Thought*, vol. i, p. 518, quoting from Royce, *The World and the Individual*: " In seeking its object, any idea whatever seeks absolutely nothing but its own explicit, and, in the end, complete, determination as this conscious purpose, embodied in this one way. The complete content of the idea's own purpose is the only object of which the idea can ever take note. This alone is the Other that is sought." " The idea is a will seeking its own determination. It is nothing else." " To say ' my idea has reference to a real Being ' is to say ' My idea imperfectly expresses, in my present consciousness, an intention, a meaning, a purpose; and just this specific meaning is carried out, is fulfilled, is expressed, by my object '."

[2] When we say that in testing by experiment we see that a theory " corresponds " with a fact, what we really mean is that the proposition

It looks, therefore, as though, as a *test* of truth, thinking was bound to proceed on the coherence theory.

But need the test of truth necessarily be the definition of truth? If we cannot show any means of establishing a relation of correspondence between ideas and things, does that mean that the *definition* of truth is found in the coherent relation of ideas to other ideas? This may be the way in which thinking proceeds, but must we *define* truth as that which we are obliged to think, relatively to the evidence at our disposal, even though admittedly this is the criterion we must follow in trying to reach it. But is the *criterion* of truth necessarily the *definition* of truth? On the radical idealist view, is it not the case, as Collingwood shows, that we cannot really ask whether absolute presuppositions are *true*, but only whether they are in fact presupposed in accordance with the necessities of thought at any given stage; and in the case of *propositions* also, it would look as though " truth " could only mean the answers to questions which we are obliged to give relative to the advance of thought and the evidence at our disposal? As a *criterion* this is surely how we must and do proceed; and it might show greater integrity in a thinker to entertain a false theory because the evidence at his disposal pointed convincingly to it (" false " here meaning that further evidence turning up later obliged him to correct it in a way he could not have foreseen at the time), than to entertain a true theory in defiance of evidence or by good luck. (There are, of course, occasions when a thinker may trust a strong instinct in defiance of the explicit evidence at his disposal. This is a kind of intellectual daring which is occasionally justified. In these cases the " hunch " probably represents a sense for implicit evidence which cannot yet be made articulate.)

describing by hypothesis what *ought* to happen agrees with the proposition describing what is perceived to happen (cf. L. A. Reid, *Knowledge and Truth*, p. 203 [London, 1923]). The proposition cannot be seen to correspond to something which is not a proposition. But the question why we attach particular weight to propositions describing perception has been considered in our preceding chapters.

But will coherence also do as a definition of truth? Or are realist theories right in so far as they maintain that truth itself must be defined in terms of some kind of relation of ideas not to other ideas, but to "reality"?[1] Yet we have seen in the last chapter that we cannot compare ideas with what is entirely other than ideas, since we can only be aware of phenomenal fact within experience. And is phenomenal fact "reality"? A correspondence theory of the relation of ideas to reality would seem to postulate some representative or copying character in symbols and ideas. And once we recognize that symbols are not representative copies of that to which they refer, it is very difficult to find a plausible way of stating what the truth relation between symbol and "reality" consists in. Hence Cassirer maintains that the development from mythical to scientific thought consists essentially in the transition from the "thing" concept, in which some realistic relation is held to obtain between our ideas and that to which they refer, to the concept of "function" in which we are left simply with the law defining the series of symbolic relations and operations. Eddington has approached still nearer to this position in his more recent work. In the *Philosophy of Physical Science* he maintains that the fundamental laws of nature and constants of physical science can be wholly derived from epistemological considerations, *i.e.* from the subjective requirements of the nature of the human mind. This results, he holds, from the following considerations:

(1) The use of the notion of probability, as in wave mechanics, emphasizes that it is *concepts* with which we are treating, not entities, since probability is an attribute not of events but of our knowledge. (We may reflect in passing how salutary it would be if all those who like to talk in a mystifying manner about things, including our-

[1] I think that Bradley was by far the greatest of the British idealists and that part of his greatness lay in his scepticism as to the identity of "truth", as a coherent system of ideas, with "reality", and his recognition that any system of ideas can only be an "appearance"; while at the same time seeing that correspondence with phenomenal fact will not do as a description of truth.

selves, being " waves of probability " would keep this distinction in mind.[1])

(2) The accepted practice in introducing new physical quantities is to define these in terms of the operations and calculations of which they are the result. (Bridgman has given a clear statement of this in *The Logic of Modern Physics*.)

This, Eddington holds, implies essential reference to our sensory and mental apparatus; and the results depend on the structure of the mental apparatus with which we order our sensations. So " The physical universe is a structure. Of the *x* of which it is the structure, we only know that *x* includes sensations in consciousness. To the question: What is *x* when it is not a sensation in any consciousness known to us? The right answer is probably that the question is a meaningless one — that a structure does not necessarily imply an *x* of which it is the structure."[2] And, more precisely, Eddington calls the " physical event " " the structural concept of that of which the sensation is the general concept ".[3] Knowledge of the physical world is then defined as the knowledge of the group structures of the whole body of interrelated actual and possible sensations. Eddington's exposition of the theory of " group structure " is too technical for a layman to follow. It describes operations which can be specified by purely formal properties, without any need for us to know anything about the intrinsic nature of the operations or the entities on which they are performed.

Eddington contends that not only fundamental laws of nature, but also the numerical value of constants, are derivable from the epistemological character of our own intellectual tools. This seems a large order, especially when we find that the number of particles in the universe ($2 \times 136 \times 2^{256}$) is among the constants and so derivable.[4] But as

[1] There are of course views which maintain that probability is an attribute of events and not of knowledge. But I confess that I cannot see what they mean.

[2] *Op. cit.* p. 151. [3] *Op. cit.* p. 149. [4] *Op. cit.* pp. 170-177.

Professor Broad has said, in a critical notice in *Philosophy* (July, 1940) to which I am much indebted, until Eddington has given his arguments in much greater detail, and until they have been scrutinized by a critic of comparable mathematical knowledge, philosophers can only treat them with caution.

In the meantime we may take a look at some of the loop-holes which Eddington himself indicates, and see whether they offer any escape from thoroughgoing idealism. " Special facts ", he says, are not deducible from the fundamental laws which depend on epistemological considerations. A universe with the same fundamental laws could contain a different set of special facts. (Such a special fact might be the number of inhabitants in Great Britain at the present time.) But if any *prima facie* special fact turns out to follow from the fundamental theory of the system, it must be regarded as part of the laws of nature. So the number of particles in the universe might have been regarded as a contingent fact, *i.e.* a universe with the same fundamental laws could have contained a different number of particles. But Eddington claims that the number of particles must follow from the total number of independent quadruple wave functions, so that " a universe cannot be made with a different number of elementary particles — consistently with the scheme of definitions by which the ' number of particles ' is assigned to a system in wave-mechanics ".[1]

Presumably as physics advances it aims at reducing more and more *prima facie* " special facts ", particular causal sequences, into correlations of laws expressed mathematically. But Eddington suggests that there is one property of the physical world which cannot be derivable from our intellectual symbolisms. This is the irreversible character of the process of entropy (a physical concept), and the irreversible character of a process of becoming (an immediate experience). " It is clearly not sufficient that the change in the random element of the world should

[1] *Op. cit.* p. 65.

deliver an impulse at the end of a nerve, leaving the mind to create in response to this stimulus the fancy that it is turning the reel of a cinematograph. Unless we have been altogether misreading the significance of the world outside us — by interpreting it in terms of evolution and progress, instead of a static extension — we must regard the feeling of 'becoming' as (in some respects at least) a true mental insight into the physical condition which determines it. . . . If there is any experience in which this mystery of mental recognition can be interpreted as *insight* rather than *image-building*, it should be the experience of 'becoming'."[1] The counterpart of this feeling of becoming in the world of scientific "laws" is entropy change — a non-reversible process towards increasing randomness. What is shuffled cannot get unshuffled. Yet the feeling of becoming, in the cases where "becoming" takes the form of a process of growth, is the feeling of a process tending towards greater definiteness and integration. How is this correlated with entropy change? Eddington does not, as far as I know, deal with this problem. But it has been stated by Whitehead in some bafflingly compressed passages where he suggests a "counter tendency" in nature.[2]

But at this point our concern is not with the nature of these processes of becoming, but solely with Eddington's recognition that we do have this immediate experience of becoming, as an irreversible process of some sort; and that this is distinct from the structure of symbolic forms which we call our knowledge of the physical world. I should like to recall the contention in my discussion of perception and thought, that we have experience of certain processes going on, as forms of activity, and that these underlie our symbolic modes of conceptual interpretation. Similarly experience of the one way character of "Time's Arrow" is distinct from mathematically formulated pro-

[1] *The Nature of the Physical World*, p. 89.

[2] E.g. *Religion in the Making*, p. 144 (Cambridge, 1927): "The universe shows us two aspects: on one side it is physically wasting, on the other side it is spiritually ascending"; and cf. *The Function of Reason*, p. 72 (Princeton, 1929).

cesses of measurement by clock time, all of which are theoretically reversible.

M. Meyerson has pointed out the significance of the irreversible character of entropy for an epistemology of science. The ideal of scientific explanation is, he says, to reduce differences to apparent differences of underlying identities, and show every process as symmetrical. (Hence the Cartesian ideal of a geometrical science.) From this point of view Carnot's principle of the irreversible character of entropy is an irrationality. There seems to be no reason why heat cannot be communicated from a less warm to a more warm body, but as a fact of observation we find that it is so, and the whole of engineering science is based upon it.[1]

The contention that scientific explanation seeks identities is corroborated by Eddington, who, however, traces it to "a very elementary and instinctive habit of thought which has unconsciously directed the course of scientific development. Briefly, it is the habit of thought which regards variety always as a challenge to further analysis; so that the *ultimate* end-product of analysis can only be sameness. . . . The sameness of the ultimate entities of the physical universe is a foreseeable consequence of forcing our knowledge into this form of thought. . . . Why does a proton differ from an electron? The answer suggested by relativity theory is that they are actually similar units of structure, and the difference arises in their relations to the general distribution of matter in the universe. The one is related right-handedly and the other left-handedly".[2]

The advantage of reducing qualitative to quantitative differences, or differences in position of identical units, is that they can then be translated into and dealt with in mathematical terms, which are "the language of science". Hence the plausibility of Cassirer's, and, we may add, Eddington's form of idealism, which Meyerson calls "panmathematicism". But Meyerson has been a chemist,

[1] Cf. *Explication dans les sciences*, pp. 205 *sq.* (Paris, 1927).
[2] *The Philosophy of Physical Science*, pp. 123-124.

and draws his illustrations from a wide range of the sciences, not, as do Cassirer and Eddington, almost entirely from mathematical physics. Hence he is acutely aware of a number of elements of science not reducible to the mathematical ideal of symmetrical intelligibility. These elements in nature are "given" to us; they cannot be deduced from, or reduced to, intelligible necessity. Carnot's principle of entropy is one; so perhaps is the "organization" of organisms in biology. Science as explanatory seeks to reduce things further and further to mathematical order; yet the presence of these "surds" in nature prevents it from being presented as a through and through intelligible mechanism. Science has therefore to be both mathematical and empirical. As mathematical, it is able to make predictions, and show that reason can to some extent penetrate nature. Yet it also comes up against elements which cannot be entirely rationalized but have to be described. Nature seems therefore both to yield to our reason and to resist it.

The criticism might be made (in fact it has been made by Professor Muirhead in his introduction to the English translation of Meyerson's *Identity and Reality* in the "Library of Philosophy") that this description of science as empirical and as seeking identities depends on the logical view of propositions as either analytic or empirical, whereas the Hegelian Logic of "identity in difference" might be able to surmount this distinction. The importance of recognizing that the Hegelian Logic depends on rejecting the logic of identity and of contradiction and on maintaining that all opposition is contrary opposition has been stressed by Mr. Church in his recent book on *Bradley's Dialectic*. Mr. Church also says that whether in the end we agree with the idealist logic or not will turn on whether we can in fact hold that there are no mere identities, and that all apparently contradictory opposition can be shown to be contrary opposition. But I consider that Meyerson has shown convincingly that the logic with which *physical science* works is that of identity, however much light the idealist logic may throw on the development of ideas in *history* or in a philosophical movement of thought. It is perhaps significant that neo-idealists such as Croce and Collingwood can only allow science to be more than " practical ", or an assertion of " abstract universals ", by turning it into a kind of history. But nevertheless science can only advance by the use of elaborate mathemathical techniques, and in this it differs radically from history. There seems no reason why rational explanation should not find different logical methods appropriate in different subject matters. (It has been suggested,[1] for instance, that possibly the Hegelian dialectic may describe a way in which ideas come to birth in creative thinking; while the logic of identity is concerned with the expository thought which gives an orderly form to the results of the process.)

But if we say that the proper logic of science is the logic of mathematical methods, we shall be left, as Meyerson shows, with elements, such as the one-way character of becoming, which are not wholly reducible to our logic. On the other hand, we have questioned whether the idealist logic is successful in showing that all empirical elements can in principle be completely exhibited as logical relations. Idealism in practice finds its empirical material to hand, and shows how certain organizing ideas can order it. The irreversible character of the process of becoming would not present a problem to idealist logic, since its key notion of the " self-development " of an idea is also an irreversible process. This is why idealist ideas have found organic and evolutionary ideas congenial company. But we have questioned whether, without the extraneous introduction of empirical material to be ordered and interpreted, there is in fact an inevitable process of self-development, *e.g.* from " Being " through " Essence " to the Absolute Idea. McTaggart was the most rigorous of the English idealists in following a strictly deductive method, but even he had to introduce one empirical premise at the outset (that " something exists "), and perhaps his most permanently interesting work may prove to be those parts

[1] By Ushenko, *The Problems of Logic*, p. 148 (London, 1941).

of the second volume of *The Nature of Existence*, where he suggests possible characteristics of relations between selves which are drawn from admittedly empirical considerations.

We must therefore admit empirical elements which cannot be exhaustively presented in terms of logical relations; and we have also said that our conceptual activity of interpretation in the symbolic forms of logic arise out of a wider experience of non-conceptual processes such as the experience of becoming. We have suggested also that these experiences have the character of responsive activities —*i.e.* responses to other interrelated processes. We are not making any assertions or assumptions about the intrinsic character of these processes, whether they are material or spiritual or both. We are only recognizing that they are the encompassing conditions within which conceptual activity takes place. We must now ask whether our interpretations into the symbolic forms of thought used by physical science enable us to say anything significant about the nature of these conditions.

We have already referred to Cassirer's distinction of three stages in the development of thought. The first is the mimetic stage, in which words and other symbols are looked on as duplicates of things, having in some way something of the potencies of the things themselves; the second is the analogical state; and the third is the symbolic stage, where we recognize that there is no " natural " meaning of symbols, but the meaning depends entirely on the ways in which they can be brought into intelligible relations with other symbols in a structural form. Cassirer has very little to say about the second, the " analogical " stage, compared with his immensely detailed treatment of the mimetic and symbolic stages. But it represents, presumably, a half-way house between " mythological " thinking and " scientific " thinking, in his sense of the term. In this half-way stage, the notions of " thing " and " cause " are hypostatized; they are analogies of our own ideas, thought of as having some independent existence. But in the third and final stage these last remnants of mythology are expunged, and we no longer think in terms of "things" and "causes" but of mathematically intelligible laws. I have already considered in what sense the notion of "cause" as distinct from law may be a legitimate and necessary one.[1] I shall now, even at the cost of preserving relics of mythology, maintain that we also need to preserve the notion of "things". We need not assume any view as to the intrinsic nature of a "thing". But we need the concept, or something like it, as a testimony to the conviction that scientific thinking is concerned with something besides a nexus of logical relations. It is concerned with seeing how conceptual interpretations arise out of a background of "responsive" activities. The "things" to which these activities are responsive transcend those activities. In their intrinsic nature they may be "material objects", "other minds", "God", or some further possibility we have not yet thought of. But we can say that their impingement on us produces certain types of responsive activity. Can we say anything significant about them from considering the types of response? Here it seems that we should explore further the possibilities of the second type of thought, the analogical, to which, as I have said, Cassirer gives comparatively scanty attention. We generally find that "analogical" thinking is dismissed very shortly by idealist writers as a relic of a primitive state of mind, except in so far as it suggests hypotheses, which, when tested and incorporated, are no longer mere analogies.[2] But if we say that we need to keep the concept of "things" as a recognition of processes transcending our conceptual forms; and if we also allow that we have no direct knowledge of the intrinsic nature of these processes, we shall have to ask whether we are not forced to try to conceive of them in concepts drawn by analogy from interpretations of experience. If we could say that our perceptual experience is some sort of "projection" of events in the external world, preserving their proportionate structure, we should have

[1] See *supra*, p. 24.

[2] Cf., for instance, Blanshard, *The Nature of Thought*, vol. ii, pp. 148 *sq.*

all we want for analogical knowledge at least of their relationships. But we have seen that we cannot say with assurance that this is so; the most we can say with assurance is that our perceptual experience, if we take all possible precautions for checking and correcting it, is a systematic distortion preserving some sort of concomitant variation with its differential conditions in the external world. But we cannot be sure that this correlation is as straightforward as a repetition of structure. Nevertheless, although even our perceptions, and still more the forms of our thinking, may not be apprehensive of the structure of things in any literal sense, and although we find empirical "given" elements not thoroughly reducible to our logical categories, yet the fact that science does continue to make correlations of experiences which are borne out by future experience indicates some sort of *rapport* between our mental processes and the nature of the world which is shaping our experience. Hence we feel justified in selecting concepts which illustrate relations within rationally connected experience, and in using them analogically to describe indirectly the ways in which "things" may be connected in the external world. The "models" of physical science are analogies of this kind. They are hypotheses symbolizing a possible way in which things may be connected, and are drawn from types of relation which seem intelligible to us in some more familiar setting. The value of the analogy lies in its helping us to conceive a possible mode of connection; it must therefore be drawn from some mode of connection which we believe to be intelligible. It may, of course, turn out that we do not really understand the connection from which the analogy is drawn as well as we thought we did. It may even turn out that the connection which had originally to be illustrated by the analogy comes to seem a more intelligible one than that from which the analogy was drawn, so that the tables are turned, and the former becomes an analogy for the description of the latter. "When Maxwell developed the electromagnetic theory by which he explained the properties of light, he thought of a medium through which these waves travelled. This was called the ether. It was supposed to have properties like those of elastic solid bodies. The reason for this choice of a model was that at that time the average man of science had been taught in great detail the theory of elasticity of solid bodies. Thus the magnetic and electric fields could be understood in terms of the familiar elastic properties. At the present time relatively few students are well trained in the theories of elasticity. The situation is thus reversed and to-day we explain the properties of elastic solids in terms of the electrical forces acting between their atoms."[1] The "ether" as a model seems to have fallen on evil days, since Lord Salisbury's famous remark that it was only the missing substantive of the verb "to undulate". Other famous "models", such as the Rutherford-Bohr planetary atom, are now said by some people to be merely conventions, crutches with the help of which our imaginations can better grasp certain mathematical relations, but totally devoid of realistic significance. But, as Miss Stebbing has remarked,[2] perhaps the most pressing need in the philosophy of science at present is to determine the scope of what are called "conventions". It seems as though the more literally minded scientists, such as Rutherford and the pioneers of organic chemistry, are often the people who make headway, rather than the more positivistically minded who dismiss models as "mere conventions". Perhaps this is because first-hand scientific work is usually inspired by some sort of realist faith; it aspires to show not simply mathematical correlations, or correlations of sense impressions, but "how nature works".

Yet its models can hardly be literal representations of "how nature works". They are rather illustrative analogies, drawn from relations which we find intelligible. The outstanding example of what seems to us an intelligible relation is that of mechanism. Hence Lord Kelvin's well-

[1] Dr. J. Langmuir, Presidential Address to the American Association for the Advancement of Science. (*Nature*, March 6th, 1943.)

[2] *Philosophy and the Physicists*, p. 283 (London, 1937).

known saying, that he could only understand a thing if he could make a mechanical model of it. But it looks as if the idea of " mechanism " was a regulative principle, that is to say, a guiding principle of method rather than an explanation in the realistic sense. " Mechanism " is an attempt to exhibit qualitative differences as quantitative differences in the spatio-temporal arrangement of ultimately identical units. If this can be done, apparently complex and diverse phenomena can be explained in terms of simpler elements which are thought to be more intelligible.

But, as Burtt remarks,[1] we must beware of turning a method into a metaphysics. Can we assume that a mechanical model is necessarily a realistic interpretation of nature? It may even be that with the extension of ideas drawn from electro-dynamics, such as that of a field of force, the conception of a mechanism, as a conception of an isolable energy system, may no longer prove fully satisfactory. (It looks as though the term " field " was already creeping into other studies, such as biology, and even psychology, though it is not clear how far those who so use it recognize that it is an analogical term drawn from electro-dynamics, where it has a precise meaning). And thinkers such as Whitehead are urging that so-called mechanical conceptions should be displaced by organic conceptions not only in biology but throughout all our thinking about nature. However, it does not look as though we had yet got concepts drawn from the new physics which can serve as ultimate methodological principles in the way in which mechanism still serves the sciences based on Newtonian physics. Meanwhile, the term " mechanism " is likely to be used in an increasingly wide sense, to mean any correlation of processes expressible in mathematical terms. But this is a looser use. As a methodological principle the concept of mechanism can be used to discipline any far-fetched analogies in terms of which speculative thinkers may seek to describe nature. The difficulty in extending

[1] In *The Metaphysical Foundations of Modern Physical Science* (London, 1925).

the idea of mechanism in its old sense to the ultimate units, the combination of which make up the mechanical system, is that it describes their properties in terms of analogies drawn from experience at other levels, where we are dealing with large-scale objects. (This necessity shows how the idea of mechanism itself is an analogical concept, in which we seek to exhibit the unknown in terms of the more familiar.) But now we are faced with the prospect that the laws of classical mechanics break down at the level of the very smallest constituents of nature. The concept of mechanism based on those laws may therefore no longer serve without qualification at this level. This does not necessarily mean the idea of mechanism will be or should be discarded, but that here the idea of mechanism should not be conceived primarily according to the notions of classical mechanics, since these may be shown only to hold of statistical averages of great numbers. In any case, it looks as though there were as yet no methodological concept drawn from the study of energy systems at the level of quantum mechanics which can provide a satisfactory alternative to the idea of mechanism. Concepts drawn from the notion of " probability " need to be used with caution, especially by the layman (as we observed above[1]). The difficulty perhaps is that these notions, drawn from relations of mathematical equations, present no intuitable content, as the notion of " mechanism " seemed to do. This may be a safeguard against adopting them in a naïvely realistic sense; but at the same time we must expect to find terms such as " field ", " pattern ", etc., given an extended use in a way which can be even less disciplined than the use of the term " mechanism " where the constructions from which the analogy was derived were more generally understood. But meanwhile some useful purpose will be served if we come to recognize the analogical character of concepts such as " mechanism " when used as explanatory principles.

But they may be none the worse for that. We have seen that we need to keep the conception of " things ", or

[1] See p. 78.

some similar term, not as a concession to mythology, but to express the fact of processes, other than our conceptually interpreted experience, which are involved in the possibility of perceptual experience. But if we try to say anything about the structure or mode of connection of these " things " or processes in themselves, we can only do so by an indirect conjecture based on analogies with structures or modes of connection within our experience. These are not realistic representations but ways of symbolizing possible modes of connection between " things ". How valuable such analogical models are depends largely on how far they play back in suggesting further systematic correlations within experience besides those from which the analogy was originally drawn. The undulatory theory of light would be a case of this, whereas the caloric theory of heat would be a case of an analogy which suggested no fruitful developments. In the favourable cases an analogy, by means of which we form a theory of the nature of something not directly given in experience, helps to make it possible to find systematic connections between observations other than those from which the analogy was originally drawn.

This suggests some sort of *rapport* between our intellectual processes and nature beyond them. But it may not go so far as an identity of structure. It looks rather as though certain structures within certain processes in nature may be projected in a systematically distorted way in our sensory experience and in the intellectual constructions based upon it. *Distorted*, since we are responding to environing processes and not reproducing them; and the response is shaped by the selective emphasis given by the character of our own sensory and mental apparatus. But that the distortion is *systematic* is borne out by the way in which we find that, if we act as if we could assume some sort of concomitant variation between our most carefully controlled observations and their differential conditions in nature beyond us, we are able to predict accurately and bring coherence into further ranges of otherwise disconnected observations.

But to assume some sort of *rapport* between nature and our intellectual processes is not to assume that the fundamental pattern of nature must be that of one particular logical method. The ancient and mediaeval science of the world was largely constructed on analogy with the Greek logic of Subject-Predicate propositions and syllogistic reasoning. Nature was conceived in terms of substances sustaining attributes, and classified into universal " real kinds ", exemplified in the individuals which were their particulars. In Cartesian science, the logical model in terms of which the world was conceived as intelligible was that of geometrical reasoning. Dialectical logic, in schools of thought deriving from Hegel, has sought to make the " evolution " of nature intelligible in terms of the " development " of an idea. The mathematical logic of functional analysis answers to a conception of nature in terms of differential equations. It may well be that there is no one pattern of rationality; we are still far from having perfected the instrument of logical thought; and different types of logical thought themselves provide analogies in terms of which we can order different ranges of experience.

The appropriateness of the logical form depends on the type of relation we seek to exhibit. This relation will be some correlation of elements within experience, considered (analogically) as throwing light on a mode of interconnection in events and processes beyond our experience. The ground for drawing the analogy is the recognition that our experience itself arises within a situation of interrelated processes. Hence we seek to give an indirect indication of their possible character in analogical terms, and we must understand the " realist " element in scientific concepts in this sense.

So nature, as Meyerson says, both is in *rapport* with our reason and resists it. The progress of physical science shows that, at least with regard to the type of process with which this is concerned, the form of thought with which it is in *rapport* is mathematical. But the existence in nature of elements not mathematically deducible, such as the one-way character of growth, shows there are limits to its complete penetration by logic. Science, therefore, must be empirical as well as mathematical. The empirical side of science consists in the elaboration of more and more ingenious and controlled methods of making more and more detailed sensory observations. From this it is generally assumed that the character of the differential conditions of these observations in an external world may be conjectured. But we must insist on the indirect nature of this conjecture. Through the extended use of empirical and mathematical methods, physical scientists are constantly extending the range of processes to which some kind of observational response can be made. On the empirical side this is done not primarily by reflecting on and developing present experience, but by devising instruments and techniques for arriving at new observational experiences.

But the theories of the physical world which are built up as constructions out of observational data so obtained are very foreign to the *prima facie* view of the world obtained from crude sense experience. Hence we have insisted on the superficial nature of sense perception. It presents us not with direct apprehensions of the nature of external events, but with clues, selected and filtered and no doubt distorted by our physiological sensory apparatus. Out of these clues some coherent theory of external events must be indirectly constructed. To quote Lord Balfour:[1] "A remote and nameless star suddenly blazes into prominence. This, says Science, is due to the fact that centuries ago and billions of miles away, a particular collection of electric charges began radiating into space with a new and catastrophic violence. As time went on an infinitesimal fraction of these radiations, which *happened* to be of the right frequency, *happened* also to reach a small planet where, and where only (so far as we know) there *happened* to be organic sensibilities rightly tuned for their reception. Thereupon there came into being a new effect, namely the direct experience by man of this old and distant cataclysm, the

[1] *Theism and Thought*, p. 111 (London, 1923).

news of which had during these many ages been wandering unnoticed through space in the shape of electro-magnetic 'oscillations'. . . ." "But there is quite another method of treating perceptual experiences, also known to common sense, but greatly and increasingly developed by science. I shall call it the indirect method. It consists in regarding perceptions not as bringing us into immediate cognitive relation with a portion of external reality, but only as supplying us with the data from which the character of external reality may (it is thought) be indirectly inferred. . . . Nature on this view is not observed; it is conjectured."[1]

So we never have mere observations of nature; we have the constructions based on them, which together form the organized body of scientific thought. It is only by living within this organized body of thought, and seeing questions to which it gives rise, that people are able to discover possibilities of obtaining new and fruitful observations.

It will not do, therefore, to speak, as phenomenalists are apt to do, of "verification" simply in terms of predicting and correlating sense impressions. Experimental verification in the physical sciences is not merely a matter of recording our sense impressions. It is a matter of devising techniques by means of which the requisite sense impressions may be obtained. These techniques involve not merely observation but productive activity, the making and use of delicate and precise instruments. It is also a matter of checking the reports of one trained observer with those of others carried out under similar conditions. Such trained observation presupposes special skilled techniques acquired through the practice of a highly developed scientific tradition. Such skill has something of the nature of a craft passed on by personal training under the practitioners of the tradition, and if the continuity of the tradition were destroyed through the breakdown of our civilization, the techniques of exact observation could not easily be recovered. So verification by the senses in any exact sense depends on

[1] *Theism and Thought*, p. 124.

a state of relationship in which the observer stands to a number of other processes and other people. By perfecting the means of detecting changes in our sensory impressions due to processes we have ourselves originated, we seek to detect ways in which our sensory impressions are likely to be due to changes in their differential conditions in processes beyond ourselves. Thus we may say that the processes beyond us are so differentiated as to produce these differences of response in us. But we can only indirectly conjecture their intrinsic modes of interconnection from studying the minutiae of the distinctions of our responsive sensations, and devising theories by which these sensations may be correlated in a systematic way. We may then hope that a systematic correlation of our sensory experiences exhibits by analogy some proportionate relation, even if only a systematic distortion, of the way in which the processes which form their differential conditions are co-ordinated. But we cannot with any assurance go so far as to claim structural identity between processes in nature and the intellectual relations between the ideas in which we symbolize them and say with Spinoza, *Ordo et connexio idearum idem est ac ordo et connexio rerum.* For mind is not a mirror, but a selective and interpretative activity which builds up symbolic constructions. But the mode of activity, which constructs symbolic forms, and which, following Whitehead, we may call the " mental pole ", grows out of the total experience of a " bipolar " being whose " physical pole " consists in activities which are not constructive but responsive to processes acting upon it. [1]

[1] The link between the two must be sought for in " conscious awareness " or " apprehension ", which, through the use of interpretative forms, takes up responses into judgments of contents and relationships. But I cannot claim to have reached a view of the nature of " apprehension " which satisfies me. I have used Whitehead's terms " mental " and " physical pole " because they are convenient for my purpose. But he would draw the distinction between them somewhat differently, and would make conscious awareness incidental in a way which I cannot believe is satisfactory. (See Appendix, p. 229.)

CHAPTER V

ANALOGIES IN RELIGIOUS SYMBOLISM

SCIENCE, we have seen, makes use of indirect analogical models by means of which possible modes of connection in nature may be symbolized. We have also seen that such models are disciplined by the regulative idea of mechanism, which secures them against being mere postulations of occult qualities, such as those assumed, for instance, in the caloric theory which represented heat as if it were an imponderable fluid. Analogies of the latter kind in effect explain nothing; they may lull our minds with the impression that we understand how a thing works, but the analogy has been drawn *ad hoc* for this particular purpose, and suggests no possible developments or correlations beyond the immediate problem which it has been introduced to explain. On the other hand the fruitful scientific analogies, such as the valency bonds in the molecular theory of matter, or the planetary model of the atom, or the undulatory theory of light, have made possible wider generalizations, and so have helped to carry forward the body of scientific thought. Such models suggest a possible picture by which our imaginations may grasp a mode of connection otherwise only expressible in the abstract form of mathematical formulae. It may be that, given the state of scientific thought at any time, and the range of observations out of which its theoretical constructions are made, only a limited number of models can be presented as plausible alternatives; though it may also be that, given the state of scientific theory at the time, two distinct models may both have to be entertained, each of which serves to co-ordinate part of the evidence to be taken into account. An example would be the holding of both the corpuscular and the undulatory conceptions of light, without there being any third " model " in terms of which these two could be co-ordinated or superseded although of course they can be co-ordinated by equations. Poincaré does indeed suggest that an infinite number of mechanical models can be made of any limited group of phenomena, provided that these explanations may be as complicated as you like.[1] But he also allows that only one or two of them present real options. The Ptolemaic model of the movements of the heavenly bodies in cycles and epicycles would be an example of a model of such complication that it became unmanageable.

So it looks as though the tests to which a scientific model must submit if it is to be of value are so stringent as to preclude aberrations of the imagination from holding sway for long. This is far from meaning that the form-creating imagination has not got a great part to play in the production of scientific models. But it means that any model has to be submitted to a drastic critical process if it is to prove of value.

Moreover, the very considerable standardization of the fundamental sensory responses in the human race means that the observations on which theoretical constructions are based can be considered as if they were "public facts" and ways can be found for detecting idiosyncrasies such as colour blindness (although actually each man's observation is a private fact). This standardization can be made still more precise by the use of instruments of measurement, photography and the like. Even where it might seem that the Theory of Relativity has introduced a necessary reference to the standpoint of the observer, it is yet possible through transformation equations so to formulate laws that they will hold of all possible frames of reference. So science can present what seems to be a completely impersonal body of thought; and its concepts can present an impression of objectivity, as though they were in no way dependent on the nature of the human mind. This, we have seen, is not really the case; but what is the case is that the character of the disciplines of scientific thinking is such as to

[1] Cf. Bridgman, *op. cit.* p. 49, and Poincaré, *La Science et l'Hypothèse*, p. 167.

exclude concepts dependent on the idiosyncrasies of any particular mind. The creative genius of a Newton or an Einstein may produce new fundamental ideas, but they can then be incorporated into the impersonal body of scientific theory.

When we turn to the symbolic forms in which religious ideas are expressed, we can find no such impersonal body of agreed thought. The fundamental data on which the symbolic interpretations of religion are built are harder to detect and determine. Those who speak of religions as based on an immediate experience, when they are asked to describe the experience notoriously do so in the terms of the religious tradition to which they belong. The original data are elusive, and the scope for the imaginative creation of symbolic forms is far greater, since there seems no agreed method comparable to the mathematical and empirical methods of physical science by which they can be disciplined. Moreover, a person's temperament and character seem to play a great part in determining his type of religious response; there is no such standardization as we have found in perceptual experience. So we may well raise the question whether we are having to do not with knowledge, but with a mere proliferation of symbolic expressions of the desires, impulses, intuitions, hopes and fears of the human mind.

Or is this religious symbolism less varied than appears on the surface? Has it even a pattern which is fundamentally the same, and only diverse in its superficial manifestations? Cassirer for one has contended that this is so;[1] he even goes so far as to speak of a universal structure of mythical thinking as one of the *a priori* symbolic forms of the human mind, and so as one of its irreducible ways of interpreting experience.[2] He describes the structure of this myth-consciousness (*das mythische Bewusstsein*) as com-

[1] See especially his *Die Philosophie der symbolischen Formen*, vol. ii, pp. 107 *sq.*

[2] Cassirer means by this that myth thinking cannot be looked on as a rudimentary and unsuccessful kind of scientific thinking. It is an *alternative* way of looking at the world, complete within its own limits.

prised of a way of thinking in which special significance attaches to particular parts of space and time and to particular numbers, so that particular times and places and numbers become sacred, instead of time, space and number being merely neutral forms of schematization. It is also the way of thinking in which particular things have their own peculiar properties and their "proper" place in space, and force other particular things to happen. These latter are perhaps the most important points in Cassirer's view for us to notice for the purposes of our discussion. For in consequence he holds that the notions of substance and cause are rationalized forms of myth concepts, carried over into the intellectual form of scientific thought, where they do not properly belong, and where they should be displaced by the purely symbolic concepts of functional relation, mass, number, law, etc. I have questioned whether it is possible to divest ourselves entirely of the notions of substance and cause if we are to do justice to the experimental as distinct from the mathematical side of science. But we have also seen [1] that it may well be true that these concepts, if they are used to indicate concrete processes or "things", and not merely functional relations, have an element of animistic thinking about them. They are animistic in an analogical sense; that is they are conceptions of processes other than ourselves, which we form through the ways in which we are aware of ourselves as acting and being acted upon. But this consciousness of acting and being acted upon is a primary datum which cannot be superseded in the "scientific" form of thought, so as to dissolve the latter, as Cassirer would do, into a "panmathematical" idealism. It provides the essential experimental foundation on which the symbolic constructions of interpretative theory are based. We have therefore said that the "analogical" mode of thought, which Cassirer notes as standing between the "mythical" and the "scientific", is far more deep-seated than he allows, and has to remain in some form as an inescapable element even in "scientific" thinking.

[1] Cf. *supra*, p. 86.

Myth thinking may be described as an imaginative picture of the world shaped in terms of the powers and feelings of man's own inner life. In creative mythical imagination these powers take on an independent life and character of their own; they become the actors in cosmogonies and theogonies, and are not thought of as mere personified abstractions. They acquire a life independent of the minds which give them birth, rather in the way in which the characters of a good drama or novel do. They are thus more than mere "projections" of the impulses of their authors; they are achievements of the form-creating imagination. Perhaps this is why modern attempts to construct mythologies, whether those of Rosenberg or of Freud,[1] can only convince those who are already disposed to believe them. Modern man has lost the innocence of imagination out of which creative myth-making can come. His myths are sophisticated, manufactured to support an ideology for political, social or therapeutic purposes. When this happens, we have already passed from myth to allegory; and allegory is a more sophisticated form of thought, notoriously difficult to handle. Allegory is a mode of expression in which the author and reader are aware that the figures are fictions — personifications of forces, emotions, virtues, temptations — and the meaning can be translated back into conceptual terms. Mr. C. S. Lewis has performed the rare achievement in *The Screwtape Letters* of handling an allegory form so as to present a modern man's sins, temptations, aspirations, in a way which carries conviction; so too with greater power, if with almost wilful complexity, has Franz Kafka in *The Castle*. But to create not only a dramatic expression of inner experience, but a mythology which carries conviction, in the face of our science and our sophistication, calls for a lost capacity to become again as little children.

Let us now return to Cassirer's contention, that the myth consciousness is a universal and *a priori* form of thought. It is certainly possible to find very considerable resemblance

[1] I do not of course put these on the same level of intellectual achievement.

between the myths of different peoples. But can we say with assurance that this is due to their being expressions of a universal *a priori* form of the human mind? It may even be that the resemblances which students of comparative religion have been eager to point out have been partly due to the presuppositions of those students themselves. When ideas and stories which are superficially the same are lived with and experienced, there may well be greater differences of feeling and meaning attached to them than appears on the surface. Words like " Immortality " may suggest a similarity of belief among different religions; and yet from closer knowledge we may find that in these different contexts they have a very different emotional and conceptual significance.

Perhaps we should say that religious symbols have been created out of forms of response of the human mind in certain basic kinds of experience which have impressed themselves as of special significance. And since the fundamental needs and crises of life are largely the same the world over, the types of experience which have formed the analogues of religious symbols are likely to be much the same. Such analogues are the idea of the Father, the Mother, the hierarchy of family relations somehow reflected in Heaven, the King, the Shepherd of the People, the Lover, the Craftsman shaping his material. These are analogues by which men endow their elemental sense of encompassing life and power with form and will. At a deeper and more complex level of experience the analogues are drawn not so much from archetypal figures as from the ways in which man himself responds to his sense of encompassing life and power. Through these responses he conceives his relation to the transcendent, and so, indirectly, the nature of the transcendent itself. Such a response is the sense of the participation of life; a breaking down of the barriers of individuality and a sense of continuity of one's own life with life and power beyond. Such a sense of continuity with environing forces is, as we have suggested,[1] character-

[1] See *supra*, p. 64.

istic of elemental experience below the level of the Subject-Object distinction. Another fundamental form of response springs from the fact that, as we also have seen, there is no direct apprehension of the intrinsic nature of the world beyond us. The transcendent is thus beyond our categories. From the deep emotional grasp of this comes the religious sense of the Wholly Other, the qualitative break between man and God, and the problem of mediation. We know that we are inescapably related to something which vitally concerns us, and yet we have no direct apprehension of its intrinsic nature. Allied to this is the consciousness of finiteness; of the limited, fragmentary, transitory, character of man's life and knowledge. In contrast with this he responds with deep feeling to the thought of the Absolute, the Unconditioned, the Perfect, the Unchanging. He is also conscious of obligation, coming from he does not fully know where; is it society, his own mind, or some Law or Word beyond these? In any case, it is something which imposes judgment and discipline on his desires and appetites. From this realization springs the sense of a Law of inexorable Justice, and the sense of guilt. From the responses in which the central feature is this sense of inevitable Law, beyond and above one's own impulses, grow the religions of resignation, which teach the peace of accepting the inevitable, whether with moral consent as in Stoicism, or with fatalism as in Islam.

But there is the form of response which springs from experiences in which Law, whether moral or natural, does not have the final word. These are experiences in which an apparently inevitable result has been transmuted by the operation of new creative resources, whether of art or of personal love. From such experiences spring, in the more moralized religions, the thought of the forgiveness of sins; in the more aesthetized, the thought of a creative process to which " the gates of the future are open," or of a final state of existence beyond Law and " beyond good and evil ". And in both the moralized and non-moralized forms we find the haunting sense of the importance of experiences in which life is renewed through death, loss and surrender.

Such are some of the fundamental ways in which man responds to the impingement upon his life of power beyond himself, whose intrinsic nature he does not know, and yet which vitally concerns him. Religions grow up through the sustained attempt throughout a living tradition to give form and significance to life in terms of certain of these basic responses. But are the religious symbols themselves more than " archetypal images " (to use Jung's word) sustaining certain forms of personal and social life? One view is that they are " collective representations ". Lévy Bruhl, with whom this expression appears to have originated, uses it to mean ways of thinking and feeling, which express the sense of participation of life with life below the explicitly logical level of thought.[1] Such ways of feeling are the common property of a social group, and express the way in which in the last resort its common life coheres. Other writers have taken the phrase " collective representation " to mean an analogical projection of social forces and ways of government on to the world beyond man and society. Hence the significance seen by Miss Harrison and Professor Cornford in *Themis* as the Mother of *Diké* — social custom producing the analogue by which the Law of the Universe is conceived. The rôle played by conceptions of *Dike* (Justice), *Eros*, *Até* (Fate), Chaos, in early Greek cosmologies shows how thinkers such as Anaximander, and Heraclitus, for all their would-be naturalism, carry over certain basic ways of thinking from the older Greek religious attitudes to the world. But should we say that these are analogues drawn primarily from the ordering of society? They are much more like analogues drawn from man's own inner conflicts, conflicts which arise and become articulate when he becomes aware of himself as not simply living in terms of the customary order of society. Then he seeks to find significance in his world in terms of these cosmological symbols of his inner life. Rather than myths having

[1] Cf. *Les Fonctions mentales dans les Sociétés inférieures*. ch. ii.

been produced as projections of forms of society, it may well be, as Cassirer suggests, that man has shaped the forms of his society in terms of his myths, or of the ways in which he has symbolized his ultimate responses to the world.

But we have still to enquire whether a myth and a symbolic expression of an ultimate response to the world are necessarily the same thing. We can see that certain forms of fundamental response are able to sustain and inspire forms of personal and social life. They express mental attitudes below the level of consciously articulated or scientific thought. But we have still to ask whether these are more than forms of inner experience in terms of which an imaginative cosmology is created. Do they in any real sense give us *knowledge* of the transcendent? This must concern us in the ensuing chapters, when we consider the nature of theological and metaphysical thinking. Meanwhile it may be noted that, in whatever sense religious symbols convey knowledge of the transcendent, it cannot be in the sense of literal and direct representation. The creatively religious mind knows this; it is rather the second-hand or conventional followers of a religion who take its symbols as literal pictures or copies of an unseen world. Hence religious thought holds together the Way of Negation and the Way of the Affirmation of Images. From the heights on which it entertains images and symbols it casts them down, and " the rest is silence ". Whenever a form of symbolic expression in thought and ritual has become dominant, Protestants will arise and claim that the symbol itself has become an object of worship, and that this is idolatry. The existence of Protestantism (in the general, not in the particular historical sense) is a continual witness to the religious conviction that symbols must only be taken as pointers to a meaning which they cannot contain. For " To whom shall ye liken Me that I am like? " Yet the Protestant himself must use symbolic forms if he is to have any positive content to his religion; a necessity which Christian Protestants have sometimes failed to recognize, because they have substituted an auditory symbolism of the

" Word " for the Catholic visual symbolism, and have failed to recognize that it is none the less a symbolism. For " The inner dilemma of Protestantism lies in this, that it must protest against every religious or cultural realization which seeks to be intrinsically valid, but that it needs such a realization if it is to be able to make its protest in any meaningful way ".[1]

So the religious mind needs both to seek expression in symbols and to deny their literal meaning. If it fails to do the latter, it falls into idolatry, the worship of its own graven images. It is always liable to fall into idolatry whenever the original response out of which the symbol is born has spent itself. Hence there will always be a place for the iconoclasts. But the iconoclasts fail to see that the impulse to give expression to experience through some symbolic transmutation is the root impulse of mind and spirit. Nor do the iconoclasts respect the sense of elation which a mind knows when it has forged a form in which its intuitive experience can be expressed with precision and a sense of inevitability.

But the religious symbol has the peculiar function of having to convey its own questionable character. It must express something positively grasped, a significant relation in experience. And yet it must point not simply to the relation within experience but to something qualitatively other which stands beyond it. Hence the ambivalent and ambiguous character of religious imagery. Such ambiguity is not the result of pious vagueness or of confusion of thought (which are the hallmarks of sentimental religious imagery). It is a precise way of conveying the fundamental dilemma of religious symbolism, which presents an analogue of the transcendent in the forms of the phenomenal, of the infinite in the finite. This may be conveyed by a cumulative use of images, mutually incompatible, as in George Herbert's Sonnet on *Prayer*.

> Prayer, the Church's banquet, Angels' age,
> God's breath in man returning to his birth,

[1] Tillich, *The Religious Situation*, English translation, p. 155.

The soul in paraphrase, heart in pilgrimage,
The Christian plummet sounding heav'n and earth;
Engine against th' Almighty, sinner's tower,
Reversèd thunder, Christ-side-piercing spear,
The six-days-world transposing in an hour,
A kind of tune which all things hear and fear;
Softness and peace and joy, and love, and bliss,
Exalted Manna, gladness of the best,
Heaven in ordinary, man well dressed,
The milky way, the bird of Paradise,
Church-bells beyond the stars heard, the soul's blood,
The land of spices, something understood.

Or a total impression of glory may be conveyed through a description the details of which ought not to be visualized severally, as in the vision of the risen Christ as the First and the Last in the first chapter of the Book of Revelation (" His head and his hairs were white like wool, as white as snow; and his eyes were as a flame of fire; and his feet like unto fine brass, as if they burned in a furnace; and his voice as the sound of many waters. And he had in his right hand seven stars; and out of his mouth went a sharp two-edged sword; and his countenance was as the sun shineth in his strength.")

Or a symbolic phrase may gather up into itself different strands of meaning and transmute them into a new unity, in which all these strands may be woven together. Pedantic scholars, who insist that the phrase must then mean one and one only of these possible alternatives, are missing the way in which the function of the phrase may be to call up all these different associations together. So Rudolf Otto, who understands if anyone does how a religious mind uses language, writes of the phrase " the Kingdom of Heaven ":[1]

[1] *Reichgottes und Menschensohn*, p. 20 (Munich, 1934). " Here the 'Kingdom' is not kingly dignity and kingly rule, not a locality or a sovereign state, not a people or a community, but all these blended together. God's might and holiness and glory, and His Throne and the power of His rule, and His angels and their ranks, and the blessed ones and saints at His throne, and the community of the righteous and the Church Triumphant, and the new Heaven and earth, transfigured existence, and heavenly blessedness, and the life everlasting, and 'God all in all' — these belong here as a whole together. And this whole should some day 'come' and we should 'enter

"Hier ist das 'Reich' nicht Königswürde, Königsherrschaft, nicht Bezirk oder Bereich, nicht Volk oder Gemeinschaft, sondern alles dieses miteinander und durcheinander. Gottes Macht und Heiligkeit und Glorie und sein Thron und Regierungsgewalt, und seine Engel und ihre Ordnungen, und die Seligen und Heiligen an seinem Throne und die Gemeinschaft der Gerechten, und die triumfierende Kirche, und der neue Himmel und Erde, und das verklärte Dasein und die himmlische Seligkeit und das Leben der Ewigkeit und das 'Gott alles in allem' gehören hier als ein totum zusammen. Und dies totum soll einmal 'kommen' und wir sollen 'hineinkommen'— (und wenn recht steht, so ist es als Vorschmack und Anwartschaft heimlicher Weise schon da, und in Glaube und Wiedergeburt sind wir 'eigentlich' schon darin). All das meint und um all das betet ein Christ, wenn er betet: dein Reich komme."

Eliot's later poems convey a sense of an eternal implicated but not held in the passage of time, through the elision from one image to another.

> The moment in and out of time,
> The distraction fit, lost in a shaft of sunlight,
> The wild thyme unseen, or the winter lightning
> Or the waterfall, or music heard so deeply
> That it is not heard at all, but you are the music
> While the music lasts.[1]

Or take Gerard Manley Hopkins' use of the symbols of sea and storm and shipwreck to convey the majesty of a transcendent, which holds us in relation to itself:

> I admire thee, master of the tides,
> Of the Yore-flood, of the year's fall;
> The recurb and the recovery of the gulf's sides,
> The girth of it and the wharf of it and the wall;
> Stanching, quenching ocean of a motionable mind;

into it' (and when things are ordered aright, then we have there already in a spiritual manner a foretaste and anticipation, and in faith and rebirth we are 'actually' already therein). All this a Christian intends, and he prays about all this, whenever he prays: Thy Kingdom come."

[1] *The Dry Salvages.*

Ground of being, and granite of it: past all
Grasp God, throned behind
Death with a sovereignty that heeds but hides,
bodes but abides;

With a mercy that outrides
The all of water, an ark
For the listener; for the lingerer with a love glides
Lower than death and the dark;
A vein for the visiting of the past-prayer, pent in prison,
The-last-breath penitent spirits — the uttermost mark
Our passion-plungèd giant risen,
The Christ of the Father compassionate, fetched in the
storm of his strides.[1]

Such imagery conveys a total impression of a transcendent which is indicated by, yet qualitatively other than, the experiences from which the imagery is drawn. The question may be raised whether this sense of transcendence is an essential characteristic of religious symbolism. I contend that it is; and that religious symbolism grows out of the feeling of the "otherness" of a transcendent which exists in its own right beyond our experience. We have no direct apprehension of its intrinsic nature, and yet it encompasses and sustains and challenges us. So far in this book we have used the term "transcendent" in a completely neutral sense, to mean that which exists in its own right beyond our own minds, and our own symbolic forms. Hence a realist reference to an object of perception is a reference to "transcendence". But it is noteworthy that as soon as we consider religious concepts, transcendence becomes a numinous word and acquires, as it were, a capital T. For religion, the sense that reality is other than our ideas about it is a sobering and awe-inspiring thought. Religion insists that, though we see the universe in the perspective of our minds, our minds are not its centre. Hence the religious response contains a reverent acknowledgment of the autonomy of "that which is". It also contains a value judgment — that which is in its own right is more important than our thoughts. Moreover, in theistic

[1] *The Wreck of the Deutschland.*

forms of religion we find the belief that there is only one existent which is an absolute existence and which can properly be said to exist in its own right. Our existence and thoughts and those of everything other than the absolute existent are finite, dependent and questionable. We shall return to this distinction, grasped emotionally in religion, when we come to the philosophy of the Analogy of Being. We should, however, point out here that the mere sense that the transcendent is qualitatively *other* than our thoughts need not by itself make it an object of worship; we do not want to worship the objects of perception. And if the transcendent were strictly unknowable it would be, as Bradley remarked concerning Herbert Spencer, mere prejudice to call it God simply because we do not know what the devil it can be.[1] Worship is related to the sense that there is not only *otherness* but also some absolute quality called " holiness " in the transcendent. It is in virtue of this that it is an object of worship, and this is the theme out of which religious symbolism grows. It may be that, as in Greek philosophy and poetry (before Aristotle), " God " (θεός) may be used in a non-absolutist sense to mean a divine power. Hence the Greeks can speak of " god " or " the gods " alternatively. But then they look to a Law or Fate or Justice behind the gods, and it is thoughts of this, rather than of the all-too human Olympians, which stir their religious emotions.

The religious symbol therefore expresses both a value judgment and an emotionally appropriated grasp of the distinction which, when the question has arisen, philosophical language indicates in oppositions such as the Phenomenal and the Noumenal, Appearance and Reality, the Finite and the Infinite, the Relative and the Absolute. If this element of awe before what is both absolute and qualitatively different is entirely lacking, it may be questioned whether it is possible to have *religion*, as distinct from ethical philosophy expressed in pious terminology. The realization of this may be one factor in that revolt against

[1] *Appearance and Reality* (2nd edition), p. 128.

liberal and modernist theologies which is characteristic of the more vigorous movements in contemporary religion. (There may be other less cogent reasons for this revolt to which we shall return in a later chapter.)

It might also be said that the upshot of Kant's criticism of Natural Theology was to prove that whatever is meant by God, He cannot be a phenomenal object. To which our reaction is to ask, what serious religious thinker has ever thought that He was? But if religion knows that its object is in some fundamental way different from the phenomenal objects and experiences from which its analogies are drawn, then it knows that these must be used in a non-literal sense. This is as true of less complex symbols as of the more complex images such as those in the passages I have quoted from Herbert, Otto, Eliot and Hopkins. Symbols such as height, depth, light, are almost universally used in religious language. Yet, as Mr. Edwyn Bevan remarks, " Height literally is nothing but distance from the earth's surface or extension of something on the earth's surface in a direction at right angles outwards. The proposition: Moral and spiritual worth is greater or less in ratio to the distance outwards from the earth's surface, would certainly seem to be, if stated nakedly like that, an odd proposition."[1] What seems to be happening is that the feeling of awe and sublimity experienced in looking up at a height is transferred by analogy as an appropriate expression for the feeling of the transcendent. So, too, in using the term " light ", " we believe that, if we could have a more perfect apprehension of God's being than we can have under earthly conditions, that apprehension would involve something analogous to the feeling now aroused in us by bright concentrated light, something which cannot possibly be described in human language except by pointing to that feeling. Thus the light metaphor would not here be the use of a figure for mere poetical or imaginative embellishment, in order to say something which we could say more precisely in other terms; it would be the most precise way

[1] *Symbolism and Belief*, p. 30 (London, 1938).

in which the Reality can be expressed in human language." [1]

Thus the test of such symbols cannot be one of com parison with that to which they refer. It can only be the test of their appropriateness as expressions of response to something whose intrinsic nature cannot be apprehended in any direct way. We therefore describe it in terms of other kinds of experience such as the seeing of light, the feeling of which is partly analogous. "Appropriateness" may mean the aptness of the comparison with other experiences; it may also mean aesthetic fittingness. These are not always the same thing. Dr. W. K. Lowther Clarke, commenting on the prayer "O Almighty God, who art a most strong tower to all who put their trust in thee", writes,[2] "The comparison of the Lord to a strong tower is not appropriate to a generation which has learned to associate safety rather with deep shelters". Perhaps in time, when we have had a few more wars, we may find it natural to talk about God as a "reinforced basement". But at present we must admit that it jars. Is this just academic purism on our part or is it that the attempt to make our symbolism too realistic may lead to a loss of the sense of the divine otherness, which it is also part of the function of the religious symbol to convey? ("A strong tower" might of course also be called realistic, but the phrase has come by association and tradition to be recognizably symbolic — we may compare the phrase "a tower of strength.")

But we may still ask whether the appropriateness of these expressions depends also on whether the responses they express are in any way shaped by awareness of reality transcending our minds, or how far they are merely symbols for our own ways of feeling, in face of a reality which is completely unknown. In other words, have we any direct knowledge to guide the selection and disciplining of our analogies?

[1] *Op. cit.* pp. 149-150.

[2] In *The Prayer Book of 1928 reconsidered* (S.P.C.K., 1943). I have taken this quotation from a review of Dr. Lowther Clarke's book in *The Times Literary Supplement*. I have been unable to consult the book itself.

There is an old tradition that man was made in the image of God; but we may ask whether the analogies in which man tries to see God do not make Him in the image of some form of man's own experience, or whether the peculiar nature of these analogies is such that they are only explicable, partly at any rate, by the active impingement on him of something other than his own experience.

> As a man thru' a window into a darken'd house
> peering vainly wil see, always and easily,
> the glass surface and his own face mirror'd thereon,
> tho' looking from another angle, or hooding his eyes
> he may discern some real objects within the room —
> some say 'tis so with us, and also affirm that they
> by study of their reflection hav discover'd in truth
> ther is nothing but thatt same reflection inside the house.[1]
>
> . . . . . .
>
> . . . and conning those large letters I AM THAT I AM
> I wonder'd finding only my own thought of myself,
> and reading there that man was made in God's image
> knew not yet that God was made in the image of man;
> nor the profounder truth that both these truths are one.[2]

Bridges' metaphor of the reflection in the darkened window recalls St. Paul's image of the mirror, " For now we see through a glass, darkly " (*βλέπομεν γὰρ ἄρτι δι' ἐσόπτρου ἐν αἰνίγματι,* 1 Cor. xiii. 12); with which we may compare the passage in 2 Cor. iii. 18, " But we all, with unveiled face reflecting as in a mirror (or R.V. marg., ' beholding as in a mirror ') [3] the glory of the Lord, are transformed into the same image from glory to glory, even as from the Lord the Spirit ". Dr. Kirk suggests St. Paul has stories of " magic mirrors " in mind. " The new Christian experience, the vision of God, is a magic mirror both because it enhances a man's knowledge of himself and *because by a mystical process it transforms him into the image of God*, ' as from the Lord the Spirit '. In this sense *man* also becomes a mirror and reflects the likeness

[1] Bridges, *The Testament of Beauty*, I, 350-357.
[2] *Ibid.* I, 401-405.
[3] For the interpretation of κατοπτριζόμενοι, cf. Kirk, *The Vision of God*, p. 103 (London, 1932); and Lietzmann, *H.N.T.* ix, pp. 113-114.

of God."[1] In 1 Cor. xiii. 12 St. Paul seems to be expressing the indirectness of our present knowledge, as contrasted with knowledge " face to face ". Is he realizing that when you look in a mirror you may see not only dimly what is behind you but *your own reflection*? He may be thinking simply of seeing some dim and oblique reflection of something behind,[2] or possibly he may also have this point about our own reflection in mind, since it is taken up in 2 Cor. iii. 18. In this latter passage the glory of God can be reflected in the image of man when man is possessed by the " spirit of the Lord " which is " liberty ". For the question is whether *we* are being transformed " as from the Lord the spirit ", so that " as a mirror " we reflect something of His likeness. In that case, we might see something of God through the image of man, especially if there are things about that image which drive us to believe that it is essentially incomplete, so that we must distinguish it from the reality which it reflects. Mr. Charles Williams, reviewing Niebuhr's *Nature and Destiny of Man* in *Time and Tide*, writes: "Of all the images which man can carry in his mind, the key image is his own. It is not necessarily the greatest, the unimaged image of Deity lies beyond it. But that greater can often only be seen by the lesser; and our chief argument is whether the image of man which man's mind holds is properly shaped as something which sees not only itself but beyond itself. . . . The image of man aspires continually to reflect the law of love, but it can neither do so nor rest content in its inability to do so."

In some such sense the mirror image may give us a clue. The concepts and symbols in which religion tries to express metaphysical truth are not " univocal " descriptions of direct apprehensions. They express something seen through forms and images of our experience; and so the question is whether the image seen in the mirror is in

[1] Kirk, *op. cit.* p. 104.

[2] The mirrors he knew would, of course, have been made of burnished metal.

the end the reflection of man himself as he looks into the mirror; or whether the study of man's own image indicates a reference to something beyond itself, since his experience is shaped by the working on him of something beyond himself. In this case, we should expect the images and symbols to be of an *indirect* character; that is to say, we must fasten not on their literal meaning as copies or representations of an unseen real world; but ask whether they are expressing the character of some actual *relation*, which is controlling the appropriateness of the symbol used. If so, the non-literal and indirect character of the terms of the symbol is not an obstacle; the question is whether such a symbol strikes us as an inevitable way of expressing a relation in which we stand to something of whose intrinsic nature we have no direct apprehension.

This position would be the opposite of any form of gnosticism — as St. Paul saw in contrasting his "riddling" perception in a mirror with Gnosis. Gnosis claims some direct esoteric information about the constitution of a transcendent world. It also tends to deny the existence of any real relation between our natural, non-esoteric experience and that transcendent world. Only the supremely abnormal is divine. "Unless ye make the male with the female neither male nor female; the right to be the left, and the left right; what is above to be below and what is below to be above; what is before to be behind and what is behind to be before, ye shall not enter into the kingdom of heaven. For the whole world is turned the wrong way, and every soul therein," Dr. Kirk quotes as a constantly recurring gnostic proverb:[1] and he remarks that it is one thing to think of God as a mirror, and another to count heaven a spiritual looking-glass country. The real issue before religion is whether its symbols are valid not as giving esoteric knowledge of another world, but as giving form to an experience which is what it is because we ourselves are being moulded "even as from the Lord the Spirit".

[1] *The Vision of God*, p. 214.

CHAPTER VI

REVELATION AND FAITH

We have been looking at religious symbols as ways in which people have expressed what they have believed to be their relation to a reality beyond themselves which concerned them in some ultimate and intimate manner. We have seen that a non-literal character is essential to these symbolic forms; idolatry might, in fact, be described as identifying this absolute reality with an image drawn from intra-mundane relationships. It is questionable whether even the heathen, on whom the prophets of the high religions pour out their scorn, do in fact make this literal identification. Rather, their idols are looked on as images in which a supernatural power has taken on itself a local habitation and a name. As Professor Hocking says,[1] "Early gods are like man and near him. But still, they were *as unlike and as remote as he could imagine them.* The differences between spirits and men, the gulf fixed between the natural and supernatural — gulf leaped in death — the exaggerations and superlatives, these are as important parts of the conception as are the likenesses and simplicities of intercourse. When man can *think* beyond the sun, and beyond the sky, — there God goes, and probably first goes." Man's images of the transcendent are, therefore, from the first not merely literal, but analogical; they are attempts to express a unique relationship in symbolic forms drawn from intra-mundane relations. But to say this raises a question rather than answers it. Is there in fact some real relationship to be so expressed; or are the ostensible analogies not true analogies, but only symbolic forms expressive of certain feeling states? For an analogy cannot claim to be significant for knowledge, unless there is some real relationship which the analogy illustrates by showing

[1] *The Meaning of God in Human Experience*, p. 327 (Yale, 1928).

how it obtains between terms which are already familiar to us. That there is such a relationship cannot be deduced simply from the analogy itself. There must be some independent grounds for asserting that a relation does obtain between our minds and reality transcending them. And this relation must be capable of being conceived in some determinate form; otherwise we must come to the agnostic conclusion that religious symbols are proliferations of feelings in face of the completely unknown.

Probably in the creative moment in which religious symbols are produced, this question is not explicitly raised. There is a state of conviction, issuing in the symbolic expression, controlled by a feeling of inevitability; we are convinced that this is the way in which what is being experienced must be expressed.

But such questions may be raised, and the need be felt to translate these symbolic expressions of religious experience into the intellectual language in which people attempt to make sense of their world. In this way religious expressions are related to other aspects of experience, intellectual, moral and social, and the claim is made that key conceptions can be derived from them in terms of which experience as a whole can be ordered and interpreted. Thus the symbols of religion are translated into unambiguous language, capable of systematic presentation. So we get theology. Theology springs in part from the form-creating impulse which we have seen to be at the root of mental activity. We cannot rest satisfied with mere arbitrary mystery; we feel impelled to construct some coherent thought form in terms of which we can order our experience and make sense of our world. But theology also springs from what have been called "paradeigmatic experiences";[1] states of mind in which a peculiarly vivid kind of awareness and responsiveness to reality beyond ourselves seems to give insight into its nature. And if we are right in suggesting that one characteristic of such states is awareness of reality as qualitatively other than ourselves, and as having some

[1] Cf. Mannheim, *Diagnosis of our Time*, pp. 131 *sq*. (London, 1943).

absolute character which impresses and challenges us, the concepts with which theology works must seek to indicate this " otherness ". This is an immensely difficult task, since it means indicating a break in our categories of explanation. And this conflicts with the form-creating impulse to seek systematic coherence and completion. This impulse may be an incentive to intellectual adventure; it may also, if the systematizing is done on too simple a level, minister to the craving for intellectual security. People like to feel they live in a " friendly universe " which makes sense; and the record of their theologies is largely (though not exclusively) a record of the intellectual houses they have built in order to come in out of the rain. But a house is also an indispensable means to civilized life. Within its shelter the arts and graces of life can grow and flourish, and standards of behaviour and sensibility are implicitly accepted. When people can feel that they live in a world which makes sense, and when their basic responses to life are assured and shared with those around them, civilized life can grow and be transmitted to the next generation. The part played by a theological tradition in building up a civilized community with standards of discrimination in manners and morals is the more easily recognized in these days when we are in present danger of seeing the latter disintegrate along with the former. So, too, we can recognize its civilizing rôle in sustaining certain fundamental ways of responding to life which can provide constant themes and inspiration to artists, poets and musicians. What would the European tradition of painting have been like without the themes of the Christian story, or of music without the structure of the liturgy, especially of the Mass, and the emotions inspired by the theme of the Passion? Would there have been a European tradition at all without these? The ages of metaphysical instability, when men are called to go out from their houses and cities, not knowing whither they go, are apt to be uncivilized ages. For civilization depends on form; on the achievement of some shape in personal and communal living.

Thus in the historical religions of the world we can see forms of civilization, social and personal morality, artistic achievement, growing up in the context of a way of living which springs out of a fundamental way of responding to the world. There is a recognizable difference of quality and tone in Buddhist, Christian or Mohammedan art and ways of life which can be directly associated with the differences of fundamental response represented by these religions. This point can be so far elaborated as to make a religion no more than the inner spiritual side of a civilization, and its theology the intellectual expression of that inner spirit, as Troeltsch saw in Christianity the expression of the inner life of Western Civilization. And there are many at the present time who look for a recovery of religious tradition mainly in order that it may provide a co-ordinating form of thought and feeling for the recovery of civilization.

But to stress exclusively its function of providing a co-ordinating intellectual and emotional form, a house secure against wind and weather within which civilized life can be lived, is to overlook the other element in religious symbolism which theology must seek to express. This is what we have called the sense of transcendence; of something qualitatively other than the forms and images which are thrown up as its analogies. Here is a disturbing element; something not to be identified with the thought forms or inner spirit of a civilization. I have said that this sense of otherness is found in first-hand expressions of religious emotion, however primitive. It is apt to be eclipsed in theology, since the character of thought itself, as seeking coherence, tempts us to present our explanatory ideas as a closed system, instead of as interpretations of a relation in which we stand to a reality other than our ideas. It is for this reason that a sound theology should, I believe, be analogical in character; it should be an elucidation of the analogies in terms of which people have expressed their relation to the transcendent, and should exhibit the nature of this relation, recognizing that we can only say so much about the nature of the transcendent itself as can be indirectly indicated in these ways. An analogical type of thought of this kind would properly be called a natural theology; we shall have to consider later its distinction, if any, from what is called revealed theology. But under the influence of Deist and idealistic types of metaphysics, natural theology during the last two centuries has come to be thought of as an exposition of a rational system of the world, in which God and world alike are defined by the explanatory principles of the system. God then becomes First Cause, or Absolute Idea, in a univocal sense, *i.e.* His nature and function are comprehended by our basic explanatory categories. As a protest against what Professor Whitehead has called "paying metaphysical compliments to God", such a natural theology has much to commend it. Nothing of intellectual clarification is gained by applying titles such as "infinite", "absolute", "eternal", "omnipotent" to God in a merely emotional honorific way. But we may question whether Whitehead has stated the only alternatives when he says that God must be presented as the supreme exemplification of our metaphysical principles, and not invoked to save their collapse.[1] The *deus ex machina* is undoubtedly a piece of metaphysical stage property with which we can gladly dispense. But it may well be that, if God is absolute while the forms of our thought are proportionate to the modes of our understanding, terms such as "infinite" may have to be applied, not as mere "metaphysical compliments", but in a carefully defined sense to indicate this break in kind. This was the aim of the Thomist theology of the Analogy of Being, which we shall consider in a later chapter.

But, as I have said, this analogical character of natural theology became obscured during the eighteenth and nineteenth centuries, and natural theology became a presentation of a relation between God and the world in terms of a monistic system of ideas, or at least in terms of ideas which minimized any qualitative distinction between God

[1] *Process and Reality*, p. 486.

and the world. So when Bishop Butler wrote the *Analogy*, he was concerned to show the likeness of religion, natural and revealed, to the constitution and course of nature; how both can be said to exemplify the same principles and point the same morals, and how belief in both can therefore be reasonably entertained on grounds of a similar balance of probabilities. So he writes, with characteristic good sense and sobriety: " Let us then, instead of that idle and not very innocent employment of forming imaginary models of a world, and schemes of governing it, turn our thoughts to what we experience to be the conduct of nature with respect to intelligent creatures; which may be resolved into general laws or rules of administration, in the same way as many of the laws of nature respecting inanimate matter may be collected from experiments. And let us compare the known constitution and course of things with what is said to be the moral system of nature; the acknowledged dispensations of Providence, or that government which we find ourselves under, with what religion teaches us to believe and expect; and see whether they are not analogous and of a piece. And upon such a comparison it will, I think, be found that they are very much so; that both may be traced up to the same general laws, and resolved into the same principles of divine conduct."[1] If our study appears to be giving some countenance to that " idle and not very innocent employment of forming imaginary models of the world ", it is because we are less confident than Butler could be either that our knowledge of the course of nature is also knowledge of its intrinsic constitution, or that we have directly revealed knowledge of the economy of Providence. We cannot therefore assume these and then go on to indicate the analogy between them. We need to see how our conceptions of the transcendent, meaning the intrinsic constitution both of nature and of the supernatural (if such there be), are formed as imaginative models, built up out of analogies from such relations as we are able to find within our experience. Hence we

[1] *Analogy*, Introduction, sect. 14.

are conscious of a break between our explanatory principles and transcendent reality, whether nature or God, in a way which we shall not find in Butler's *Analogy*. Moreover, in the case of God, if we realize what is implied by saying that He is *absolute*, we shall see an additional reason why we cannot apply our categories univocally.

It is the recognition that natural theology had lost the sense of " the endless qualitative distinction between God and man ", and that in consequence " the Absolute has gone out of life " (to use two phrases of Kierkegaard's) which has been largely responsible for the anti-philosophical revolt of Karl Barth and his followers in contemporary theology. This at least seems to me to be the most profound impulse behind that revolt; there are other, and, in my opinion, less profound impulses ingredient in it, among them one which we have said is very often present in theological thought: the desire to live in a familiar house secure from wind and weather. This desire is more characteristic of certain of Barth's followers than of Barth himself, the cutting edge of whose prophetic criticism can in principle be turned against all theological forms whatsoever. Moreover, the reassertion, not only of a belief in divine transcendence, but of belief in authoritative theology, can serve not only as a house fortified against the tensions and perplexities of modern intellectual life, but also (and more reputably) as a base from which to attack its false gods of nation, race and class. The impressiveness of such witness on the part of those whose theology enables them to articulate their relation to the transcendent has been evidenced by both Catholics and Protestants in the continental church struggle.

But let us now examine the attack made by the resurgent neo-orthodoxy on the possibility of a natural (or, more broadly, a philosophical) theology. If this attack be right in principle, then it would spell the end of one time-honoured attempt to sustain a form of metaphysical thinking. But it also claims that there can be *revealed* knowledge of transcendent reality. We shall have to ask whether it is thereby able to escape the epistemological problems which beset metaphysical thinking.

The attack started from Kierkegaard, who unlike some of his followers knew just what he was attacking. It fell almost unnoticed at the time, while the Hegelian System reigned in almost undisputed sovereignty over the philosophical schools. Kierkegaard saw that the claims of the System could only be justified if the philosopher occupied the place of a transcendent mind or of " consciousness in general ". And he rubbed this into his Hegelian contemporaries with all the resources of his ironic wit. " Who then is to write or to complete such a system? Surely a human being; unless we propose again to begin using the strange mode of speech which assumes that a human being becomes speculative philosophy in the abstract, or becomes the identity of subject and object. So then, a human being — and surely a living human being, *i.e.* an existing individual. Or if the speculative thought which brings the systems to light is the joint effort of different thinkers: in what last concluding thought does this fellowship finally realize itself, how does it reach the light of day? Surely through some human being? And how are the individual participants related to the joint effort, what are the categories which mediate between the individual and world process, and who is it again who strings them all together on the systematic thread? Is he a human being, or is he speculative philosophy in the abstract? But if he is a human being, then he is also an existing individual. Two ways, in general, are open for an existing individual: *Either* he can do his utmost to forget that he is an existing individual, by which he becomes a comic figure, since existence has the remarkable trait of compelling an existing individual to exist whether he wills it or not. . . . *Or* he can concentrate his entire energy upon the fact that he is an existing individual. It is from this side, in the first instance, that objection must be made to modern philosophy; not that it has a mistaken presupposition, but that it has a comical presupposition, occasioned by its having forgotten, in a sort of world-historical absent-mindedness, what it means to be a human being. Not indeed, what it means to be a human being in general; for this is the sort of thing that one might even induce a speculative philosopher to agree to; but what it means that you and I and he are human beings, each one for himself." [1]

Hegelianism presupposes that there is nothing which cannot in principle be mediated through the categories of philosophical thought, and that the individual thinker is but a medium through which these ideas seek their fulfilment. This means that for such idealism metaphysics is identified with the development of its own type of philosophical logic. But Kierkegaard claims that the transcendence of one existing being by another means that, though there may be a system of ideas, there can be no system of existence. Each existence has its own inner subjectivity opaque to objective thought, which cannot be mediated in any direct communication. It can only be responded to in passionate "inwardness" by another existing being from his own subjectivity. Any direct relationship, by which Kierkegaard appears to mean the direct conveying of truth from one spiritual being to another, is impossible, unless one of the parties has ceased to be "spirit". For "spirit" exists in making decisions, and decisions cannot be externally induced. (The most even a terrorist can do to a person is to provide him with exceptionally strong inducements to decide to do something himself.) Communication between spiritual beings is, as Socrates knew, indirect communication. A teacher cannot directly convey a truth to another; he can only confront the other with teaching which puts questions to him on which he must himself decide.

Hence existence cannot be mediated in any system of ideas. "Existence" means for Kierkegaard individuals confronting one another as centres of will. The essential nature of an individual is thus hidden and inaccessible to external observation. The relation between one existence

[1] *Unscientific Postscript*, p. 109 (Translation by Swenson and Lowrie, O.U.P., 1942).

and another can never be one of understanding, in which the essential nature of the other can be grasped in thought. It can only be a relation of faith; a decision of will in which one individual acknowledges the being of another. The thinking which issues from such inner decisions Kierkegaard calls " existential thinking ".

In such an inner decision the faith of one individual can call to the faith of another; but it cannot be communicated or expressed through mediating ideas. If such be the relation between individual finite existences, the relation between a finite and an infinite existence is *a fortiori* " a paradox " which cannot be mediated in thought. For all commensurability of the finite and infinite, Kierkegaard says, is paganism. Yet Christianity, he sees, stands and falls by its claim that the infinite has been mediated in the finite, not in ideas, but in a particular historical existence. Such a fact would doubly defy any " objective " rational expression, and could only be embraced by the believer with passionate inwardness, that is with faith, so that the believer is " crucified upon the paradox of the absurd ". Kierkegaard is at the opposite pole from the type of Christianity which appeals to the words and acts and quality of spirit of Jesus as " evidences " of the divine nature. On the contrary: " The historical fact that God has existed in human form is the essence of the matter; the rest of the historical detail is not even as important as if we had to do with a human being instead of God. . . . If the contemporary generation had left behind them nothing but these words: ' We have believed that in such and such a year God appeared among us in the humble figure of a servant, that he lived and taught in our community, and finally died ', it would be more than enough." [1] " Hiddenness " (Kierkegaard's word) could not well go further. Kierkegaard may be said to have pressed it almost to the point of perversity; as also when he insists that, far from religion being something which can be " expressed " in life, to the outside observer there can be no discernible

[1] *Philosophical Fragments*, p. 87 (Translation by Swenson, O.U.P., 1936).

difference between the believer and the unbeliever. The believer enters, just as the unbeliever does, into all the relative obligations of life; the only difference is that secretly he knows that in the light of the absolute they are all utterly questionable; and he has " the edification of the thought that before God we are always in the wrong ".[1]

Kierkegaard has raised in an acute form the question of mediation. He is saying " *Finitum non capax infiniti* ": there can be no way of awareness or insight into the finite that can make it in any way a symbol or a vehicle through which something about the transcendent can be mediated. Confronted with the Christian faith in the Incarnation, he does not follow after the faithless generation who ask for a sign. He could have said " He hath no form or comeliness, and when we shall see him there is no beauty that we should desire him ". Could he also have said " We beheld his glory . . . full of grace and truth "?

He is concerned above all to contend for the incommensurability of the finite and the infinite; and if this be the whole truth, there is no place for analogies drawn from experience, for we can only recognize that we are faced by a radical discontinuity. So Kierkegaard's attack is directed against any systematic philosophy which fails to recognize this discontinuity. It is not directed against philosophy as such — witness his love for Socrates. But if the transcendent is not only outside our categories but also in every way beyond our experience, if it is to be mediated to us at all, it could only be in some way completely distinct from either reason or experience — by the God-man, says Kierkegaard, in whom we can only have faith " in virtue of the absurd ". This is the point where Kierkegaard's contention has been taken up and emphasized by the Barthian School.

The liberal movement of the last two generations had looked to a synthesis between philosophy, science and theology through the method of critical reflection on religious experience, asking what light, if any, such experience when examined could throw upon our knowledge of

[1] *Entweder-Oder*, p. 295 (ed. Schempf).

the world. In such a synthesis theology, when fully developed, would lose such accidental characteristics as were due to its having arisen within particular historic religions, and approximate to a general philosophy of religion. But in the neo-orthodoxy of the Barthian school we are witnessing a reaction against the idea that theology is a rational, scientific study built up inductively from the examination of experience. Instead, theology, it is claimed, is concerned with the exposition of *revelation*, which is something *sui generis*, to be distinguished alike from religion and from philosophy. Its proper correlative is not experience, nor the reflection on experience, but *faith*; and faith must be distinguished from any insight of reason and conscience, and understood as a divine gift, the *testimonium intus spiritus sancti*. On this view it might be said that philosophy of religion and theology start from different ends, the one working inductively from reflection on experience, the other deductively from faith in a revelation which it seeks to interpret. On the one hand, we should have *intellectus quaerens fidem*, understanding in search of faith; on the other, *fides quaerens intellectum*, faith in search of understanding. But if we think of this distinction as though it represented two parties, digging a tunnel from different ends, and hoping to meet in the middle, the dialectical[1] theologian tells us this cannot happen. For each party is doing its digging on a different level. Theology, he will say, is working from a revelation which enables it to see the world from the point of view of the transcendent mind of God; philosophy is digging with the instruments of human reason and conscience, which are warped along with the rest of man's nature, so that philosophy cannot even dig its part of the tunnel straight.

Then we may ask whether there can be any relevant relation between them. Here the dialectical theologian

[1] The Barthian school describes its method as " dialectical ", by which it means the setting of ideas against each other in irreconcilable oppositions. This leads to a plentiful sprinkling of its works with the word " paradox ". Some of these " paradoxes " seem largely rhetorical and capable of being resolved on closer analysis.

answers that although a philosopher cannot reach faith (he could only do so by submitting in obedience to revelation, and so becoming not a philosopher but a theologian), yet he has his value as a " negative critic ". He cannot attain to any positive statements which can contribute anything to the theology of faith; but he can presumably use his trained critical faculties to expose any apparently positive statements advanced by non-dialectical (*e.g.* natural) theologians or by other philosophers. He thus has a certain function to fulfil, although he cannot in the nature of the case attain to " saving faith ".

But the suggestion that the function of philosophy is to be purely negative criticism needs examination. Can any criticism be relevant and effective without some point of contact with that which is criticized, or some positive grounds from which criticism can be made? That " *omnis negatio est determinatio* " has been generally recognized by logicians ever since Plato in the *Sophist* demonstrated the impossibility of making absolute negative judgments. We can only say that a thing is *not* something on the basis of some positive knowledge about it. So criticism which has no positive point of contact with that which it criticizes cannot even make significant negative statements about it. It is not possible to be, *e.g.*, an art critic without some positive inner appreciation and knowledge of art.

But what point of contact does philosophy have with the faith in relation to which, according to dialectical theologians, it plays its rôle of " negative critic "? Is there some *Anknupftungspunkt* (to use a word of Barth's), some point at which both ways of thought can meet and speak in a way relevant to one another ?

The claim that theology is concerned with the exposition of revelation makes it very difficult to find this point of contact. For in order that philosophical criticism may be relevant and pertinent, it must raise the question of the criterion of revelation. What is the evidence on which theology claims to have to do with revelation? A criterion suggests some touchstone of judgment, by which an alleged revelation may be validated as genuine revelation or invalidated. And this suggests some principle of discrimination more ultimate in authority than the alleged revelation. It is this which the upholders of the latter deny. For a revelation cannot be judged by any higher authority than itself. " What are the reason and conscience of sinful man to judge the Word of God "? we are asked. And if God speaks, it is not for us to judge or criticize; we can only obey. A philosopher may be left asking how we know that God has spoken; if a particular religious tradition claims that He has done so, must we accept the claim at its face value? The theologian may appeal to an inner state of conviction, but this, he says, must be sharply distinguished from the assent of reason and conscience, those all-too human and perverted tools. It must be the work of the Holy Spirit, the *testimonium intus spiritus sancti.* How this *testimonium intus spiritus sancti* is related, if at all, to the strivings of reason and conscience, is a question to which the neo-orthodox give, in my opinion, no satisfactory answer. The controversy between Barth and Brunner over *imago dei*, the question of whether there is any faculty of the natural man left uncorrupted enough to discern the truth of God, is couched in terms of an *a priori* psychology, which also presupposes belief in the theology of the Fall and Redemption, and is thus not of much help to an enquiry which cannot take this scheme for granted, but is examining its credentials.

I cannot help thinking that the antitheses between philosophy and theology, drawn by continental theologians of the Barthian school, are due in part at least to the fact that their conception of the nature of philosophy is formed in terms of the particular types of radical Hegelianism and of radical Kantianism which dominated the German universities in the last generation. Whereas in England Kant and Hegel could be domesticated by the Cairds and T. H. Green in a way which emphasized their moral content, and presented them as philosophical pillars of a kind of Christian faith, in Germany their more radical elements were stressed in a way which made them exclusive alternatives to such faith. Hegelianism became a form of philosophical imperialism, an all-conquering monistic system. (We have already examined the claim of radical idealism, that there is nothing in principle which cannot be completely taken up into its categories of thought, if these be sufficiently developed, and we have seen that this claim breaks down not only when we come to " revelation ", as the Barthians would say, but at the most elementary level of sense perception.) On the other hand, schools such as the Marburg School developed the sceptical side of Kant, according to which the understanding is enclosed within the limits of the phenomenal world, and nothing can significantly be said about the nature of what transcends these limits. The transcendent becomes not only outside our categories, but also in every sense outside our experience. In contrast to these dominant influences in Germany, the notion that in all experience the mind is holding commerce with something other than itself is characteristic of the realist and empiricist strain in the British philosophical tradition. So Brunner[1] distinguishes philosophy, as concerned with the systematizing of universal ideas, from revelation, as concerned with " concrete fact ". But on the view that philosophy is interpretative of what is given in experience from the level of sense perception upwards, this distinction will clearly not do. There is an element in every " given " which is concrete and individual, and so opaque to discursive reason. It could not be exhaustively described even in an infinite number of propositions, for such propositions are abstractions from the total experiential situation in which the thinker, as an individual, is confronted by other individuals, and acts and is acted upon. We have seen that this is the case in judgments based on sense perception, so that, as Professor A. E. Taylor says, " *Sense* itself is a kind of natural revelation ".[2]

Brunner himself elsewhere recognizes that this distinc-

[1] *The Philosophy of Religion*, ch. i (English translation, London, 1937).
[2] *The Faith of a Moralist*, vol. ii, p. 89 (London, 1931); cf. also p. 212.

tion between philosophy as abstract and revelation as concerned with concrete historical fact will not stand, and writes,[1] " Our critics have not realised that if we accept the point of view of an ' historical event ', the event of revelation has become subordinated to a universal order, that of history, whereas it is in reality a category by itself. It is neither Idea nor History — just because it is the decisive event — but the unique (*Einmalige*) which, as such, cannot be part of history, but which means the judgment on or fulfilment of history. Those who have seen how historical positivism has obscured the meaning of the Christian witness just as disastrously as non-historical idealism, will only be thankful for Barth's obstinacy upon this point. An ' historical event ' can also be perceived like other historical events. It is thus never a matter of faith." We shall return to this conception later on when we come to consider the interpretation of history.[2] At this point I quote Brunner's statement as showing that the gulf is here fixed not only between revelation and idealism, but between revelation and any form of realism or empiricism. Revelation is *sui generis* in such a way that neither a philosophical nor an historical enquiry can be strictly relevant to it. Nor can there be any analogies between revelation and any form of thought and experience, even of religious experience.

If the claim of theology must be upheld in this sense, so be it. But we must face the result; it must mean that there can be no real communication on ultimate questions between theologians and the historians, philosophers and scientists who are pursuing their own methods of enquiry, unless the historians, philosophers and scientists are prepared to adopt a purely positivist attitude towards their own enquiries, and deny that they are in any way concerned with metaphysical questions. It is perhaps no accident that the neo-orthodox dogmatic theology has gained ground at the same time as logical positivism has been the dominant philosophical movement. If we are not allowed to say

[1] *The Mediator*, p. 391, *note* (English translation, London, 1937).
[2] Cf. *infra*, p. 156.

anything significantly about the transcendent, it would appear that the only escape from complete agnosticism would be for the transcendent itself to declare itself to us in some way recognizably distinct from our own forms of thought. That revelation is distinct from our own forms of thought is shown, it may be said, by the fact that the precondition for the faith which can receive it is a confession of our own utter ignorance and incapacity before the ultimate questions which concern us. So Brunner writes,[1] "The negative point of contact is a consciousness of vital need which is at the same time a consciousness of guilt". But he continues, "Faith is certain that revelation alone enables us rightly to apprehend that need, that vital incapacity, which is the presupposition of faith; and that thereby revelation itself begets its own presupposition in the crucial sense". In this case, we are still left without any real point of contact between the mind to which faith in revelation has been given and the mind to which it has not. Barth has put what may be the same point in deeply moving language:[2] "Thus God's revelation is precisely his revelation as the *hidden* God. And therefore faith in God's revelation can only give a very *humble* answer to the question 'Who is God?' and it is faith which will confess God as the God of majesty and therefore as the God unknown to us. It is faith in God's revelation which is deadly fear of God's mystery, because it sees how God Himself veils Himself in mystery. Scepticism, which thinks it also knows that God is hidden, has not reached the point of being such fear unto death. Scepticism has not been taught by God Himself that He is hidden, but is a human answer to a human question. One must know the darkness of Sinai and of Calvary and must have faith, to know the God who is *above* us and His hidden nature."

But what is this faith which can respond to revelation? In this passage it is very clear that Barth does not mean by "faith" an intellectual assent to propositions. It is an

[1] *The Philosophy of Religion*, p. 20.

[2] *The Knowledge of God and the Service of God*, p. 28 (London, 1938).

"existential" act (to use a much abused phrase [1]) in which we commit ourselves in a positive response to a demand which meets us. "This unknown God above us who is known to faith, is not an unknown natural law, or an unknown cosmic riddle or unknown fate. He *deals* with man in the very act of confronting him in the darkness of Sinai and Calvary." [2] That the essence of faith lies in a positive response to something which calls out a "yes" from our whole nature, I believe to be profoundly true. It is not even rightly expressed as a "decision" to believe (a term often used in such discussions). I believe that Calvin was right when he saw, perhaps in a distorted way, that if you had to decide whether to believe or no, you did not really have faith. When faith is present, it holds with a sense of inevitability. You cannot choose whether to give or withhold consent any more than a trained musician can choose whether or not to play the right note. In the abstract, in cold blood, he may say he is free to play whatever note he likes; but when his whole being is absorbed in the playing, he will only be able to go where the music takes him.

But can we take the fact that we sometimes find ourselves impelled to make this positive response of faith, to say "yes" from the depths of our being, below the level of conscious reasoning, as in itself an assurance that that which calls out such response is a "revelation"? Professor A. E. Taylor has described something very much akin to this in our experience of the "surprises" of a great artist. He quotes from Sir Walter Raleigh, writing about Shakespeare.[3] "He is most natural when he upsets all rational forecasts. We are accustomed to anticipate how others will behave in the matters that most nearly concern us; we seem to know what we shall say to them, and to be able to forecast what they will say in answer. We are accustomed, too, to find that our anticipation is wrong; what really happened gives

[1] See *supra*, p. 124, for the meaning of "existential" in this regard.
[2] Barth, *loc. cit.* p. 29.
[3] *The Faith of a Moralist*, vol. ii, pp. 92-93.

the lie to the little stilted drama that we imagined, and we recognize at once how poor and false our fancy was, how much truer and more surprising the thing that happens is than the thing we invented. So it is with Shakespeare. His surprises have the same convincing quality."

Something like this is also described by those who write of the experience of creative inspiration, such as Henri Poincaré, writing of mathematical ideas in *Science et Méthode*, and, more generally, Dr. Rosamond Harding in her *Anatomy of Inspiration*. Creative inspiration cannot be described simply as an extrapolation from theories or ideas held hitherto. It may come rather as a leap to a new level of apprehension, in the light of which we see the pettiness of our former ideas. Yet although the new idea is a leap, and no mere deduction from what we have thought before, creative thinkers unanimously testify to the importance of hard preparatory work. If the creative idea comes, we can see the place of the previous thinking in the light of it. Is there something analogous to this in the experiences described as "revelatory"? We have illumination which is no mere deduction from previous knowledge; but the illumination is at the same time like a leap of recognition. This may throw some light on the problem we noticed earlier — the relation between faith described in terms of the energizing of the Holy Spirit, and man's efforts of reason. We have a leap to a new level of apprehension, and yet we can say that what is so apprehended is something we have been dimly groping after. If such analogies with experiences of creative inspiration hold, then there would seem to be something peculiarly artificial in the controversy between Barth and Brunner over the "*Imago Dei*."[1] Must God, they ask, create a new nature in man to respond to revelation, or is there already something in man's nature which revelation fits? Barth maintains that there must be just as much a new creation as if God were to give the power of discerning His will to stocks and stones; Brunner maintains that man has retained the "form" but lost the

[1] Cf. Baillie, *Our Knowledge of God*, pp. 17 *sq*. (London, 1939).

" content " of the image of God (whatever this distinction means). The controversy seems to me to depend on a static conception of " man's nature ", whereas growth in thought demands a previous condition of fumbling and search, and then a leap to a new level of apprehension which may call for descriptions such as " a new creation ", and even " a gift of grace ", and yet is not unrelated to the fumbling efforts of the previous stage. To ask whether the distinction between the two modes of apprehension is one of " degree or of kind " is but another abuse of those much abused words.[1]

But this analogy between " revelation " and the experiences of creative thought would be reiected by dialectical theologians. As one of them says, " In revelation something is disclosed to me that no eye has ever seen — not even mine! I hear something that no ear has ever heard — not even my ear! Something is prepared for me which has entered no human heart — not even my own heart! Only the phenomenon, as such, can appear to my reason; but it is impossible, owing to the essential conditions of the situation, to understand revelation, since a revelation comprehended would not be one. Any ' insight ' I may have, even if it comes to me suddenly and with coercive clearness, is therefore far from being a revelation, but is at best the ' appearance ' to me of some phenomenon; so that all reports about ' illumination ', or of connections disclosed to us ' like a revelation ', are mere metaphor and a bad one at that."[2]

In this passage the effects of a radical insistence on Kant's distinction between phenomena and things in themselves is clearly shown. All " appearance " is mere appearance, telling us nothing whatever about the nature of what appears. Such knowledge could therefore only be conveyed by some entirely abnormal method of revelation. More-

[1] Cf. Baillie, *op. cit.* p. 101.

[2] Van der Leeuw, *Religion in Essence and Manifestation*, p. 565 (the English translation [London, 1938] of his *Phänomenologie der Religion*, Tübingen, 1933.)

over, Van der Leeuw is using the phenomenological method of Husserl, a method which advocates " bracketing " any metaphysical interpretations of the subject of discussion, and describing it as it appears in all its aspects, in the belief that thereby its essence as a pure psychical experience may become evident. We cannot here enter on a discussion of the blend of idealism and a kind of Platonic realism of pure Ideas in which Husserl's Phenomenology consists. As a method, it had the rare and undoubted merit of suggesting to German philosophical students that they should *look* at a subject in all its aspects and manifestations before launching out on a metaphysical theory about it. But to elevate the phenomenologist's self-denying ordinance of " bracketing " metaphysics into an insistence that no insight or illumination can ever tell us about anything save mere appearance is an example of what has been called making a metaphysics out of a method.[1] The result is to to put the transcendent not only outside our categories, but also outside our experience, so that nothing whatever can be significantly said about it, unless it be communicated to us from the side of the transcendent itself by a revelation which can bear no relation whatever to our ordinary methods of apprehension. But we have contended that, although all theoretic knowledge of the transcendent from the level of perception upwards is an interpretation cast in symbolic forms, and thus far it must be indirect, yet nevertheless these interpretations are conditioned, and to some extent can be controlled, by an actual situation of relatedness together with awareness of a relation between ourselves and what is beyond ourselves. This relation can be spoken of in terms of interaction or of encounter and response; its character in the case of religion has yet to be determined more precisely. But if this view, or anything like it, be correct, no experience can be called merely phenomenal; it is conditioned by the nexus of relations out of which it arises.

If it be conceded that all experience is constituted by

[1] Cf. Burtt, *The Metaphysical Foundations of Modern Physical Science.*

relations to the transcendent, yet nevertheless it might still be said that the differentia of revelation should lie in its being a kind of direct knowledge not conditioned by the various symbolic forms of interpretation which underlie other kinds of knowledge. This may be what is meant by those who contrast the " objectivity " of Christian dogma with the " relativism " of human forms of thought. If by this is meant that revelation consists of certain absolute propositions, this has been admirably discussed by the Archbishop of Canterbury in his Gifford Lectures.[1] He notes that through the greater portion of Christian history it has been held by Christians that " the kind of knowledge which Revelation gave consisted in exact, clear-cut truth statements. It was an immediate communication of truths as they existed in the Divine mind, even though their communication might involve some measure of accommodation to the human mind's power of reception."[2] But, the Archbishop urges, the typical *locus* of revelation is not propositions, but *events*; awareness of a divine activity may be mediated through the interaction between minds and events in the world process. " There is no imparting of truth as the intellect apprehends truth, but there is event and appreciation; and in the coincidence of these the revelation consists."[3] Thus we should not properly speak of " revealed truths ", though there may be " truths of revelation ", that is to say, propositions which express a correct appreciation of events in which a divine activity has been working.

Such a view of revelation has far more to commend it than any view which implies that faith is a matter of entertaining propositions which are immune from the conditions of interpretation which beset other forms of mental activity. The experience of living through certain events might bring home to a person a consciousness of being judged, guided

[1] W. Temple, *Nature, Man and God*, ch. xii (London, 1934).

[2] Cf. the scholastic saying, " *Quidquid recipitur, recipitur ad modum recipientis* ".

[3] *Op. cit.* p. 314.

and sustained by power beyond himself, so that he found himself driven to using phrases like " the hand of God ", and such consciousness might then be described as faith in revelation.

That divine activity was at work finally and definitively at a crucial point of history in the particular events of one human life cannot, as far as I can see, be proved or disproved by any metaphysical study; though the interpretations of the significance of that life can indeed be shown to be conditioned by the thought forms of a certain period of history, and by certain traditions of belief and expectation. Hence the difficulty of elevating either the documents of Scripture or the decisions of Œcumenical Councils to the status of revelation. The best that can be said of these (and it is a great deal) is that they have their treasure in earthen vessels. They are interpretations of the conviction that revelation was given; if we cannot go behind them and reconstruct a plain tale of the events thus interpreted, historical criticism can only, through meticulous scrutiny of the interpretations, raise the question of sufficient reason; what manner of man was this, on whose behalf his followers were driven to make such astounding claims? We shall return to this question again in considering the relation of theology and metaphysics to *history*.

Meanwhile, let us return to the contention that the correlative of revelation is faith, and that these two are *sui generis*, and demarcated from any other form of insight or apprehension. If we agree with the Archbishop that the *locus* of revelation is not propositions, but events appreciated as the vehicle of divine activity, then it is clear that no body of Scriptures or dogmatic formulations can be taken as finally authoritative, except in the sense that they are the classical documents of a religious tradition.

It would seem that the Reformers themselves were far from holding that the words of Scripture were infallible in any mechanically exact sense. Luther could indeed be surprisingly free in his criticisms of the text. They did of course hold that the Scriptural books taken together were the authoritative vehicle of divine revelation. But the Word of God was not just the written text; it was contained, or even hidden, in Scripture, and could flash forth from any passage through which the reader became convinced of the reality of the forgiveness of sins and of justification by faith, as was Luther in reading Romans iii, 16-18.[1] The Word of God is therefore always contemporary with the believer; the passage of Scripture is the medium through which God speaks to his condition in present immediacy. The power that the Bible has shown of being contemporaneous with the experience of successive generations has made the claim that it contains the " Word of God " no mere idolatry of a book. Its passages have brought home to successive generations a sense of a relation in which they stand to the transcendent. But were the Reformers, and especially Luther, right in seeing this relation, as shown in the Bible, as exclusively that of justification by faith and the forgiveness of sins? Is this the one fundamental idea in Scripture? Be that as it may, *how* the Reformers believed that the Word of God is contained in Scripture is illustrated by a fine passage of Calvin's in the 1539 French edition of the *Institution of the Christian Religion*.[2]

Nous ne cherchons point ou argumens ou verisimilitudes, auxquelles nostre jugement repose : mais, nous luy submettons nostre jugement et intelligence, comes à une chose eslevée par d'essus la necessité d'estre jugée. Nompas comme aucuns ont accoustumé de recevoir legierement une chose incougneuë; laquelle apres avoir esté cougneuë leur desplaist. Mais pource que nous sommes trescertains d'avoir en icelle la verité inexpugnable; nompas aussi commes les hommes ignorans ont acoustumé de rendre les espris captifz aux superstitions: mais pource que nous sentons là une expresse vertu de la divinité monstrer sa vigueur, par laquelle nous sommes attirez et enflambez à obeyr sciemment et voluntairement, neantmoins avec plus grand' efficace que de volonté ou science humaine. C'est donc

[1] For another such experience, cf. Bunyan in *Grace Abounding*, " As I was passing in the field . . . suddenly this sentence fell upon my soul, 'Thy righteousness is in Heaven'. . . . Now did my chains fall off my legs indeed."

[2] Ch. i, p. 21.

une telle persuasion, laquelle ne requiert point de raisons: toutesfois une telle cougnoissance, laquelle est appuyée sur une tresbonne raison. . . . Finalement c'est un tel sentiment, qu'il ne se peut engendrer que de revelations celestes.[1]

This passage from Calvin shows that the kind of response the Reformers called " faith " was a positive response of the whole nature, involving emotional and volitional as well as cognitive elements. It is rightly described as an act of self-commitment, since it is a " yes " which is said with the whole being. It is therefore distinguished from discursive and analytic knowledge, and it is not properly described as the readiness to entertain the most probable hypothesis. To believe that something is likely to be true on a balance of probabilities is not faith, but a strictly rational affair.[2] The theory of probability is an important part of the logic of evidence; it is not an analysis of faith. This does not mean that faith consists in believing against evidence; the praise lavished in certain quarters on Tertullian's sayings *credibile est quia ineptum est* and *certum est quia impossibile* is not warranted nor supported by the main consensus of Christian thought. Those who make the virtue of faith directly proportionate to the logical impossibility of its object had better keep company with the White Queen. (" I can't believe *that*! " said Alice. " Can't you? " the Queen said in a pitying tone. " Try again: draw a long breath, and shut your eyes." Alice laughed. " There's no use trying ", she said; " one *can't* believe

[1] " We are not looking for arguments or analogies on which our judgment can rest; but we submit our judgment and intelligence to (Scripture) as to something lifted above the necessity of being judged. We do not act like people who are accustomed to accept lightly something unknown which would offend them if they did come to know it: but we so act because we are very certain of its being the unshakable truth. Again we do not act like ignorant men who are in the habit of enslaving their minds to superstitions; but we act like this because we feel there the very essence of divinity showing its power, by which we are drawn and inspired to obey in full knowledge and of our own will, and yet with a greater efficacy than comes by human will and knowledge. Thus this is a conviction which requires no reasons; but all the same such knowing is founded on a very good reason. . . . Finally, such a mental state can only be the result of divine revelations."

[2] Cf. Keynes, *A Treatise on Probability*, ch. i.

impossible things." "I daresay you haven't had much practice", said the Queen. "When I was your age I always did it for half-an-hour a day. Why, sometimes I've believed as many as six impossible things before breakfast.") But faith is distinguished from the entertainment of a probable proposition by the fact that the latter can be a completely theoretic affair. Faith is a "yes" of self-commitment, it does not turn probabilities into certainties; only a sufficient increase in the weight of evidence could do that. But it is a volitional response which takes us out of the theoretic attitude. Hence the common saying that faith is that on which we act. The decision of the British Government to continue resistance in the summer of 1940 can rightly be described as an act of faith. The chances of success might have been estimated at 20 per cent, 50 per cent, 51 per cent — I do not know. But what constituted the decision an act of faith was not a calculation that the chances of success were on the balance favourable, and so that it was reasonable to act on the most probable hypothesis; nor was it a blind assertion that although the balance of probabilities was against us, nevertheless we should succeed all the same. Faith is not a matter of acting either according to or against the balance of probabilities; and even in estimating probabilities in some circumstances we judge that we should act according to the favourable balance, and in other circumstances we judge that we should act even on an unfavourable balance according to what, taking the whole situation into consideration and having regard to what is at stake, we judge to be "justifiable risks". This can still remain a purely logical and theoretic procedure. But faith is the positive response of "yes" to something which challenges our decision. The element of faith in the decision to continue resistance in 1940 lay in the conviction that *whatever the balance of probabilities* (and these could be soberly and objectively estimated as far as possible), here was a challenge which we could not refuse to meet; and the country rose in spirit with a "yes" to meet it. The fact that by the grace of God it had the faith to say " yes ", and that it had the leadership which could evoke the latent faith, may appear in retrospect to have made that moment one of the turning points of history.

The distinction between a judgment of faith and a judgment of probabilities may be further elucidated in terms of a distinction drawn by the late Professor Stocks between " total " and " partial " assertions.[1] A partial assertion is either a proposition stating matter of fact, verifiable in sense experience, or a logical proposition which can be brought into a coherent system with other logical propositions of the same type. So we could make a number of partial assertions about a man, *e.g.* that he is bald, aged 55, keeps chickens, is an A.R.P. warden, etc. But if we say that he is a *good* man, we are making a total assertion which cannot be exhaustively analysed into any number of partial assertions of matters of fact. If we were asked why we think he is a good man, we might say that he looks after his old parents, gives away some of his eggs, spends his spare time on A.R.P., and the like. But it might be possible to make any number of partial assertions of this kind, and yet they would not mean the same as we mean when we say that so-and-so is a " good " man. For it might be possible to enumerate a whole series of estimable acts, and ways of behaving, and yet at the end of it all we might not be willing to say that so-and-so was a " good " man. (" Though I bestow all my goods to feed the poor, and though I give my body to be burned, and have not charity, it profiteth nothing." To say someone " has charity ", as distinct from doing charitable acts, would appear to be a total judgment of his character, like saying that someone is good.)

The total assertion expresses a judgment of the man's character as a whole. It is therefore akin to what we described as the " adverbial mode " in perception, whereas " partial assertions " would be akin to the " accusative

[1] Cf. his Riddell Memorial Lecture, " On the Nature and Grounds of Religious Belief ", reprinted in *Reason and Intuition*, pp. 38 *sq*. (edited by D. M. Emmet, Oxford University Press, 1939).

mode ", in which we are aware of differentiated contents.

Whereas the judgments of probability would be " partial assertions ", judgments of faith appear to be of the nature of " total assertions ". They are our conscious responses to the character of something as a whole. They can be partly analysed into partial assertions; a literary critic may give his reasons for judging a poem or play good or bad. But the power of a poem or play to hold us, to arouse a conviction of inevitability, so that we say " Yes " to it, seems to be something more than the sum total of the reasons we may give for thinking it a good poem or play. In fact this positive response may be elicited before we have begun to analyse reasons.

When we make a positive total judgment with our whole being, we say that we have faith in the object concerning which it is made. " Total ", therefore, can also be taken as referring to the fact that the judgment is an act of the whole man. I have said, following Professor Stocks, that it is an assertion about the character of its object as a whole. But we may of course be mistaken in thinking that we have grasped the character of the object as a whole. Nevertheless, the attempt to do this, and not merely to give assent to those of its aspects which can be analysed in terms of discursive reason (or " partial assertions "), calls for an integrated response of the whole man, and therefore the term " total assertion " can be taken to refer both to the intended object of this judgment and to the way in which the judgment is made. Such judgments can be distinguished, as we have seen, from beliefs based on estimates of probabilities, and also from judgments of the self-evidence of logical arguments which could, of course, also be described as examples of assent given freely and at the same time seen to be necessitated. The latter judgments consist in intellectual assent given to arguments the steps of which are clearly articulated. The total assertion is not an argument, but an act of evaluation, and so includes emotional response. The capacity to make such a response is not something we can command at will; if the object holds us, it holds with conviction. If it ceases to hold us, we do not say that the balance of probabilities has been decreased, but that we have lost our faith in it. Hence there seems something incalculable about faith, and we can understand why Calvinists and others have spoken of it as a " gift of God ". It may come, and it may be withheld. It is, to use Newman's phrase, a matter of " real assent ", which logically may not add anything to " notional assent ", but which is an appropriation on the part of our emotional and volitional nature. Yet, as Newman says, notional assent may long precede, or never in fact be consummated in " real assent ". We may believe something is real, but not, as Arthur Balfour said, that it is " really real ".

If faith is to be described as a positive total response, we may ask whether there is something distinctive in kind about religious faith. The examples I have given have been those of response to a moral challenge; a belief in a person's character; a judgment that a poem or play is convincing. I cannot myself see that religious faith is something different in kind *toto caelo* from these; that the *testimonium intus spiritus sancti* is something wholly distinct from such intuitive convictions. If the theologian insists that it must be wholly distinct, since intuitive judgments are highly fallible, while the Holy Spirit can lead us into all truth, I can only plead invincible ignorance. The feeling of conviction is certainly no guarantee in any sphere that we are not mistaken; yet our " total judgments " of conviction are those to which we commit ourselves, though we may come to re-cast them later in the light of experience and fuller knowledge. The distinction of religious faith seems here to consist not in a different type of apprehension, secure against mistakes, but in the fact that the matters on which the total judgment is made are those which most intimately and ultimately concern us. A poem may carry conviction as the reconstruction of a certain mood or as a way of responding to life. We can give it " real assent " as a convincing expression of a way of feeling and may make what we may call a " total judgment " of the imagination, without also committing ourselves to accepting its " philosophy of life " when we are not reading the poem. So we can observe what has been called " psychic distance " from the poem. It does not express feelings which we ourselves necessarily have; but it symbolizes feelings to which we can give imaginative assent because it convinces us that they are feelings which someone must have had at a certain time and in a certain mood. But the religious total assertion is not compatible with this attitude of " psychic distance ", of " believing and not believing ". It is our response in what we believe to be a relation to transcendent reality; it may be expressed, as we saw in Chapter V, in symbols and analogies, but underlying these is a conscious responsive relation in which our whole nature is somehow committed. It may be, as we have said, that at certain times and in certain moods we find we can respond positively better than at others; that faith seems to come and to be withdrawn. But this is looked on as a sign of weak or unstable faith; in the mature religious person faith becomes a stable, lasting disposition. This sense of commitment to something calling out a " total assertion " about what concerns us most ultimately and intimately is the hallmark of religious faith. It is the theme of religious literature and of religious worship.

Nevertheless, I do not think it can be said that the movement of religious faith is the result of the operation of something completely different from the cognitive and conative powers we exercise in other forms of total judgment. The distinction lies in its having to do with what concerns us most deeply; our final attitude and way of living in relation to reality beyond us. It has its analogues in the " existential " attitudes of faith which underlie all serious moral and intellectual effort, or indeed all creative work. The followers of these also know the call to scorn delights and live laborious days, to discipline their natural inclinations so as to follow a search which claims their devotion. Hence for some people these may well take the place of religious faith. The religious person may believe that without religious faith these will lose the self-abandonment of worship; he may say that their lives may be built so much into the pursuit of their creative activity that if its possibilities were shattered, all but the greatest and most courageous of them would lose any power of living positively at all. But that the way of the creative worker is not a way of faith, an exacting task of discovering the way of grace for him — this, I believe the theologian may not say. If, however, he insists, as certain of the orthodox do insist, that faith can only properly be said to be present when the power to submit to revelation has been supernaturally created in us, then those who know themselves impelled to follow the inner call of one of the growing points of the spirit in creative thought and work must go their way without the blessing of theology. There might then be a "costing choice" (to use a phrase of von Hügel's) between these ways, but there could not, as far as I can see, be any real synthesis between them. The need for such a choice is a very real possibility; it is the theme of the question of the relation of theology to philosophy, which has been constantly debated, in lives as well as in logic, throughout the history of thought. On the answer we give to this question depends our view of the nature of theology. To this we must now return.

CHAPTER VII

THEOLOGY, PHILOSOPHY AND HISTORY

THE story of the relations between theology and philosophy would be almost co-terminous with the history of thought. The relation of either to science is of course another important chapter in that history. But whereas science has achieved its own freedom of enquiry by discovering its determinate methods and its determinate subject matter, the question of the right relation between philosophy and theology remains a present one. This is partly because, unlike science, neither of these has a determinate and generally accepted method. Perhaps part of the reason why philosophy and theology are to-day further apart than they were a generation ago is due to this *malaise* concerning method. Each is in process of trying to discover its appropriate method, and in the meantime, in the effort to become conscious of its methods, each insists on its own distinctiveness, rather than on the possibility of contributing in co-operation with the other to a common truth. But another reason why it is difficult to determine their relationship is one not of method, but of subject matter. Neither can be confined to a departmental subject matter, since both are concerned with the presuppositions which in the end colour our thinking about everything else. But whereas philosophy on its critical side is concerned with the examination of presuppositions, theology springs from faith in certain presuppositions, in the light of which it sets out to interpret the world. It is therefore inevitable that philosophy and theology should continually confront one another uneasily, since philosophy claims the right to question any presupposition, whereas theology claims that in the end everything, including philosophy, must be brought under the judgment of its own ultimate authority. (Not necessarily under the authority of *theology*, but under the authority of the presupposition from which theology springs.) This may become clearer if we look at some of the principal ways in which philosophy and theology have been related, some of which will be seen to be compromises, which fail to do full justice to the claims of either or of both. Such a study may help to clarify what we mean by metaphysical thinking, since our view of the relation between theology and philosophy must have close bearings on what we think about the nature of metaphysics.

1. Philosophy may be subordinated to theology by allowing reason to move only within bounds defined by revelation. Philosophy can then become a preparatory stage for theology. This is done positively in Catholicism, negatively in dialectical theology. In Catholicism, especially in Thomism, philosophy can build up a natural theology preparatory to revealed theology; but it is then bounded by the authoritative doctrines of the Church, received through Scripture, the writings of the Fathers, the decisions of the Councils and the *ex cathedra* pronouncements of the Popes. Accepting this body of dogma, it then carries out an extensive study of historical philosophy, and interprets and systematizes philosophical problems in terms of its own fundamental principles. None but a fool can fail to be impressed with what Catholic philosophers have achieved in this way. Nor need such philosophers necessarily be making a *sacrificium intellectus*; they may hold that the limits assigned to natural theology are wide enough to leave reason free to investigate all that it is competent to know, and that the fundamental principles of Thomist natural theology are the only possible principles of an intelligible metaphysics. We shall return to this question in a later chapter in considering Thomist metaphysics. At this point we can only note that, even if the claim that the principles of Thomist natural theology are a *philosophia perennis* could be upheld, the distinction between two bodies of thought, a natural substructure and a supernatural superstructure, could not satisfy the radical claims of a philosophy which seeks to investigate *any* body of doctrine whatsoever. Hence

the Catholic solution cannot be acceptable to any one who is impelled to undertake a radical criticism either of Scripture or of Aristotelian metaphysics.

Dialectical theology[1] limits philosophy not by assigning to it a subordinate sphere of natural theology, but by maintaining that it can only end in a confession of ignorance on all the questions of ultimate concern. It says in effect " There can be no philosophical knowledge of the Transcendent; but we believe the Transcendent itself has revealed itself to us in the Word of God. Accept this in faith, and you can escape scepticism; but you must then cease to be a philosopher and become a theologian."

2. Instead of subordinating philosophy to theology by allowing philosophy only within the bounds of revelation, we may subordinate theology to philosophy, and only allow " religion within the bounds of mere reason ".[2]

This is the solution which found its most famous expression in Eighteenth Century Deism. There are, it is said, certain truths concerning the nature of God and the world, which human reason can apprehend and demonstrate. Religion then becomes the practice of a virtuous life, on the basis of these demonstrable propositions. But a more sceptical philosophical criticism may question whether these propositions of natural theology are thus demonstrable. Moreover, does such a natural theology face the distinction of kind which has to be drawn between absolute actuality and interpretations relative to the forms of our thought? We have seen that religious symbolism grows out of the consciousness of this distinction; but it was lost in rationalist natural theology. As Professor Gilson has pointed out, in the Seventeenth and Eighteenth Centuries, the proper name of God became no longer " He Who Is ", but " The Author of Nature ".[3] Such natural theology is therefore in effect likely to be a myth of a

[1] For this use of the term " dialectical ", cf. *supra*, p. 126.

[2] The title of a work of Kant (who, of course, did not hold that the ideas of Natural Theology were demonstrable, except by the Practical Reason).

[3] *God and Philosophy*, p. 89 (Yale, 1941).

Demiourgos, more mythical than the older orthodox philosophical theology because less conscious of the analogical character of its language.

3. Instead of philosophy being a preparation for theology, theology may be a preparation for philosophy, and looked on as an undeveloped form of philosophy. Theology, it may be said, is a symbolic form of thought, midway between art and philosophy. It is bound to its own symbols; but philosophy can take these symbols and discover their meaning in univocal language. This meaning may be very different from what the theologian thinks it is. Such is, on the whole, the conclusion of left-wing Hegelianism; and it is not without reason that theology sees a life-and-death struggle for its very existence in its struggle with this form of idealism. But such a view is subject to the objection we raised against idealism, from its interpretation of perception upwards. We saw such idealism contends that there is nothing in principle which cannot be exhaustively taken up into univocal categories of thought. But if reality, even in the objects of perception, transcends the categories of thought, which are interpretative abstractions, its nature cannot be completely taken up into thought. Theology must uphold this sense of qualitative otherness, and also springs from the religious evaluation of absolute actuality as *holy*; its final aim, therefore, is to point not to philosophy but to worship, as St. Thomas knew when from writing the *Summa* he passed to the *Lauda, Sion, Salvatorem.*[1]

4. The tension between philosophy and theology may be avoided by delimiting the scope of both. Theology becomes a translation into intellectual language of religious symbols, which are expressive of ways of feeling, but are neither true nor false. Philosophy becomes purely analytic and positivist, analysing the meaning of propositions, but excluding questions of metaphysical truth and falsehood. In this way there need be no conflict, if both keep off the demilitarized zone of metaphysics, where conflicts might occur. But this is to acquiesce in the view that nothing can significantly

[1] Cf. Temple, *Nature, Man and God*, p. 317.

be said about the transcendent; it is also to evade the questions raised by the existence of the thinker himself.

5. The inner side of a philosophy may be identified with the intellectual expression of religion, so that it becomes a form of theology. That there can be such an inner side to a philosophy was the experience of some of the greatest philosophers, Plato, Aristotle, Plotinus, Spinoza. Philosophy becomes for them far more than merely an intellectual or critical activity. It becomes a "turning of the soul" (literally a "conversion"), "from becoming to being";[1] the attainment of a god-like state of contemplative activity;[2] the discovery of "that which matters most" (τὸ τιμιώτατον);[3] "the intellectual love of God".[4] That philosophy has been able to become a religious faith for some of its greatest masters is a fact which can sustain and encourage its students. But their faith grew out of the whole spirit in which their philosophy was carried on. We must, therefore, distinguish the *religion* of Plato or of Spinoza from the *conclusions* of either Plato or Spinoza taught as a religion. When the views of philosophers are taught by their followers as though they were a collection of religious or ethical maxims, we soon find them treated in a dogmatic spirit which destroys their real character. This happened to the Stoics and later Platonists of the Roman Empire.[5] They lost the spirit of free critical enquiry, and their philosophy consisted largely in quoting the *placita philosophorum*, or maxims of the great men of the past. Philosophy, in so far as it is itself a venture of faith, can and does issue in religion for some of those who are themselves philosophers, but their conclusions cannot provide a second-hand religion for their followers. When the views of a philosopher are treated in this way, they are likely to become bad philosophy. A philosopher can only allow himself to be turned into a popular prophet at his peril. We may add that a philosopher can only found an

[1] Plato, *Republic*, 518 c.
[2] Aristotle, *Nicomachean Ethics*, 1177 b.
[3] Plotinus, *Enneads*.
[4] Spinoza, *Ethics*.
[5] Cf. the fact that the later Greek philosophers are called θεολόγοι.

esoteric sect at still greater peril.

But if philosophy can itself issue in a form of " total assertion ", this assertion, we have seen, is of the nature of faith. In this case, there would be no conflict in principle between theology and philosophy, though there might be, and indeed are, conflicts in practice between theology and philosophy as actually pursued. Moreover, if they pursue their characteristic functions, we have no reason to suppose that they will necessarily come closer together, for they are both incomplete, and incomplete in different ways. But we are now perhaps better able to see wherein this difference of function consists. Theology is bound up with the life and existence of a *Church*, in the sense of an historic religious tradition, expressed in liturgy, dogma, and forms of corporate and individual piety. Such a tradition springs from the life and message of a Founder, in which some archetypal " total assertion " about the nature of reality became articulate. From this source has sprung a tradition in which the significance of that " total assertion " has been elaborated in the symbolic forms of liturgy, and dogma; and in which ways of life have grown up shaped by the quality of feeling which these express. These ways of life may further have given form to society through the institutions the construction of which they have inspired. A theologian is a thinker whose roots are in such an historic tradition, or who deliberately puts himself within it by an act of faith. He seeks to give expression to its basic faith in terms of the intellectual language of his day, but he brings his work to the touchstone of the archetypal total assertion by which his tradition lives. His work is liturgical, both in the sense of a *λειτουργία*, a service given to the life of his church, and also as interpreting the response to the transcendent which is expressed in the worship of his church. He therefore consciously works as a thinker of a religious community. This need not mean that his freedom of thought is limited by any authoritative body of propositions, such as formularies, though in practice it does generally mean this. But the formularies and documents expressing the " total assertion " out of which the tradition has grown form a standard which he must treat with the most serious respect. They are the classical grammar of the form of thought and life of the tradition within which his work is done. Of course, the more the theologian is driven to question these standards, the more his work may approximate to that of a philosopher; and there can be few theologians who are not driven by the urge to clarify their faith through critical thought. Purely dogmatic theology, like purely abstract philosophy, probably only exists as a piece of Barthian folklore. (Barth himself is well aware that he cannot completely avoid philosophical language and methods.) But a theologian is conscious that his work is devoted to clarifying and carrying forward the faith and life of the tradition to which he belongs, and he can thus speak not only from his individual insight but from the authority of the collective wisdom of the tradition.[1]

A philosopher, on the other hand, can speak from no authority save that of the intrinsic cogency of his thought. He may have grown up in some historical tradition; it may be the rock whence he was hewn and the hole of the pit whence he was digged, but he must win independence of mind over against it. His concern is to build up a way of thinking through critical clarification. What he can achieve in this way may seem thin in comparison with the massiveness of an historic tradition. But he may achieve some first-hand perception or piece of criticism which may contribute indirectly to the life and thought of the tradition itself.[2] The besetting danger of such independent thinking is that it may attain superficial clarity through disregard of experience other than that of the thinker. The individual thinker, therefore, needs to be conscious of the massiveness

[1] It may be as well to remind certain modernists that a tradition can embody collective wisdom as well as collective prejudice; in practice it probably combines both.

[2] It may be that a certain " Quality of Disbelief ", to use Mr. Charles Williams' phrase about Montaigne, is one of the modes which, as he suggests, " our Lord the Spirit " uses in certain periods. (See *The Descent of the Dove*, ch. viii.)

of the historic tradition, with its accumulated experience, although he must keep his independence of mind over against it. Criticism, of course, simply means judgment; it can be appreciative and not merely destructive. But it can appeal to no authority save the inherent persuasiveness of its own argument. Whether a philosophical critic has a specific function within the life of an historic religious community will depend partly on whether he can himself see his work as his contribution to that common life, and partly on whether the community is prepared to suffer him. It may well not do so; Athens could not suffer Socrates, and Spinoza was cast out of the Synagogue. But a philosopher on his part must observe the principle of justice, minding one's own business, *τὸ τὰ αὑτοῦ πράττειν*, and not claim to be a spokesman of the tradition, unless he is prepared to become one of its theologians. If he does claim to speak for the tradition, and the claim be quite properly disallowed by its leaders, then he ought not to form some schismatic sect of his own. His proper work is to search for clarity and understanding, if it may be, within the life of the religious community; but if it may not be, he must go his way, without bitterness, outside. Here Socrates showed the right way; he recognized the legitimate right of the laws of Athens to condemn him, and was prepared to abide by their verdict; but he would not give up his call to go on enquiring and questioning. His death witnessed, as Professor Nock has said, "not to a doctrine, but to a vocation".[1]

A word in passing concerning claims of intellectual humility and accusations of intellectual pride, which are sometimes somewhat rhetorically made by both philosophers and theologians. In my judgment neither pride nor humility is specifically characteristic of either activity; they are characteristics of human nature and may come out in both of them. The argument that the refusal to submit to authority is a sign of intellectual pride is a curious one; the refusal may be due to an inner urge to seek truth

[1] *Conversion*, p. 165 (Oxford, 1933).

which comes out of a profound sense of one's own ignorance, and of the complexity and mystery of things.[1] There can very well be arrogance in the claim to dogmatic certainty as made by the orthodox (or perhaps more often by the neo-orthodox). On the other hand, the spirit of obedience in which a theologian devotes himself to the life and thought of his community may produce a freedom from pre-occupation with self out of which a deeper understanding of truth may be won; while the advanced thinker who insists that a religious community should give him the right to be one of its preachers, even if he questions its presuppositions, may be simply a tiresome individualist. There is no immunity against pride in either theology or philosophy, in orthodoxy or in original thought. Pride can only be escaped when the followers of each activity of the spirit are conscious that their work is but a part within a larger whole, and so can be informed by the charity that seeketh not its own. Nor can either of them claim to be an absolute mode of thought. We are sometimes told that philosophy is merely human, whereas theology " sees things from God's point of view ". I do not believe that this distinction can be upheld. Theology does not occupy the place of the transcendent mind of God. It is the interpretation by men of their faith in the impingement of divine activity upon them. Philosophy, moreover, can be very conscious of the partial and fragmentary nature of our knowledge; that " the wisdom of the world is foolishness before God "; and yet not let this deflect it from realizing the imperative need for " large draughts of intellectual day " in the dark corners of the human mind, which may remain dark under the aegis of theology, just

[1] Cf. the following sentences from Reinhold Niebuhr, *The Nature and Destiny of Man*, vol. ii, p. 230 (New York, 1943). " Luther's contemptuous attitude towards philosophy is therefore without justification; more particularly because in practice philosophy sometimes achieves a greater spirit of humility than theology. It is saved from *hybris* by its lack of any quick means of escape from the obvious limitations of all human knowing. It has no Jacob's ladder upon which the angels of grace rightly ascend and descend; but which is used falsely when the theological Jacob imagines it an instrument for climbing into heaven."

because of theology's rightly conservative function.

Rightly conservative, because theology is, as we have seen, not simply an insufficiently clarified form of philosophy. It is bound up with the life of an historic religious tradition. And it is not true that, as Fichte said, " It is the metaphysical element alone and not the historical that saves us ". A writer as close to the idealist tradition as Professor Hocking, who sees religion as a way in which an idea " takes upon itself existence in some here and now ",[1] also sees how such ideas are bound up with the life of the historic religious community. " For truth is never truth in general; it is answer to question. Now questioning is historical; or to put it conversely, the history of any group is a corporate questioning process. Each community has its own frontier of perception, its own region of groping. It has what we may call its world-line of religious searching. . . . Now the mystic is a bearer in his own person of the questioning out of which he was born. When he joins his community in worship, he joins in its questioning — for worship when it is alive contains a new groping of the soul, not a wearing deeper of old ruts. And if he finds an answer, he must bring it back into the context of the questioning to which the answer applies. He must vest his insight in that particular historical campaign."[2] We may go further. A religion may not be only one particular " world-line of religious searching ". It may be a " world-line of religious searching " which has its source in certain experiences in history. In the great positive religions, and pre-eminently in Christianity, the life of the founder is directly relevant. The religion does not simply grow from developing the content of the founder's teaching; the life of the founder is held to be one of the crucial moments, perhaps the crucial moment, of history, in which some new relation to the transcendent has been established. The historic religion seeks continually to re-affirm and express this relation; in rite, celebration, meditation, way of life;

[1] *Living Religions and a World Faith*, p. 62 (London, 1940).
[2] *Ibid.* pp. 45-46.

and its theology makes it the key to an interpretation of the world. Thus the community whose way is defined by Torah looks to the moment when Moses stood on Sinai; the Christian Church sees its life as continuing God's act of reconciliation of the world to Himself in the life and death of Christ; Islam receives its commission from the Prophet as the community of the faithful, committed to God in submission to the stark majesty of His Transcendence; Buddhists look to the moment of illumination under the Bo tree, when Buddha saw the way of release from the restlessness of finite existence. From these moments of history something new has come into the world; new ways of living in relation to the transcendent, which have given form to new ways of feeling and of thought. These were not reached by general reflections on the general character of experience; they were born out of particular kinds of experience at particular times. One way, therefore, of defining the distinction between "natural" and "revealed" theology is (as Professor Webb has suggested) by the distinction between ways of thinking about religion which are confined to reflection on the *general* characteristics of the world and of experience, and ways of thinking which take *historical* experience seriously. The latter see in history a way through which something new may be given, not only as insight, but as achievement, as *opus operatum*. It is for this reason that the thought of a theologian must be integrally bound up with the life of an historic religious community.

Religious communities are historic communities; and their ways of thought are not philosophical speculations; they grow out of the interpretation and celebration of historical events. But the idea of "historical experience" needs further elucidation. Although the "historical element", however this should be understood, does distinguish Christianity radically from (say) Platonism, it will not do merely to contrast the "objectivity" of Christianity, as presenting historical events, with the "subjectivity" of Platonism, as expressing only man's aspirations. Those who make this comparison certainly do not mean by "objectivity" the plain tale of events. In fact the claim is made most persistently by those who have abandoned the hope that the Gospel records can be made to yield "historical truth" in the historian's sense of the term. They are from the outset theological documents, presenting not just events, but the interpretation of events. This can be taken in two senses: (*a*) the interpretation is something given along with the events, and inherent in them; (*b*) the interpretation is people's attempt to read the significance of the events. Most of those who speak of the "objectivity" of dogma must mean "interpretation" in sense (*a*). The word "objectivity" is meant to stand in opposition to the "subjectivity" or conditioned nature of the interpretations made through the forms of human thought. But for any interpretation to be "objective" in this sense, it would have to be given by some revelation, or word of God entirely absolved from the conditions of our ordinary modes of apprehension. We have considered this view of revelation already. If it is adhered to, it means that in the end the historicity of events will be decided on doctrinal grounds. The doctrinal interpretation would be a primary datum, behind which it is said we cannot go. As a comment on this I may quote Professor Manson, in a review of A. Richardson's, "The Miracle Stories of the Gospels" in the *Journal of Theological Studies* (vol. xliii, p. 93). "If once we admit the distinction between meaning that is inherent in the event and meanings foisted upon it — with the further possibility of events created to be the bearers of the meaning it is desired to convey — it becomes the more urgent to discover what did happen in any given case. If the heavenly meaning really is in the earthly event we cannot have too clear a picture of the event as it actually took place; and if this be an impossible demand, it is a matter for profound regret, and not (as seems to be the tendency in these days) for mild theological jubilations."

The difficulty lies in getting clear this conception of a "meaning" inherent in an event. "Meaning" is a term properly used of some type of symbolic relation. Does an event in *itself* have meaning, or does it have meaning potentially in relation to interpretative thought? Thought constructs some interpretation in the symbolic medium of language; and if that interpretation shows reason why the event is judged important, and the difference its occurrence made to other events, we say that we apprehend the " meaning " of the event. When it is said that certain events are " charged with meaning ", this presumably means that when we are confronted by them we are stimulated into interpretative activity. The event produces a shock in the smooth flow of experience and hence we judge that it is important. " History " is made up of events which have been differentiated from the countless other events which occur because of some judgment of importance. So history, as Professor Dodd says, is not a mere record of the temporal series of events indifferently; it is the record of such events as have been selected because " they have a meaning related to the concerns of man and society "; an historical event is an " occurence and its meaning for the persons involved in it ".[1] This is to say that history as we know it is always ideal;[2] it is a thought structure in which certain sequences of past events are reconstructed according to judgments of importance and significance. But this is history *a parte subjecti*, the thoughts in which we seek to reconstruct the course of events. Should we also say that behind this there is history *a parte objecti*, the actual course of what really happened? The difficulty is that the latter can only be seen in terms of the former; the course of events in itself is a form of transcendence, an object beyond our minds. The status of the transcendent object which constitutes history in this sense is hard to determine. It may be said to be the " past ". But the past presumably no longer exists. What exists is present events, which constitute certain " sources ", traces in the present from

[1] *History and the Gospel*, p. 26 (London, 1938).

[2] Is it necessary to remind the reader that " ideal " here is used in its epistemological, not in its moral sense?

which the historian seeks to reconstruct the past *ideally*, in thought. There can be no test of "correspondence" between present judgment and past fact, since past fact cannot be an object of observation. So the historian's test of truth is coherence; his view must make a convincing pattern out of all available evidence (records, archaeological finds and other sources). "Historical truth" is thus, as Mr. Oakeshott has said, not "what really happened", but *what the evidence obliges the historian to believe*.[1] Mr. Oakeshott indeed allows no meaning to history beyond this. "The distinction", he says, "between history as it happened (the course of events) and history as it is thought, the distinction between history itself, and merely experienced history, must go; it is not merely false, it is meaningless." This is because he does not admit that there can be anything which transcends experience. We have questioned this in our discussion of idealism; we contended in the case of sense perception, that sense perception demands a situation of interacting events out of which thought constructions are built up as symbolic transformations. A similar contention might be made concerning history. History *a parte objecti* is the nexus of interrelated events in their bearing on man and society. The last words suggest a qualification and an abstraction. Ought we not to say that history is the whole process of events? It may well be that, if nature is process, science is concerned with the life histories of organisms and even of electrons, and the histories of the larger scale nexūs of these which make up physical objects. But "natural history" can be distinguished from what is more narrowly called "history", even *a parte objecti*, in that the latter arises with the appearance of a new factor in the process. This is the human will, with its purposes and aspirations. History is then the nexus of events which issues from men's purposes and aspirations, interacting with the purposes and aspirations of other men, and with the "senseless agencies"[2] of natural processes. A natural

[1] Cf. *Experience and its Modes*, ch. iii, "Historical Experience".
[2] Cf. Whitehead, *Adventures of Ideas*, p. 6.

event becomes an historical event when human thoughts and purposes are affected by its occurrence (*e.g.* the eruption of Vesuvius which destroyed Pompeii and Herculaneum is for this reason an historical and not merely a natural event).[1] The proper categories of historical explanation are therefore not those of cause and effect, but (to use Professor Toynbee's phrase) " challenge and response ". We are interested in studying the ways in which men have acted in response to situations which have presented them with problems; the non-human circumstances are only of interest in defining the circumstances within which human action takes place. The situations studied by history are thus non-recurrent situations; they cannot be even approximately repeated, as can a scientific experiment. For each move creates a new situation in which new problems arise and new solutions need to be found. So history is concerned with interactions between human purposes and other human purposes and between these and natural events. It is sometimes said that history only begins when human purposes have attained to the level of rational distinction which we call " civilization ". Before this, the interaction between men's crude purposes and the " senseless agencies " of nature is written off as " prehistoric ". (Africa, — Hegel said, — is no proper subject for history.) But I doubt whether this distinction can be rigidly upheld. It is true that the type of evidence available concerning " prehistoric " or even primitive man is not of the type which the historian can best handle. There are no records, or charters; and such evidence as there is, is likely to be sporadic and separated by long periods of time: a skull here, a cave-drawing there, an encampment there. But even if we say that " prehistory " is archaeology rather than history, yet archaeology is in method an historical rather than a scientific study. It is concerned with non-repeatable situations, and seeks to establish enumerative generalizations (*e.g.* " Pottery of this type is not found after such and such a date ") and not universal or statistical generalizations.

[1] Cf. Dodd, *History and the Gospel*, p. 26.

It might also be said that for an event to be historical, it must be concerned not simply with the interaction between men's purposes and their circumstances, but be an instance of such interaction as has affected the course of " public affairs ". So a " private " event (*e.g.* the length of Cleopatra's nose) becomes an " historical " event only because it has affected public affairs. This is certainly a criterion by which an event is judged " important " enough to be taken up into the record of history *a parte subjecti*. But again, I doubt whether the distinction can be upheld absolutely. Much historical research is concerned with exhibiting the nexus of events in human lives in greater and greater detail. It might be said that mere " fact " as such is not of historical interest unless we can show that it has some interest in a wider context. Who is going to engage on historical research into what Queen Victoria had for breakfast on the day after her accession? But supposing it could be argued that Queen Victoria's relations with Lord Melbourne were affected by her losing her temper because she was suffering from acute indigestion. Then the question of what she had had for breakfast might be of historical interest. Moreover, a good deal of what is called " social history " is concerned with describing not only political and military events, but the kind of lives lived by obscure peasants and artisans and private persons during a certain period. How much do we learn about the Napoleonic Wars from the novels of Jane Austen? Is the fact that the war seemed to cause hardly a ripple on the surface of life as it went on in Mansfield Park and Longbourn itself a matter of historic interest concerning the England of the Napoleonic Wars?

Events, we can say, are only taken up into the record of history *a parte subjecti* as a result of some selective judgment of importance. But who is to say absolutely that the selection has been rightly made? Much historical discussion is occupied with questioning former judgments of importance, and bringing out the relevance of events hitherto overlooked.

> Say not " a small event "! Why " small "?
> Costs it more pain that this, ye call
> A " great event ", should come to pass,
> Than that? Untwine me from the mass
> Of deeds which make up life, one deed
> Power shall fall short in or exceed! [1]

History *a parte objecti* is, thus, the nexus of relationships between events formative of man's life in society. Of these, certain events are more " important " than others, meaning here by important that they are in some way creative of spiritual reality. This can only be baldly stated here: I use the phrase to mean those events which either constitute decisions, or are elements in situations within which decisions have been made, which have defined in some way men's form of life in relation to others and to society. History *a parte subjecti* (which is history as we know it) is built up on judgments of importance; it seeks threads of co-ordinated events which exhibit the forms of life of man in society in its respective periods. It is of the nature of a " composition ", a coherent pattern of " significant events " abstracted from the vast background of all the events which have occurred. In this sense it can be said that history is " events and meaning "; [2] but then we must recognize that we are speaking of history *a parte subjecti* — the " composition " constructed by man's thought in the endeavour to make sense of the " past ". We cannot speak of the pure " objectivity " of the total complex of event and meaning.

There is, moreover, the danger that this ideal composition of events and meaning may become (to use a term borrowed from Mr. Oakeshott) the " practical " and not the " historical " past.[3] The practical past is a " tradition " which constitutes part of the form of people's present beliefs, such as their patriotic or religious beliefs. It forms for them a kind of illuminated track through the darkness of past events, in terms of which they can make sense of

[1] Browning, *Pippa Passes.*
[2] Cf. Dodd, *op. cit.* p. 27.
[3] *Experience and its Modes*, p. 103.

their faith and their world. Such "practical pasts" are extolled in sagas and in sacred legends. They are histories seen through a form of faith; such are the histories of "chosen people", whether the Biblical history of the "old" and of the "new" Israel; or the sacred mission of Rome seen through the eyes of Virgil;[1] or the histories of the oppression of the working classes during the last 2000 years. Such histories nourish the forms of life of communities, and are celebrated in their festivals, holidays and holy days. Their main function is to uphold a form of life and make it intelligibly significant. "And it shall come to pass, when your children shall say unto you, What mean ye by this service? That ye shall say, It is the sacrifice of the Lord's passover, who passed over the houses of the children of Israel in Egypt, when he smote the Egyptians, and delivered our houses."[2]

It is doubtful whether life can be significantly lived without conscious relation to some tradition. Those who do live without it live as a kind of moral proletariat, without roots and without loyalties. For to be significant life needs form, and form is the outcome of a quality of thought and feeling which shapes a tradition. The "practical past" is history co-ordinated by a form of faith. What is its relation to the "historical" past? It is frequently urged, in reaction to what is called *Historismus*, or historical positivism, that a form of faith gives us the spectacles through which we can see events, and that without spectacles we could not see at all.[3] The analogy is not a very good one. The function of spectacles is to correct distortions or blurring due to our personal defects in vision, so that we can see objects in sharp focus as they appear in "standard" vision. Spectacles thus would only provide an analogy

[1] Dante brings these two "practical pasts" together; he sees Roman History as the preparation made by divine Providence for the temporal power of the Holy Roman Empire, parallel to Hebrew History, which was the preparation made by divine Providence for the spiritual power of the Church.

[2] Exodus xii, 26, 27.

[3] Cf. *e.g.* A. Richardson in *Theology*, vol. xlvii, No. 277, p. 161.

with the forms of faith in terms of which history is interpreted, if we could only see things by selecting one of a number of different pairs of coloured glasses, or one of a number of pairs of glasses each of which magnified, reduced or distorted objects in a different way. The truth behind the contention that there can be no purely "objective" history is the fact which we have recognized, namely, that history as we know it consists not of mere sequences of events, but of events co-ordinated by some selective judgment of "importance". In the case of the "practical past" this selective judgment is determined by the faith which the tradition sustains. But those concerned for the "historical past" are aware that the tradition is a "composition" built up by this selective judgment out of a wider context. "Very deep is the well of the past", runs the opening sentence of Thomas Mann's *Tales of Jacob*. And he goes on to describe how the sacred stories, such as those which have gone into the making of *Genesis*, are but "coulisses", pieces of scenery on the sides of a stage on which the eye can rest, where memory can pause and find a hold. But the historian who presses further back finds "a whole vista of time coulisses opening out infinitely as in mockery".

Moreover, the historian treats the tradition not just as a coherent pattern, but as a storehouse of problems awaiting investigation. On this investigation he brings to bear every piece of evidence he can find and which he judges to be relevant; not only the evidence of the tradition but such evidence as can be drawn from secular history or from the discoveries of the archaeologist. An outstanding instance of the attempt to translate a "practical past" into an "historical past" is the way in which certain scholars since Wellhausen have treated Biblical history, and especially the New Testament. As Schweitzer rightly says, German research upon the New Testament "is a uniquely great expression of sincerity, one of the most significant events in the whole mental and spiritual life of humanity".[1] That

[1] *The Quest of the Historical Jesus*, p. 397 (English translation, London, 1926).

it has been frustrated in its high hopes of giving a reconstruction of " what really happened " is (in the words I have already quoted from Professor Manson) " a matter for profound regret and not for mild theological jubilations ". Whenever a decision as to what was historical fact is made on doctrinal grounds, we are being confronted not by the " historical " but by the " practical " past. The conclusion may in fact turn out to be correct; or, in default of historical evidence, a decision on doctrinal grounds may be the only alternative to a suspense of judgment. But those who so decide must not try to have it both ways and claim that their faith rests on the sheer objectivity of what is " given " in history. The " history " with which they are dealing is an ideal world of the *interpretation* of events.

So, we have allowed, is all history in so far as we can know it. But history for the historian is " what the evidence obliges him to believe ". And he must, I think, be continually conscious of the possibility of new bits of evidence being drawn out of the deep well of the past, in the light of which he must recast his story. He must be conscious not only of the " illuminated track ", but of the vast wastes of darkness surrounding it. Nevertheless, history as he presents it, *a parte subjecti*, can never be the mere plain tale of events. It can only be threads of events co-ordinated into certain patterns. Events indeed must not be selected because they fit into a pattern or substantiate an historian's judgments of importance. The historian must seek as far as possible to find the pattern which is suggested by the events he is studying. But without some tentative sense of " pattern " or some judgment of what is important he would not have any questions to ask or know how to begin to look for evidence. His " view " as it takes shape must be a dialectic between his sense of pattern and such evidence as he can find. In the history of the more distant past, the mere fact that a source has survived is enough to make it *ipso facto* part of the evidence of which any pattern must take account. In the history of the recent past, and still more in contemporary history, the mass of potential sources is so vast that the historian has the greater responsibility of selecting those which will exhibit important threads of co-ordination. Hence we must doubt whether even the most impartial of historians can escape entirely from the practical past. He cannot merely recount events. He must create out of his " sources " a coherent pattern of events and meaning. " The tradition yields us only ruins. The more closely we test and examine them, the more clearly we see how ruinous they are; and out of the ruins no whole can be built. The tradition is dead; our task is to revivify life that has passed away. We know that ghosts cannot speak until they have drunk blood; and the spirits which we evoke demand the blood of our hearts. We give it to them gladly; but if they then abide our question, something from us has entered into them."[1] Moreover, events must be distinguished from one another by discontinuities which are to some extent arbitrary. And in order that we can speak of events at all they must be organized into wholes, the continuity and limits of which are to some extent conventional. These complexes of events are given names which are analogical terms drawn perhaps from natural processes, physical and biological — " periods ", " revolutions ", " movements ", " renaissance "; or are analogical personifications, such as " France ", " Britain ", " The Roman Empire ". Or events are organized under names describing their status from a particular point of view — the " Middle Ages ", the " Ancient World " (which, as Bacon long ago pointed out, was really the youth of our western world). The historical researcher is continually discovering the fictional element in these terms; the " Middle Ages " are now said to begin in the fifth or even the third century; the " Dark Ages " not to be so dark after all; the Renaissance to reach back to the thirteenth century.

Nevertheless, as we have seen in connection with the other forms of thought, such analogical terms provide the " models " by means of which we can make a mode

[1] Wilamowitz, quoted by A. D. Nock, *Conversion*, p. 270.

of interconnection between events intelligible to ourselves. They are ways in which an historian can give shape to our knowledge of an epoch, by exhibiting what he judges to be its important continuities and discontinuities. And as with the models of scientific and metaphysical thought, such analogical forms are of service if they symbolize some important mode of connection. But, again as with the models of scientific and metaphysical thought, we cannot claim that they are realistic representations. They are symbolic forms in which we grasp a mode of connection between events; but the pattern must comprise all known events which are judged to be relevant and sufficiently important to be recorded. The words "relevant" and "important" show that we cannot escape from selective judgment; but here, as in perception, the judging subject must be alert to receive new data coming to him from his actual interrelation with the manifold processes of events transcending his own mind. And in this latter sense — the actual interrelations between natural events and human purposes, and of these with one another — history is no symbolic or analogical form. It is the field of real relationships into which we are cast (for, to use Heidegger's word, to be actual is *Geworfensein*). Yet history as we know it is a symbolic form interpreting certain aspects of this process, based on selective judgments of relevance and importance made by historians. Sometimes an historian, or more probably a theological historian steeped in the "practical past", claims that his judgment of relevance and importance has given him the clue to the significance of the process as a whole. He then writes a "philosophy of history", or a sacred history (*Heilsgeschichte*). So St. Augustine sees, interwoven with the history which is the dark record of the crimes, the follies, the misfortunes of mankind in the *Civitas Terrena*, the drama of man's redemption, the history of the *Civitas Dei*. Hegel sees history as the progressive realization of the Idea, the March of God on earth; Spengler sees history as the morphology of the growth and decline of civilizations; Henry Ford sees it more simply and succinctly as " Bunk ".

A philosophy of history, or a *Heilsgeschichte*, is based on a " total judgment " of significance. It claims to be more than a finite perspective; it claims to be an estimate of the significance of the process as a whole. But such a " total judgment " could only properly be made by a transcendent mind which could evaluate it as a whole. This may be why the most searching philosophies of history have been eschatological; they have pointed to a " Day of Judgment ", conceived of as beyond history, when the significance of history will be declared. There are two games being played says Shaw's Blanco Posnet: the game we play together and the game that is being played on us. We go on trying to imagine the pattern of the big game through the analogies of our little games. And if our historical experience in our little games leads us inevitably to draw these analogies, they may have a similar type of status to other " total judgments " of a theological or metaphysical kind. But it is as analogies of this type that they must be judged. And it is to the closer scrutiny of analogies of this type that we must now return.

CHAPTER VIII

ANALOGIA ENTIS

We are approaching the question raised at the outset: the nature of metaphysics, and the sense in which it may be held to be both analogical and significant. This question can hardly be longer deferred. Science and history, we have seen, both employ analogical concepts in the form of models or fictions, and if it were possible to confine our attention to science and history as positivistic disciplines, such analogical concepts might be no more than convenient ways of organizing correlations of empirical data. But science and history cannot be adequately described as purely positivist disciplines; the working scientist is not generally content to regard his models as merely conventions. He believes that they serve to make the nature of the physical world intelligible in some more realistic sense than can a mere convention; and in support of this he can point to the way in which the good model suggests further correlations of empirical data. The historian can rest still less securely in pure positivism. For though he may claim only to be telling us what was the case, he must in fact give us selected patterns of events organized and interpreted according to judgments of relevance and importance. And some justification for such judgments may be demanded.

When we looked at religion and theology, the question of metaphysical justification arose still more acutely. We considered religion as taking its rise from certain crucial moments in which expression is given to what claims to be a response to reality beyond our minds. Theology, in its service to the life of the historical religious community, translates this response into intellectual terms. But theology is thrown back continually on the faith that the initial response from which the life of the religious community grows expresses some actual relation to reality beyond our minds. Philosophy must raise this question explicitly and face it squarely; some may try to answer it in terms of a view of a direct apprehension of the nature of reality. But this course is not open to us, since we have maintained that ideas are not direct apprehensions of objects, but abstract and symbolic constructions built up out of some more primary situation of relatedness. And since the process of symbolic construction is also one of "transmutation" (to use Whitehead's word), neither can the relation of ideas to what is other than ideas be one of literal representation. This would not need to disturb us if we could maintain that some analogical relation held; ideas would then be transmutations expressing a similarity of relation in terms which are different. If it could be held that there can be likeness of structure not only between percepts, but also between concepts and that which they symbolize, we should have such an analogical relationship. But we have seen that there are only a few cases in which we can say with any assurance that this obtains. In other cases, some looser form of analogy must be sought, expressing appropriateness of response in non-literal symbolism. The criterion of "appropriateness" would have to be sought in the nature of the relation to be expressed. So we are thrown back on the necessity of seeing whether we can maintain *some* form of non-analogical knowledge in the nature of the relation to be expressed, if we are to justify the analogies in which we seek to express it. This is a question which we shall take up in the next chapter. But before doing so we must pay our respects to a famous and carefully formulated attempt to give a justification for an analogical method in metaphysics. I am referring, of course, to the Thomist philosophy of the Analogy of Being.

The writings of neo-Thomists such as M. Maritain and M. Gilson show that this philosophy is not merely of historical interest but is capable of an impressive contemporary statement. If we would maintain that metaphysics and theology are in *some* sense analogical ways of thought, and if we cannot accept the Thomist position without qualification, it is important to try to make clear just where our divergence lies.

Thomism starts from the belief that the object of metaphysical thinking is to understand the nature of Being; that Being is prior to ideas about it, and that we must therefore start not from *essences* (definitions in conceptual terms), but from *existence*. The problem of philosophy is then to express the essence of existence in conceptual terms. This is why Thomism parts company with the Ontological Argument in its Anselmian form. The Argument so stated holds that we can pass from the idea of a perfect being to its existence. Thomism claims that *existence* (not the *idea* of existence) is prior to essence, and that the problem of metaphysics is not to see how, starting from ideas, we can deduce existence, but how, starting from the prior fact of existence, we can transpose it into conceptual terms. That there is existence is known, it is held, empirically. It is an empirically given fact that *something* exists; and the task is to elucidate its nature and the conditions on which its existence may be explained. Hence the central importance given to the Cosmological Argument. We start from empirically given existence — our own selves and the objects of our perception. These are contingent, in that their essences are distinct from their existence; their essences can be thought of, *i.e.* the idea of their non-existence can be logically entertained, without falling into self-contradiction. "Contingent" beings can also be described as essences-in-becoming, *i.e.* they are processes, in which the actualizing of their essential nature depends not simply on their own activity but on environing and limiting conditions. So we start from the belief both that existence is prior, and that any empirically given existence can be thought of as contingent. But if all existence were contingent, there would be no reason why there should be a world at all. Hence, it is argued, there must be some non-contingent existence whose essence is inseparable from its existence. This is *ens realissimum*, necessary Being, on the prior actuality of which all contingent and relative being is dependent. That is to say, Thomism maintains that the sufficient reason for the existence of contingent things is to be sought by reference not to a system of laws or logical grounds (which would be ideas), but to a necessary *Being*. For law and logical grounds are essences, statements of possibilities; and the first premise of Thomism, as of Aristotelianism, is that no world can be derived merely from possibilities; actuality is prior, so that if anything exists, something must necessarily exist.

We may notice in passing that there is a difficulty here in the term " necessarily ", which is a term of modality, properly applied to logical relations. A conclusion follows necessarily from its premises. Can we say that something exists " necessarily ", or can we only say that it exists? Professor Broad has raised both these objections to the Cosmological Argument.[1] " Necessity " as a term of logical implication is always hypothetical; it is applicable to propositions of the type " If p is true, then q is necessarily true ". But Broad reminds us no existential proposition is of this form. Moreover, if the relation of God to the world is thought of in terms of ground and consequent, the consequent must follow necessarily from the ground (as Spinoza saw). The phrase " *necessary* Being " is therefore unfortunate (and we would observe that the proper Thomist term is *ens realissimum*). What Thomists are seeking to express is not a relation of logical implication, but of existential dependence. This is the idea of " creation ", the bestowal of existence on contingent beings by Absolute Being, Who Himself simply " is ", and is under no " necessity " of causing contingent beings to exist. Whether the idea of creation can be made intelligible is another matter. Thomists would point out that since it expresses a *unique* relation, it cannot be given a generic, but only an analogical, description.

The point is that Thomism is combining the conviction

[1] In the *Journal of Theological Studies*, vol. xl.

that existence is prior to essence (being to concepts) with the conviction that there should be a sufficient reason for the existence of the world. If the essence of the world is thinkable apart from its existence, then the world must depend on an *ens realissimum* in which essence and existence are one, *i.e.* which cannot not exist. All contingent existences and ideas must depend in the end not on a supreme idea, but on an absolute existence. Calling this absolute existence " First Cause " has not been altogether happy for Thomism, since it has led to such ignorant and ill-informed criticism as assumes that all the Cosmological Argument says is, " The world exists, therefore somebody made it ", and at once rejoins, " Then if God exists, someone must have made Him, and who did? " The expression " First Cause " should not be taken to mean the first term in a temporal causal sequence, but the ground on which the whole series depends. So the question before the Cosmological Argument is whether the sequence of contingent beings can only be explained rationally with reference to a necessary being on which the sequence depends. This relation, since, as we saw above, it is a unique relation, cannot be described as a proper *instance* of a causal relation. The term " First Cause " can therefore only be used analogically. Thomism is thus maintaining both that there should be a rational explanation of the world, and that, according to the principle that actuality must be prior to idea, this explanation must be by reference to an *ens realissimum* and not by reference to an idea. I should like to observe in passing that if we accept the two premises, that there must be a sufficient reason for the world, and that actuality must be prior to possibility, something like the Cosmological Argument to an *ens realissimum* seems cogent, however difficult it may be to define a relation of dependence which is not a relation of logical implication nor of causation in the ordinary sense. But might it not be possible merely to accept the fact that " something given exists " with what Alexander called " natural piety ", and then seek to elucidate its character? Alternatively, might it be said that, although any given empirical fact may be contingent, yet the whole system of such facts, when fully understood, would be seen to be a necessary system? We should then have the *Deus sive Natura* of Spinoza, the *ens realissimum* conceived not as an absolute being on which relative beings are dependent, but as the "necessary" system taken as a whole. It may be that these three positions present the main metaphysical alternatives.

But to return to the Thomist *ens realissimum*. M. Gilson says[1] that the original contribution of Christian thought to philosophy was the notion of absolute existence, of One *qui non aliquo modo est, sed est*. In Greek thought either the existence of all things is held to be eternally necessary; or the gods or divinities are non-absolute beings; or the world is to be explained with reference to an Idea, such as Plato's Idea of the Good, which "transcends being".[2] But in Christian philosophy we have the idea of an absolute existence, "He Who is". The act by which "He Who is" causes to exist something which of itself is not is called in Christian philosophy "Creation". The problem of Christian philosophy has been to use the Greek philosophical technique and terminology to express an idea which Greek philosophy did not contain. Where the idea was contained was in the Hebrew scriptures. Gilson,[3] following St. Thomas, refers to the story in Exodus iii. 13, 14, where Moses "instead of engaging upon deep metaphysical meditations to discover the true name of God, . . . took a typically religious short cut. Moses simply asked God about His name", and got the answer, "I AM THAT I AM". "Hence the universally known name of the Jewish God — Yahweh, for Yahweh means 'He Who is.'" Hence in the Jewish-Christian religion the proper name of God is "He Who is". Put metaphysically, this says that all contingent existences and ideas depend in the end, not on

[1] In *God and Philosophy*, ch. ii (Yale University Press, 1941). I am glad to record my indebtedness to this brilliant study.

[2] Cf. *Republic*, 509 B.

[3] *Op. cit.* p. 40. Cf. *Summa Theologica*, Ia, qu. 13, art. 11.

a supreme idea, not even on the *idea* of being, but on being itself.

But can we go on to say anything about absolute being beyond that "He is"? And why "He is" rather than "It is", or τὸ ὄν? Can we say not only *an sit* but *quid sit*? Here the Thomist philosophy of the Analogy of Being (*analogia entis*) claims to have established a method whereby we can. Being, if it is not a mere formal, is an analogical notion. We cannot describe pure being in itself, since we should not know how to differentiate it. Hence to Hegel "pure being" is the lowest and not the highest of the categories. And Mr. Collingwood, arguing against the possibility of ontology, says, "The science of pure being would have a subject-matter entirely devoid of peculiarities; a subject-matter, therefore, containing nothing to differentiate it from anything else, or from nothing at all".[1] We can only know being as it is realized in determinate modes of being, and then describe it analogically. These determinations are particular finite beings with generic and specific characters. But Thomism holds that there are certain qualities of being which are not peculiar to any genus, but can be predicated of anything of which we can say at all that "it is". These are called "transcendentals" because they "transcend every genus". All being, considered in itself, is *essentia*, *i.e.* it is a thing with unity; it is what it is. All being, considered in relation to other being, is distinguished from it; it is not what it is not. All being, considered in relation to the satisfaction of desire, is *good*, because it fulfils the tendency of something to become that which it potentially is. All being, considered in relation to knowledge, is true. Thus we have six transcendentals, *ens*, *res*, *unum*, *aliquid*, *verum*, *bonum* (being, thing, unity, distinction, true, good). These can be predicted univocally of anything including the *ens realissimum*, of which we can say that "It is".

But do these transcendentals take us any further in speaking about the nature of the *ens realissimum* than we

[1] *Essay on Metaphysics*, p. 14.

were in saying simply that " It is "? We can say that it is what it is, and is distinguished from what it is not. But this does not tell us anything about its character (*quid sit*). What about the transcendentals " true " and " good "? These are used honorifically of *ens realissimum*; but, given the strictly defined meaning they hold in this context, how much do they in fact tell us? " True " means that the nature of being is to be that which makes propositions true; but does this say anything about the character of what is true? " Good " is generally understood as bearing a moral connotation. But Thomism follows Aristotle in making " good " an analogical conception, meaning the realization by anything of its end. But if we are to say that " the *ens realissimum* is good " means " the *ens realissimum* is a complete realization of being ", this seems a tautology. We seem no further, then, in predicating the transcendentals of the *ens realissimum* than we were in saying " It is what it is ".

The next assertions which we can make about being, according to Thomist philosophy, depend on the " Analogy of Proportionality ". We can say that the properties of anything are related to its being in a way proportionate to the relation of the properties of another thing to its being. So

$$\frac{\text{Man's properties}}{\text{Man's being}} :: \frac{\text{A stone's properties}}{\text{Stone's being}}.$$

This analogy of proportionality holds of the relation of absolute being to its properties, so that we can say:

$$\frac{\text{Properties of created being}}{\text{Its being}} :: \frac{\text{Properties of uncreated being}}{\text{Its being}}.$$

This does not mean that the properties of uncreated being are related to its existence in a way *similar* to the relation of the properties of created being to *its* existence; but that, as the properties of created being are related to its existence in the manner *appropriate* to the existence of a created being, so the properties of uncreated being are related to its existence in the manner *appropriate* to the existence of uncreated being. But we do not know the modality of the properties of uncreated being; we can only say that it is such as to be appropriate to the existence of uncreated being.

But if the analogy of proportionality cannot tell us the modality of the properties of uncreated being, does it in fact tell us anything? How do we even know that there is an analogy of proportionality? One possible answer may be given in terms of the Thomist view of the nature of properties as universals. Such universals can only be predicated of dependent and created being in virtue of their derivation from absolute being, which contains the exemplars of all universals *formaliter* (and moreover is the actual ground in virtue of which possibilities are possible). Hence the perfections proper to all created beings are contained formally in the absolute being, on which they are dependent for the actualization of their proper perfections. This means that terms drawn from the relative perfections of created things can be used as analogies to say something about the absolute being on which they are dependent for their actualization. They will not tell us the proper essence of absolute being, but they will tell us that there is a proportionality between the relation of absolute being to that property as realized in it, and the relation of created being to that property as realized in it according to its own mode of being. But although there is this analogy, there is also a fundamental difference; the properties of the creature are realized according to its own mode of being; in uncreated being they are realized absolutely.[1] So as soon as we begin to draw analogies to say something about

[1] Cf. St. Thomas, *De Potentia*, qu. 7, art. 7, ad. 2. "Similitudo creaturae ad Deum deficit a similitudine univocorum in duobus; primo quia non est per participationem unius formae, sicut duo calida secundum participationem unius caloris; hoc enim quod de Deo dicitur praedicatur de Deo per essentiam, de creaturis vero per participationem, ut sic talis similitudo creaturae ad Deum intelligatur qualis est calidi ad calorem, non qualis calidi ad calidius. Secundo quia ipsa forma in creatura participata deficit a ratione eius quod Deus est, sicut calor ignis deficit a ratione virtutis solaris per quam calorem generat." (Quoted by Pénido, *Le Rôle de l'analogie en théologie dogmatique*, pp. 55-56.)

God's properties in terms derived from the properties of creatures, the terms cannot be used univocally. We cannot attribute characteristics known in the particular modal being of the creature to that which is their unconditioned ground without making this distinction. But with this distinction, qualities drawn from the modes of perfection of created beings can be used analogically to say something about uncreated being. For the creature exists in virtue of a relation to uncreated being; and its properties, in so far as they are relevant to the essential perfection of the creature, are what they are because of its dependence on uncreated being which contains the archetypal idea of that perfection.[1]

On this count the proper perfection of any created thing should serve as an analogue to say something about absolute being. All modes of being, in so far as they realize their natures, are analogues of absolute being. As Father Przywara writes,[2] " The whole hierarchy of stages rising from dead matter to pure spirit is a hierarchy of stages *inside* the process of becoming; so that in consequence, since dead matter and pure spirit are both (as ' process ') equally distinct from the pure Being of Deity, any stage rising *to* God is impossible, and only that relationship counts which is shared by all the various stages of evolution between the creaturely ' becoming ' and the Divine ' Being '. It follows directly that the highest grade in the process (that of pure spirit) is not, as compared to the others, the *nearest* to God, but that the hierarchy of stages in its total complexity of union, and in its network of ' prehensions '[3] from dead matter upwards to pure spirit and from pure spirit downwards to dead matter, is *the whole of it* in the highest degree near to God and in the highest degree the similitude of God."

[1] Cf. St. Thomas, *de Potentia*, qu. 9, art. 5. " Omne quod est perfectum in creaturis oportet Deo attribui secundum id quod est de ratione illius perfectionis absolute non secundum modum quo est in hoc vel illo." (Quoted by Pénido, *op. cit.* p. 190.)

[2] *Polarity*, p. 69 (English translation, London, 1935).

[3] The English translator, Dr. Bouquet, has taken this word of Whitehead's to translate *in seinen Beziehungen.*

According to Thomist principles, therefore, all modes of being should form a hierarchical economy of things pursuing their end, without essential mutual frustration, and in their degree all things should be similitudes of God. We ought to be able to draw similitudes not only from pleasant and beautiful things, but from good liver flukes and good mustard-gas. " Good ", it will be recalled, means the realization by anything of its proper end. We cannot therefore say of anything that it " ought not to be ", since being, as a mode of realization, is as such good; and evil is described in terms of a deprivation of being. It is therefore right to speak of liver flukes and mustard-gas as " good " in so far as these are realizing their own nature. (It might of course be argued that man's sinful ingenuity discovers unnatural uses for good mustard-gas.) These can also provide analogies of uncreated being. Hence the futility of the charge of " anthropomorphism " so often levelled in ignorance against Christian Theism of the Thomist type. This charge often goes along with a simple-minded hylomorphism or mechanomorphism on the part of those who bring it. They assume that the nature of things as a whole is a replica of the model their minds have formed of the nature of matter. They are quite unaware of the *caveats* and qualifications which classical Christian Theism has drawn against applying literally to absolute being conceptions drawn from any of the modes of being as we know them.

We may even go so far as to say that the Analogy of Proportionality leans towards an agnostic rather than an anthropomorphic conception of the nature of God. It enables us to say that the properties of *anything* (not merely of a man) are related to its being in a way analogous to (but not identical with) the relation of God's properties to His being. But it does not enable us to select certain properties as especially characteristic of God, beyond the properties named in the " transcendentals ". And these, we have seen, are no more than an analysis of the Aristotelian conception of actuality. This is in effect all that we can get out of what are called " properties which signify perfection *simpliciter* ".

But when Thomist theologians speak more descriptively of the attributes of God, their analogies are drawn in a selective way from relations which are in some way judged to be appropriate. In such analogies, instead of only saying that the properties of *any* created thing are related to its being in a way proportionate to the relation of the properties of uncreated being to its being (" Proportionality "), the attempt is made to attribute particular characteristics to uncreated being. To do so, recourse must be made to the Analogy of *Proportion* or attribution,[1] whereby characteristics of one thing are attributed by analogy to another. This is a weaker form than the Analogy of Proportionality, and may come near to metaphor (as in the analogies of the head and members, and the vine and branches). Its value, in so far as it says anything positive, is to illustrate a relation which we say obtains between God and creatures by using terms drawn from creaturely relations. Hence to call God " Father " is not to speak anthropomorphically, nor is it to speak merely symbolically. It is to illustrate the *relation* of dependence which obtains between creature and creator by means of the analogy of the relation of child to parent. But the appropriateness of the analogy depends on the reality of the relation which it exemplifies. The existence of the relation cannot be established by analogical argument; but if there are independent grounds for asserting it, it can be described analogically. Such a relation of dependence St. Thomas claims to have established in the Five Ways: these are arguments from the relations of potential motion to an unmoved mover; of efficient causation; of contingent to necessary being; of exemplarity; and of final causation.[2]

Since the Analogy of Proportion attributes particular names or properties to God, it traverses a precarious path between the pitfall of anthropomorphism on the one hand and that of mere " symbolism " on the other. " Anthropo-

[1] Cf. Pénido, *op. cit.* p. 227.

[2] *Summa Theologica*, Ia, qu. 2, art. 3.

morphism" uses terms of absolute being in the same sense as of creatures, and in speaking of God as "Father" thinks of Him as a human father *in excelsis* raised to superlative degree. This misses the distinction in kind between absolute being and all modes of being. "Symbolism", as condemned by Catholic theologians, looks on such concepts as imaginative expressions of feeling, while remaining agnostic as to whether there is some real metaphysical relationship which they exemplify. This was the position of some (not indeed all) of the Roman Catholic Modernists condemned in the encyclical *Pascendi*. (The position has been aptly caricatured in the phrase "There is no God and the Virgin Mary is His Mother".)

So far we have been concerned with what, I hope, is a straightforward exposition of the Thomist metaphysics of *analogia entis*. We must now turn to comment and question.

In the first place, why does the dependence of contingent on necessary being mean that the former can provide analogies for the latter? St. Thomas would probably say because they are related as the effects to the cause. We have seen that "cause" is properly used of some one of the necessary conditions of a given event, by producing or preventing which the given event can be produced or prevented.[1] The relation of "First Cause" to contingent beings cannot be conceived in this way. It is conceived rather on the analogy of ground to consequent; except that in the relation of necessary being to being in particular modes, the modes do not follow inevitably from the nature of the ground (as *e.g.* in Spinozism). In Thomism the ground itself alone is "Necessary Being" and the modes of being depend on it not as following by logical necessity but as produced by creative act. Hence we have a unique type of relation of dependence, which is only spoken of analogically in such expression as "First Cause" and

[1] See *supra*, p. 24. Even if this particular definition of Cause be not acceptable, our difficulty remains in principle that of taking *any* definition of Cause, which is drawn from a relation between intramundane events, and extending it to the world as a whole.

" World Ground ". This presents a difficulty when we consider St. Thomas' Five Ways of inferring the existence of God.[1] These imply the validity of causal analogies when applied to the relation of God to the world. It may be said [2] that the expressions *uncaused* cause, *unmoved* mover are a recognition that the word " cause " is only used of the " First Cause " analogically. But if " cause " itself, when so used, can only be used analogically, then can we point to the fact of a causal relation between God and the world as a basis for the drawing of analogies?

In any case, even if we could allow that there is a relation between God and the world analogous to the relation of cause to effects, would this mean that we can derive analogies of the nature of the cause by studying the effects? St. Thomas would probably say yes, because the effects must resemble the cause. This difficulty was raised as long ago as Maimonides. Maimonides asked why God must be good or wise in order to cause goodness or wisdom rather than be matter or plant in order to cause matter and plants. St. Thomas answers: [3] " Effectus in suis causis sunt virtute ut calor in sole. Virtus autem huius modi nisi aliqualiter esset de genere caloris, sol per eam agens non simile sibi generaret." (" The effects are in their causes virtually, as heat in the sun. But unless the virtual power of this kind were in some sense of the nature of heat the sun acting through it would not generate what was like it.") So whatever is necessary to the perfection of matter and plants exists in God " virtually ". God is not a body, because a body is not a perfection.[4] But He possesses " virtually " such properties as are necessary to bring bodies to perfection. On the other hand, attributes such as goodness and wisdom, which imply perfection simply, exist in God formally and not only virtually. That is to say, they say something about His nature, and not only about a power he possesses to produce a certain effect in the world.

[1] *Summa Theologica*, Ia, qu. 2, art. 3.
[2] As by Pénido, *op. cit.* p. 92.
[3] I. *Summa c. Gentiles*, c. 31
[4] Cf. *Summa Theologica*, Ia, qu. 13, art. 2.

But there is a difficulty in St. Thomas' illustration of the causal relation of God to matter by the analogy of the way the heat of the sun produces effects. The sun and the effects its heat produces are within one and the same energy system. This, if anything, must be what is meant by the saying " Like causes like ". As a statement that there should be a literal resemblance between causes and effects, the saying is a mere superstition. There is no literal resemblance between, *e.g.*, pressing a button and the illumination of the room with electric light. But these two events form a single energy system. And in such systems the relation of cause and effect is not one of resemblance, but of functional dependence or concomitant variation. Is this description applicable to the relation between absolute and derivative being? It looks as though what we needed was not causal analogies so much as analogies illustrating this relation. The modes of being need not necessarily resemble that on which they depend. The important question is whether we can formulate the relation of dependence in which they stand, or find analogies which will express it.

We must of course recognize that the thinkers who have handled the Thomist *analogia entis* have been very well aware that their analogical thinking was concerned not with literal resemblances of *terms*, but in showing how the same principle or structure of relations could be discerned in different media. They have shown considerable skill in detecting such transpositions. So M. Maritain, for example, points out to such Catholic sociologists as look for a reproduction of the forms of the feudal, hierarchical society of mediaeval Christendom that the Thomist philosophy of analogy seeks not to re-establish the social forms of a former age, but to see how the fundamental principles of its sociology can be realized in a mode proper to the very different political and economic conditions of our own age.[1]

[1] *True Humanism*, p. 133 (English translation, London, 1938, of *L'Humanisme Intégrale*).

The real question here is obviously what these fundamental principles are, and how far they dictate a certain structure of social relations as exhibiting the " natural law ". Mediaeval thinkers interpreted the doctrine of analogy in this way. The relation of God to the universe, and also the structure of the " natural " group of the family, provided analogues in terms of which the right ordering and relation of other things could be deduced. The structure of the family was taken to be the patriarchal family, exhibiting relations of monarchical justice (father to children), aristocratic justice (husband to wife) and democratic justice (brothers to brothers), as described in Aristotle's *Politics*. Such an order reflected the " natural justice " of the order of the world. The order of the world, as dependent on the monarchical power of God, was the macrocosmic analogue from which the right "natural " order of the microcosms within the world could be deduced. Arguments deducing the structure of the microcosm from the macrocosm abound in mediaeval writers; they are beautifully exemplified, for instance, in Dante's argument for a universal empire in the *De Monarchia*. His papal opponents also used arguments drawn from the allegorizing of Scripture or of nature, such as the arguments for the temporal supremacy of the Papacy drawn from the statement that two swords were given to Peter, and from the fact that the moon (representing the empire) shines by light reflected from the sun (representing the Papacy). Such allegorizings were not merely pieces of special pleading to support a political point of view. They rested on the interpretation of *analogia entis* as meaning that there is a fundamental structure of being to be discerned in every part of the universe, so that the right structure of a certain part, such as the political relations of Empire and Papacy, can be inferred from the structure of another part, such as the relation between sun and moon.

The presuppositions of this type of argument are clearly (*a*) that there is a fundamental structure of being, repeated in each mode, and (*b*) that this can be formulated in terms of the structure of the macrocosm, the relation of God to the universe. My first difficulty over these presuppositions is that, according to the Thomist theology of analogy itself, the relation of God to creatures is unique and different in kind from any relation of creatures to one another. Can the relation of God to the universe, therefore, be taken as an argument for the monarchical character of society? In any case, in mediaeval political thought kingship is a non-absolutist *officium*, not an analogate of the absolute dependence of the world on God. It would be hard to see an analogate of the latter in St. Thomas' formulation of the principle that monarchy ultimately rests on consent, a principle preserved in the Roman Civil Law, and never lost sight of in the Middle Ages. In effect, what we find has happened is that the principle of the analogy of being has been united with the sociology of Aristotle's *Politics*, so that the latter is taken to exhibit the " natural " order of things. And mediaeval thinkers could well have done worse. The problem, however, before contemporary Catholic sociologists such as M. Maritain is to see whether certain general principles of relationship can be distinguished from the accidental features of the structure of a particular type of hierarchical society.

Another question which we may well raise is whether we can suppose that the same fundamental patterns are exemplified both in nature and in human society, so that the former can provide analogues for the latter. This assumption rests on a conception of nature as an economy of beings all in process of seeking their proper ends in concourse with one another. This may well be the ideal for a human society; can we say that nature provides its analogue? If so, all things, by fulfilling their own ends, should contribute to the good of one another and the whole, which would thus form one harmonious system of ends, co-ordinated and subordinated to one another. But does nature in fact bear this out? Is it borne out, *e.g.*, by the life cycle of the malaria parasite? We find in nature a proliferation of beings seeking to live not only by mutual support, but also at the cost of mutual frustration.

The conception of nature as an economy of ends probably derives in great part from the conception of nature as made up of a limited number of real kinds, each having its proper end and proper place in the series. Hence the conception of process as the actualization of a possibility, which already exists as a form, or exemplar. But if we look on evolution as a study not of the procession of forms, but of the forms of process (to use a phrase of Professor Whitehead's), we cannot look on the relation of the process to an *ens realissimum* as consisting of the actualization within the process of fixed possibilities, already existing formally as archetypes in the *ens realissimum*. It may rather be that the process is such that new possibilities continually emerge from the forms of interrelation within it. These possibilities may often be mutually conflicting and frustrating.

But to conceive the relation of finite beings to an absolute being in terms of processes developing towards the realization of their archetypal exemplars may not be the only way in which such a relation can be conceived so as to provide the foundation for an analogy of being. The relation in the form in which we have questioned it may be the form also questioned by Father Przywara as " exemplarism ".[1] But the relation of archetype to particularization is not the only way in which the metaphysical relation required can be conceived. It may be conceived as the dependence of finite on absolute being.[2] Taken in this form, it indicates why there must be a radical break in our categories when extrapolated from finite to absolute being; and, as we saw in an earlier chapter, it is characteristic of religious symbolism

[1] Cf. *Polarity*, p. 31. Cf. also A. M. Farrer, *Finite and Infinite*, p. 40: "The notion of God as *Ens Realissimum*, if that means a pool of all possible predicates somehow synthetised into one being, is the most abjectly vulgar of theological ideas. We do not know how these predicates are contained in the mode of perfection which is somehow their archetype, and to enumerate them is to give an inventory of the world from which we have drawn them, not of the God to whom we know not how we should assign them." The Divine mind cannot merely be the " kaleidoscope of infinite possibility ". (Cf. *ibid.* p. 270.)

[2] Cf. Farrer, *Finite and Infinite*, for a detailed analysis of the " essence-existence " argument in this sense.

to mark this break. Hence the rational theology of the *analogia entis* finds the proper end of its austere path not in a " definition " of the Divine Essence, but in worship of " Him Who is ", " the ground of being and granite of it, past all grasp God ".[1]

We may summarize the conclusions of this chapter as follows:

1. Thomism rightly sees that the metaphysical problem starts not from essence, but from existence. We are conscious of empirical existence, of processes of acting and being acted upon; and then we seek to formulate their character and conditions in conceptual terms.

2. The Thomist conception of the nature of Being is drawn in terms of the Aristotelian analysis of the relation of possibility and actuality. It is therefore tempting to ask whether Thomists are not formulating the idea of what, according to Aristotelianism, would constitute perfect rationality, namely, an eternal activity of free and complete self-realization, and then interpreting the universe in terms of this.[2]

3. If we try to abstract the general, univocal character or structure of Being as such, pure Being, considered as a universal, becomes, as Hegel saw, the lowest and emptiest, and not the highest category. But this is the very opposite of what Thomist writers intend. Pure Being to them is not an abstract universal, or indeed any universal *idea* at all. It is *ens realissimum*, necessary or absolute, as opposed to contingent, existence.

4. The notion of "necessary" Being needs examination.

5. The " Transcendentals ", unity, distinction, good, truth, which purport to say something about the universal character of Being, in effect tell us no more than that " It is what it is ". And since we do not know how the divine attributes are realized in the divine existence, the Analogy of Proportionality in effect tells us no more.

[1] Cf. *supra*, p. 108.

[2] If so, their philosophy furnishes a perfect example of the theory suggested in our next chapter.

6. Any characterizing of Being beyond this depends on analogies of attribution, which select certain types of relation within the world as analogues. But we cannot assume that these exemplify a universal structure of Being, as was assumed in the mediaeval analogies.

7. There may yet be some fundamental relation or relations of finite actuality to absolute reality transcending it. But to describe this relation as that of things to a " First Cause " will not do, unless more explicit recognition than we find in St. Thomas' Five Ways is given to the fact that the word " cause " can here only be used analogically. And if the word " cause " is here only used analogically, can it define the relation in virtue of which we draw analogies?

Our main divergences from the Thomist philosophy follow from an epistemological difference of a deep-seated kind. We have allowed to mind a spontaneity in the creation of symbolic forms which makes the problem of the objective reference of ideas more difficult for us to answer. We must now consider what significance might be given to metaphysical analogies in terms of our own epistemology.

CHAPTER IX

METAPHYSICAL ANALOGIES

In earlier chapters we have considered experience as arising out of a nexus of relationships and as shaped by interpretation into symbolic forms. All experience, we said, was shaped by the impulse towards the creation of form, which is at the root of mental activity, and possibly of life. But experience is not merely symbolic form, driven forward and controlled by the principles of its own inner development. We saw reason to reject those kinds of speculative and epistemological idealism which would have us identify reality with the immanent development of the forms of thought, maintaining that there is nothing in principle which these cannot permeate, so that the final goal of experience would be a state in which thought and being were one. Beyond experience would then be nothing which could significantly be called real; the only distinction which could significantly be drawn would be between a vague and inchoate experience and an articulate experience, fully mastered by the forms of thought. But we have been unable to accept this idealist presupposition. We have looked at experience not merely as creation of form, but as creation of form arising out of an initial situation of interrelated processes. The experiencing subject is a responsive centre within this nexus of relationships. Thus we hold there are things existing in their own right out of response to which experience is constituted. At the level of conscious awareness " response " can become not merely reaction to stimulus, but a modification of activity directed by a judgment concerning the nature of a relationship.

We have metaphysics whenever we use symbols with transcendent reference; that is to say, when we are not simply concerned with the patterns of our symbols, in their internal functional relations, or with the ways in which they can be transposed or translated into other symbols, but ask whether they can be referred to " things " which transcend symbolic forms. Cassirer has said that the retention of the concept of " things " is a relic of myth thinking, whereas in fully logical scientific thinking we require not " things " but functional relations between symbols. We have been prepared to grasp this nettle, and accept the need to retain this much (and perhaps much more) of myth. We need some concept — " things " if you will — to express the otherness of existences impinging on us from beyond our own experience. Metaphysics is concerned with relating symbolic forms to that which is not symbolic form, but in some sense substantival being. The difficulties in doing this, once we have recognized the objections to any " correspondence " or representional view of the relation between our symbols and reality beyond them, are such as to make denials of the possibility of metaphysics seem at the least plausible. But we cannot escape from metaphysics if we allow weight to the contention that forms of experience can only arise out of situations of interrelation. Even sense experience bears this out. There are no purely ostensive judgments reporting sense data, except as abstractions from a wider context of activities through which data are obtained. Moreover, verification by sense perception at its most exact is no mere straightforward affair of reporting sense data. It depends on elaborating techniques for obtaining observations; and these depend on the observer being no mere isolated experiencing subject, but on being related to other people within a tradition of scientific work, within which skill in these techniques may be acquired and imparted, and instruments for obtaining observations made. And in types of thinking other than science, it is doubtful whether purely private experience could mean anything. The possibility of our being able to say anything at all depends upon some medium of communication. There must be some agreed or presupposed context within which what we say can have meaning. Hence any view of language which reduces it to indicative signs breaks down. Language becomes meaningful, an expression of thought, because it grows out of communication, which can establish contexts within which non-indicative terms are significant. But this is only possible if a mind can enter into some responsive relationship with other minds. The nature of this relationship is a question to which we must return. We need only note at this point that the possibility of the development of language as a symbolic form depends on the possibility of some kind of communication.

Experience, then, grows out of situations of relatedness; and metaphysics must be concerned with the attempt to elucidate these situations, both in respect of the character of the relations themselves, and in respect of what can be conjectured through these as to the nature of that to which the experiencing subject is related. The experiencing subject interprets its experience through symbolic forms; but the question remains as to how these are to be related to that which it is experiencing.

One possible view, which we have seen Whitehead takes in his theory of perception, and which also comes out in *Gestalt* theories, is that the symbolic forms of experience to some extent repeat the pattern of that which they symbolize. If this could be maintained, they would then be " analogies " in the original and proper sense of the word. For analogy (ἀναλογία) in its root sense is a proportion, a similarity of relation between two sets of different terms.[1] If, therefore, it could be maintained that the structure of perceptual experience is proportionate to the pattern of the structure of the external field, we should have such an analogical relationship. The differences of the terms — a perspective prehended in consciousness on the one hand and the objective external field of events, whatever that may be, on the other — could be disregarded, and we could concentrate on the identity of structural pattern. Unfortunately we have seen reason to question whether we can go so far as to claim that there is a *repetition* of

[1] See *supra*, p. 6.

structural pattern. All we can say with assurance is that there is some close concomitant variation between changes in the pattern of the external field and changes in the pattern of perceptual experience. The critical control of observations tries to discriminate between such changes in our perceptual patterns as arise out of changes in their external differential conditions and such changes as arise out of changes in their internal conditions in our own physiological states. To do this may call for communication with other observers; and the fact of communication indicates some degree of resemblance of the structural pattern of the experience of one observer and that of another. But we cannot define propositions about physical objects merely in terms of the identity of structural pattern between the experience of different percipients (which would be a phenomenalist interpretation) if, as we have urged, a percipient's experience, including his experience of other percipients, arises out of his response to an environing field with which he is continuous through his body.[1] So the structural likeness which communication discovers between the experiences of different observers can be taken as evidence of some systematic character in the environment within which they are related. Hence we take the corroboration of our perceptual experience by other observers as additional indication that there is some close relation of concomitant variation between our perceptions and their differential conditions in an external world. But this does not give us knowledge of the intrinsic nature of events in the external world, independent of our perceptual experience, and this, it seems, is a limitation we must accept. We can, however, say that if we can establish structural relations within perceptual experience and formulate them accurately, there are likely to be structural relations in the external world which they do not necessarily repeat, but to which they bear some systematic proportion.

We might illustrate the different levels of interpretation by a pyramid of different levels of abstraction. Each level

[1] Cf. *supra*, Chapter III.

is built up by a selective activity dependent on the level below, and this selective activity transposes the relationships at the lower level into a new unity which is a high degree of simplification.

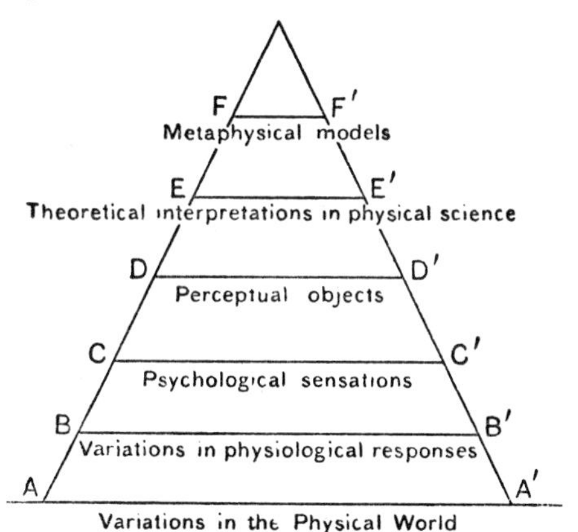

The relation of AA′ to BB′ and of BB′ to CC′ we have described as a relation of systematic concomitant variation. BB′ does not repeat the structure of AA′, nor does CC′ repeat that of BB′. But each is an organized structure related systematically to the level below (though the nature of the correlation between BB′ and CC′ is an unsolved problem). The perceptual object at level DD′ is a simplified organized whole which is a transformation of the sensations at level CC′, and through these related systematically to levels BB′ and AA′.

The types of connection indicated by level EE′ have been discussed in our Chapter IV. They are constructive descriptions of possible modes of connection between the entities or events which are postulated as the constituents of nature, these modes of connection being described in terms of an analogy with some relation within our experience (*e.g.* the planetary model of the atomic structure of matter).

Our special concern in this chapter is to consider the types of construction indicated by FF′ and their relation to the subvening levels. On levels B, C, D it is plausible to suggest that some kind of systematic structural relation obtains between each stage. The value of the analogical models represented by EE′ is gauged by the extent to which they illustrate a mode of connection between phenomena at level DD′, which is capable of exact mathematical formulation, and leads to predictions which can be brought within the same general pattern.

But when we come to metaphysical constructions (FF′), we are not dealing with theories which can be described as ways of symbolizing structural relations of a homogeneous type between physical events. In so far as a *prima facie* metaphysical theory is of this nature, it can be written off as a physical model of wide generality. A metaphysical theory proper contains analogical conceptions which not only symbolize certain structural relations, but also certain qualitative distinctions. Hence they are closely connected with the type of theory we have described in considering religion and theology; we have seen how these grow out of certain attitudes to the world having a certain qualitative character. Like the religious judgments, the basic metaphysical judgments are of the nature of total assertions; they are judgments of importance and significance which govern the development of a theory. If you ask from whence are these basic judgments derived, I should suggest that they are derived predominantly from some particular type of experience, *e.g.* intellectual, aesthetic or moral, which has seemed to provide a clue in terms of which a *Weltanschauung* or philosophical attitude could be developed. The theory must then be developed according to canons of consistency and comprehensiveness; but the basic impetus to the creation of that particular interpretative theory comes from a particular kind of experience which gives rise to a judgment of importance. The basic insight or judgment of importance provides an impulse to achieve some coherent and wider co-ordination of experience with reference to it. How far this is successful depends on the driving power of the original experience, and on the metaphysician's power of sustained constructive thought. If both of these be strong, some real measure of penetration may be achieved. But such penetration as is achieved is always from the perspective of a judgment of what is the important relation to develop. Metaphysics should, and perhaps may, be an attempt to see life steadily; but it cannot see it as a whole, *sub specie aeternitatis*. No metaphysical system is drawn up from the point of view of a transcendent mind, "spectator of all time and all existence".[1] Metaphysical theories can only be "compositions", products of the mind's form-creating power, and born in particular types of selective experience. The most that can be hoped is that the power of the composition may be sufficiently strong, and the initial experience sufficiently significant, for some important co-ordination to be achievable in these terms.

We have spoken of "importance"; and the notion clearly calls for defence and elucidation. The word suggests a subjective feeling of emphasis, and perhaps for that reason has received but scanty attention at the hands of logicians. Yet it is a notion fundamental to every kind of mental activity. This has been brought out by Whitehead, in one of the few philosophical discussions of the notion.[2] He says, "There are two contrasted ideas which seem inevitably to underlie all width of experience, one of them is the notion of importance, the sense of importance, the presupposition of importance. The other is the notion of matter-of-fact."[3] The notion of importance has sometimes been treated as though it were at odds with the notion of "matter of fact". "A sound technological procedure is to analyse the facts in disregard of any subjective judgment as to their relative interest. And yet the notion of importance is like nature itself: Expel it with a pitch-fork, and it ever returns. The most ardent upholders of objectivity in scientific thought insist upon its importance. In truth 'to uphold a doctrine' is itself such an insistence. Apart from a feeling of interest, you would merely notice the

[1] Plato, *Republic*, 486 A. [2] Cf. *Modes of Thought*, ch. i.
[3] *Ibid.* p. 5.

doctrine and not uphold it. The zeal for truth presupposes interest. Also sustained observation presupposes the notion. For concentrated attention means disregard of irrelevancies; and such disregard can only be sustained by some sense of importance." [1] "Importance" is here connected with the notion of "relevance". And "relevance" is determined with reference to some interest, problem or purpose. Our concern is rather with the notion of "importance" as governing the initial judgment from which a theory is developed. Here we may take up a suggestion of Whitehead's, that one characteristic of "importance" is that it imposes a "perspective".[2] Without some judgment of "importance" we are presented with mere multiplicity of detail, or at best a dead level catalogue of facts. A judgment of what is important brings form into multiplicity, whether in presenting an intellectual theme, or in the practical conduct of life. There is, of course, always the danger that it may impose preconceptions; but a preconception can at least sustain interest and later be corrected, whereas a mere manifold of undigested matter of fact can tell us nothing.

So we have said that a metaphysical theory develops a perspective, an outlook on the world in terms of some co-ordinating relation which is judged to be the important relation. If we ask for justification for the judgment, it is evident that no direct demonstration can be forthcoming. But there are certain criteria which can be applied. First, it must be possible to show that a coherent perspective *can* be developed in terms of this idea or group of ideas. Next, a judgment of importance can claim support from the fact of its comprehensiveness. It must be able to show that a wide range of diverse facts and experiences can be co-ordinated in a coherent form from that perspective. Beyond this, there is a further suggestion of Whitehead's,[3] that a metaphysical theory, while not capable of demonstration, should commend itself as self-evident to the civilized minds of the age. I am not sure what "self-evidence"

[1] *Modes of Thought,* ch. i. p. 12. [2] *Ibid.* p. 15. [3] *Ibid.* pp. 66 *sq.*

means in this context. It cannot be meant in the rigorous sense of the perception of logical necessity. It may mean what Mr. Gilbert Ryle has called somewhere the " Of course " with which we greet an important logical discovery. Or it may mean that the theory uncovers what Mr. Collingwood has called " absolute presuppositions ", those principles and assumptions which underlie and make possible the pursuit of intellectual enquiry at the stage it has reached in any age. In this case there may be a shift in the principles which commend themselves as self-evident in different periods (as in the Newtonian period it was self-evident that all events had causes; now it is not self-evident). In these cases we might describe such judgments as judgments of " methodological importance ". Or a metaphysical analogy may be developed from the ideas which are having a creative and stimulating influence on the intellectual imagination of the age, in its literary, religious, political and social life, and so exhibit what are for that age the important types of relation. Here again there may be a shift from the analogies which make sense in one age to those which make sense in another. It is even possible that at the same time there may be alternative metaphysical theories, co-ordinated in terms of different fundamental relations. These may not be logical contraries, but even in some sense complementary, exhibiting perspectives of the world co-ordinated from those standpoints. We may well feel dissatisfied with a view that different perspectives, developed from different fundamental judgments of what is important, may have to be allowed at the same time; but at certain stages in thought this may be the best that can be done. It may indeed be possible that there is some relation or group of relations of adequate generality and applicability to provide a universal metaphysics, a *philosophia perennis*; but, in our opinion, they have not yet been formulated.

What the metaphysician does, therefore, is to construct a theoretic model drawn from analogy from some form of intellectual or spiritual relationship which he judges to be especially significant or important. We have suggested some criteria to which such a judgment will have to be submitted in the development of the theory. But the initial impulse for the thinker himself may be derived from the fact that it is in this relation that he has found a creative point of growth. And at the creative point of experience there comes an inevitable power of positive response; the thinker finds himself saying " yes " freely with his whole being. I do not believe that any of the great metaphysicians have cast round looking for some interesting idea in terms of which they might be able to construct a theory. They have been charged with the sense of importance and significance in some spiritual or intellectual experience, and the excitement of this has driven them on to attempt to give intelligible form to other vague reaches of experience with reference to this basic insight. So Plato finds his metaphysical key in an intuitive perception of the intelligible beauty of form, the road to which leads through the austere discipline of mathematics. Hence for Plato the " real " is to be sought for in the formal elements of experience, separated from the irregularities of sense perception. The excitement inspired by the contemplation of the beauty of pure form is not describable in cold abstractions, but takes on the imaginative clothing of myth, and becomes Eros moving between earth and heaven.

Aristotle is the most austerely scientific of metaphysicians; yet would we be wrong in suggesting that his interest in tracing processes of biological development gave him the judgment of importance which led to his analysis of the structure of the universe in teleological categories? He draws his analogy from the drive to completion found in physiological desire; in terms of this every microcosm within the universe becomes an analogy of the macrocosm, which is held in being by the Prime Mover because the Prime Mover is the supreme object of desire (*κινεῖ ὡς ἐρώμενον*).

Spinoza writes his metaphysics to explain the peculiar kind of peace which comes from accepting what you see to be necessary. Descartes finds his model of a world divided into thought and extension by extrapolating the kind of thinking which produced his discoveries in co-ordinate geometry. Leibniz (I suspect) is working on an algebraic model; and is it fanciful to see in his views on continuity an analogical extension of the theory of the calculus? Hegel finds the creative moment in experience in Reason, of which philosophical thinking is the supreme manifestation. This becomes for Hegel the channel through which the universal Reason thinks in us; and " reality " takes the form of a movement of philosophical argument in the pattern of thesis–antitheses–synthesis, a pattern which Hegel contrives to find illustrated throughout nature and history. For Kant, pure reason is not the creative element in experience; its spontaneity is confined to the principles which order the phenomenal world. But practical reason, in its consciousness of moral law in which it freely legislates for itself, is to Kant the point of contact with the world of reality; and it is therefore to practical reason, and to this alone, that religion can properly belong. The moral experience of obligation is therefore for Kant the key experience in which we are confronted by the real world.

To come to illustrations from among the moderns. Alexander finds a clue to the nature of things in terms of the " restlessness " of Space-Time and in the " nisus " towards higher forms of organization which emerge from it. The analogical character of all these expressions — " restlessness ", " nisus ", " emergence ", perhaps even " Space-Time " as Alexander conceives it — is apparent. Whitehead sees the process of the self-formation of actual entities as the " appetition " towards a form of satisfaction, conceived through the analogue of an aesthetic composition of a formal, even mathematical, kind. Bradley finds his clue in the unity of sentience. McTaggart might be suggested as a test case. Here if anywhere is the attempt to construct a rigorously deductive and demonstrated metaphysical system. But even here, as Professor Broad has shown,

McTaggart had not really *proved* that the only kind of series which could form a determining correspondence hierarchy must be a series of minds perceiving each other. I suggest that the decisive factor leading McTaggart to this view was his mystical sense for affection, conceived as the perception of one mind by another, and that the body of his system in *The Nature of Existence* is an analogical argument from this experience.

Then is a metaphysical system after all simply a creation of aesthetic imagination, or an attempt to dominate the world in theory from the standpoint of a merely personal impression governed, as William James would say, by whether we are temperamentally " tough " or " tender " minded? May not such attempts deserve the stricture Bradley passes on those who claim to find a sense of significance in the experience of volition? " Volition ", he writes, " gives us, of course, an intense feeling of reality; and we may conclude, if we please, that in this lies the heart of the mystery of things. Yes, perhaps; here lies the answer — for those who may have understood; and the whole question turns on whether we *have* reached an understanding. But what you offer me appears much more like an experience, not understood but interpreted into hopeless confusion. It is with you as with the man who, transported by his passion, feels and knows that only love gives the secret of the universe. In each case the result is perfectly in order, but one hardly sees why it should be called metaphysics." [1]

What then should be called metaphysics? What, if anything, does a metaphysical theory achieve? To begin with, as we have said, it achieves the creation of an intellectual form. Without form, nothing can be grasped; there is mere vague multiplicity of confused impressions. There is exhilaration and satisfaction about achieving a form in which to express experience, even if the form must needs be a simplification and even a distortion of the original experience. Secondly, a metaphysical theory is

[1] *Appearance and Reality*, p. 115 (2nd edition, London, 1897).

prevented from being a merely subjective impression by the need to achieve some measure of comprehensiveness. It must be possible to show that the world can be ordered from that perspective; and that when it is so ordered, light is thrown on types of experience other than that which forms the matrix from which the metaphysical view is developed. If the attempt to order experience from this perspective leads to distortions of an obvious character, the theory will not commend itself. If the attempt leads to dislocations and inconsistencies within the theory itself, it will not commend itself either. The demand for systematic unity is in itself a check on the vagaries of "mere subjectivism". Systematic unity need not mean, as the anti-systematizers take it to mean, that everything in the universe is forced into the strait-jacket of a preconceived body of ideas which admit of no further development. It may be quite in order for a metaphysical system to be "open" — to indicate unsolved problems, or even aspects of reality which cannot be brought under its categories — provided that it can show that the reason why these "open" questions must remain open lies in the interpretation which the theory itself is giving. Moreover, in any interpretation of experience on a wider pattern, such as metaphysics undertakes, there are certain sub-patterns, as it were, of which account must be taken. These are the patterns elaborated by the various specialized empirical enquiries, working in their own restricted fields. A metaphysical theory cannot dictate to these empirical enquiries what patterns they shall find (we raised this suspicion against Hegel's *Philosophy of Nature*). Violence must not be done to the empirical propositions of science and common sense *within their own limits*. That is to say, there must be no dictation of the conclusions of empirical enquiries working according to their own experimental methods. The metaphysical theory may give its own interpretation of the status of these empirical propositions *in toto* — for instance, such an interpretation as that of Berkeley's phenomenalism — but it cannot dictate to the experimentalist what these propositions in particular shall be. This we saw to be the objection to metaphysical analogies of the deductive type, which claimed to dictate, *e.g.*, the number of the planets or the number of the Gospels. This criterion is of a negative character; that is to say, no metaphysical theory can be sustained which does not respect empirical propositions in their own sphere. A metaphysical analogy must therefore take account of the patterns, the *phenomena bene fundata* which empirical enquiries do in fact find, and if it can set these patterns in a wider context of interpretative theory without distorting their essential character, some gain in synoptic vision may be achieved. It is perhaps in this way that we should answer the problem which arose over the relation ot theological and philosophical to historical judgments.[1] These former were described as " total assertions "; *i.e.* they are derived not only by logical implication or by empirical evidence, but depend on an estimate of character. And historical judgments, in so far as they depend on judgments of " importance ", are also more than purely logical or empirical judgments. Nevertheless, we maintained that the fact that there is a subjective element in historical thinking does not mean that there is not an essential difference between the attempt to answer questions in a way which gives full weight to historical evidence, and the attempt to answer them on, *e.g.*, theological considerations alone. We might now put the difference in this way. Any view which attempts an estimate of the significance of events, whether philosophically or theologically, cannot be merely empirical. It implies some qualitative evaluation. But there is a distinction between those views which convey their evaluation only through some imaginative picture, and are thus philosophical or theological myths, and those views which take up into a qualitative evaluation patterns which have been constructed out of empirical enquiries. The latter kind of view is a way of looking at these patterns as a whole, without distorting their internal structure.

This may be illustrated by some of the figures used by

[1] See *supra*, p. 168.

the *Gestalt* psychologists.[1] It is possible to see two or more meanings in the same pattern of lines by switching the attention from one way of evaluating it as a whole to another, *e.g.*

This figure can be seen as a goblet, or as two profiles facing one another. Which form we see depends on an act of mental decision, and we can switch from one to the other of the two alternatives. There are, however, as far as can be seen, no further ways of seeing significance in the figure as a whole which would leave its pattern undistorted. Applying this analogy to metaphysical views, we could say that they depended on an initial conviction, an evaluation of the patterns represented by the conclusions of empirical enquiries. There may be two or more ways in which the patterns as a whole may be looked at and seen to make sense; but there cannot be a large number of interpretations which would be possible without distortion. Respect for the structures built up by empirical enquiries is therefore a check on the proliferation of merely fanciful metaphysical interpretations.

But the analogy of the *Gestalt* figure breaks down when we apply it to the relation between metaphysical and empirical assertions, in so far as in the *Gestalt* figure we know that we have the *whole* pattern in our field of observation. No metaphysical theory can be more than highly selective. It can only take account of such among the innumerable patterns produced by empirical enquiries as the metaphysican's own aptitude and training enable him to appreciate. Also the patterns produced by empirical enquiries are but fragments torn from a wider background

[1] I owe the above illustration to Professor M. Polanyi.

which has not as yet been mastered by any methods of orderly enquiry. The metaphysician must be conscious of this vague background; but he can only penetrate it through the analogy provided by the form of experience he has taken as his clue. His view seeks to express some characterization of reality, but necessarily with omission of a vast range of detail, and necessarily also with some distortion due to his selective judgment of what is important. Perhaps a better analogy of the kind of relation a metaphysical view may bear to the real, if it is successful, is not the *Gestalt* figure, but a Fougasse cartoon. Fougasse can convey certain important characteristics of a whole subject through a very few lines — the tilt of an eyelid, perhaps, or the curve of a neck. There is distortion; there is a high degree of selectivity; there is certainly the artist's personal way of seeing; yet the result conveys an important character of the situation.

If a metaphysical view can achieve this much, and enable us to appreciate better some character of experience, it is more than justified. However simplified its form, compared with the complex multiplicity of detailed experience, it need not be a strait-jacket confining that experience into a narrow framework of ideas. Its simplification may, like that of the cartoon, enable us to detect some important character or thread of co-ordination. The achievement of an intellectual form in which this can be exhibited is not the same as the hardening of a preconception, or the rationalizing of a purely private impression. For we have seen that the mental activities of constructing symbolic forms arise within a prior situation of relatedness in which the subject is a responsive centre. We may look here for a link between metaphysical analogies as " co-ordinating " analogies of experience, and metaphysical analogies as " existential " analogies of being.[1] The experiences which have stimulated a thinker into making judgments of importance, and which have set the tone and direction of his metaphysical thinking, have been experiences in which he

[1] See *supra*, p. 14.

has had the strongest impression of contact with reality other than himself. The impression may not be substantiated; perhaps part of the necessity he finds for developing the metaphysical view comes from an urge to see whether it can be substantiated. Even Hegel, the prince of systematizers, can only make the claims he does make for philosophical reason because he believes that in philosophical reason he experiences the spearhead of universal reason thinking through him.

But Hegel, like other idealists, did not recognize the analogical character of his metaphysics. He could thus see his system as the complete articulation of the Absolute in conscious thought. By no means all metaphysicians have made so grandiose a claim. The anti-philosophical polemics of dialectical theologians [1] should be directed not against reason, but against the pretensions of reason in the Hegelian system.

If the dialectical theologians are right, our metaphysical analogies could in no sense give insight into the nature of reality; they could only (as Barth has more than hinted) tell us something about the nature of the human mind. Even that need not mean they were lost labour; the symbolic forms in which man finds himself drawn to order his experience will always be part of his proper study. But it would mean explaining away the conviction by which we have seen that the first-hand metaphysical thinker is impelled — the conviction that some particular form of intellectual spiritual experience has given him insight. Insight into what? If into experience, then may not experience again be simply the expression of the nature of his own mind?

This can only be answered, as far as I can see, if it can be maintained that experience is not only a spontaneous process of form creation, but arises out of a relation to that which transcends the subject. The transcendent may then be outside our categories; but that does not mean that it is entirely outside our experience. It is the environment

[1] See *supra*, p. 126.

in which we live and move and have our being. We have seen that even sensory verification depends on there being more in the environment than is disclosed through the senses; it depends on the possibility of the enquirer entering into some kind of communication with other minds both as collaborators and in order that language may have meaning. Hence some measure of communication and relationship is a condition for any way in which experience can be significant.

But perhaps we are wrong in imagining that it can be significant. Perhaps no relationship is possible, either between one mind and another, or between a human and an infinite mind. Perhaps such experiences of relationship as we seem to have always turn out nugatory. We are conscious that there is a reality transcending us. We are conscious of an imperative demand that we enter into a right relation with it. But what if every attempt at relationship with other people or with the powers above is frustrated? There may be a perversity in the nature of things like the perversity of dreams, when we feel that it is vitally important that we should do something, but cannot discover what it is; that we should reach some destination, but it seems as though the machinery of a whole Circumlocution Office were working to frustrate our efforts; we feel we are guilty of something, but we cannot find out what it is, nor can we find the judge who is condemning us. Such a condition of metaphysical frustration is expressed with unforgettable power in Franz Kafka's psychological allegories. It represents one of the profoundly serious metaphysical possibilities, divided by a gulf from any form of positivism or mere agnosticism. The transcendent is there; it makes its demand on us. But we cannot enter into communication with it.

For those who find themselves driven to this conclusion, metaphysical thinking can only be a negative dialectic, the criticism which discloses some romantic fallacy in any thought or experience which claims that we can enter into any fundamental communication with that which transcends our own minds. And I do not know of any demonstrative argument by which such a position can be refuted. For we have said that there is no direct apprehension of the intrinsic nature of transcendent reality. We only know it through relationships interpreted in the symbolic forms of our thinking. Yet even Kafka's allegory of frustration itself presupposes some relationship — that reality is such as to make demands on us, though we cannot fulfil them or even discover what they are.

But besides the metaphysics of frustration, we may also have the metaphysics which fastens on such possibilities of positive relationship or communication as our experience itself may also suggest. For instance, there is the kind of responsive awareness which makes possible a work of art. Works of art are no mere realistic representations; they are symbolic forms, expressive of a way in which the artist has felt and perceived his subject. Yet the genuine work of art has a quality of independent life; we can contemplate it as something which has achieved being-for-itself; it gives us a feeling of completion and harmony, so that extraneous notes and information about the artist, or the circumstances of its production, are not necessary in order that we may enjoy it. The possibilities of so entering into responsive awareness of other people and of things that we are conscious of their *being* in their own right is a question on which those who are thinking with discernment about the nature of " non-propositional knowing " may be able to throw more light.

Meanwhile a pioneer work, which looks already like becoming a classic, is Martin Buber's philosophical meditation, *Ich und Du*.[1] A good deal has been written elsewhere by others[2] about Buber's distinction between " primary word " signified by the expression " I-Thou ", and the " primary word " signified by the expression

[1] English translation, *I and Thou*, by R. Gregor Smith (T. & T. Clark, 1937).

[2] *E.g.* H. H. Farmer, *The World and God* (London, 1935), and J. H. Oldham, *All Real Life is Meeting* (Christian Newsletter Books, 1943).

"I-it". In the relation "I-it" we have the subject's relation to objects apprehended as existing contiguously in time and space, and bounding one another.[1] In the relation "I-thou" we are conscious of being confronted by another centre of experience. We cannot include the "Thou" merely as an object within our own experience; we must respect it as an independent centre of experience from which the world is apprehended from a perspective which is not our perspective.

Professor Karl Heim has tried to express the relation between two fields of consciousness, each of which is an independent and infinite system, in terms of relations between "dimensions". In this he has been widely followed, *e.g.* by Professor H. H. Farmer and Dr. Oldham. I cannot feel that this is altogether fortunate. "Dimension" is a term fraught with emotional suggestion to the unmathematically minded. We have all heard dimly of a fourth dimension, and the term suggests occult mysteries. Professor Heim describes a dimensional relation as a difference between two manifolds each of which is a separate and infinite system.[2] For instance, a plane of infinite extent can be erected at right angles, intersecting any given plane. This definition is then taken to express the relation between different perspectives. When we look at a thing from different aspects, each perspective is a distinct spatial plane, yet each comprises the whole object.[3] The definition is then extended to the relation between one *percipient centre*, seeing the world from his perspective, and another percipient centre seeing it from his. "For, if another is there at all, then everything that is there for me, everything that can come within the domain of my consciousness — houses, people, animals, plants, stars — must be there for the other person as well. They must come within the sphere of his

[1] This, of course, may not be the last word about "physical objects", especially if we accept the principle of Whitehead's denial of "simple location". But Buber's description may perhaps be allowed to stand as stating the usual mode in which we apprehend physical objects.

[2] *God Transcendent*, p. 58 (English translation, London, 1935, of *Glaube und Denken*, 3rd edition).

[3] *Ibid.* p. 64.

consciousness too. My world is also his world. Then, if the other is there at all, he must be everywhere. I cannot escape into any part of my objective world into which he cannot follow me. For every place into which I may flee lies no less within the horizons of his consciousness. That follows from the inapprehensible dimensional unity of the two infinitudes, which both claim to embrace the whole of reality." [1]

Two infinite dimensions can be related to one another if they have an element in common, *e.g.* the point from which a line is drawn vertically to any given line, or the angle at which two planes intersect. So there may be contact between one world of consciousness and another world of consciousness if they have a common content. This means, presumably, that I become aware of some element in my experience as also an element in your experience. This does not mean that I recognize that an object I see from my perspective is also an object you see from your perspective; but it means that we are conscious of an experience as a shared act. "I know that the very same performance which in my consciousness-space is passive, is active in the consciousness-space of the other person, and *vice versa*. I *hear* the word which you *speak*: I *speak* the word which you *hear*. We make contact when I know that the same act which for you is speaking is for me hearing, and *vice versa*." [2]

This description of the relation between two centres of consciousness in terms of "dimensions" may be a useful analogy as bringing out the distinction of such a relation from one of mere contiguity in space. But the word is dangerous because, as I have said, it has an emotional penumbra of mystery about it, which makes people think that by using it we have not only an analogy, but a definition of the relation we are considering. "Dimension" is strictly a term of measurement, applied to the number of co-ordinates up to *n* which may be necessary to locate a point. To talk of time as the "fourth dimension" is

[1] *God Transcendent*, p. 100. [2] *Ibid.* p. 169.

therefore simply to treat it mathematically for purposes of locating a point as though it were another linear dimension. Can "dimension" be used to express what is meant by "perspective from a certain standpoint of conscious experience"? We seem to have an example of a *μετάβασις εἰς ἄλλο γένος*.[1]

The confusion becomes even worse when the term "dimension" is applied to the relation between the world and God. Heim makes a great deal of what he thinks was the pre-Copernican conception of transcendence, in which he says the universe was thought of as a finite, enclosed system, and God was quite straightforwardly "beyond" it. But now, he says, we know that the Universe is infinite,[2] and what therefore can be meant by saying that God is "beyond" it? He then gives us an elaborate account of "dimensional boundaries" to describe how it is possible for two infinite spaces to be related. But we are left wondering how far all this throws any light whatever on what is meant by the "transcendence of God". In the first place, it is doubtful whether philosophical, as distinct from popular, theology ever literally thought of God as inhabiting a region "above the bright blue sky". The notions of "above" and "below" could be seen by very little thought to be symbolic. But the word "dimension" sounds sufficiently impressive to deceive even the more sophisticated (as it seems to have deceived so careful a thinker as Professor Farmer[3]) into thinking that it gives an explanation and not a mere spatial analogy for something

[1] In a note on p. 233, Heim, in replying to a critic, says, "According to Diem, therefore, it is permissible to use the term 'co-ordinate' even of the fourth, or up to the *n*th dimension of non-Euclidean geometry, where we have passed beyond the possibility of demonstration. In order to be known as a co-ordinate, *it is necessary only that a relation should be capable of algebraic expression*." [Italics mine.] "If this is admitted, then there is no case for withholding the term from other relations which cannot be directly demonstrated. These also must be regarded as co-ordinates of a higher order." But the point is, surely, that the co-ordinates *are* capable of algebraic expression, and so can be represented on a graph. This is not the case with Heim's so-called "higher" co-ordinates in an "I-Thou" relation.

[2] Do we?

[3] See, *e.g.*, *The World and God*, pp. 103-105

non-spatial. It may be less misleading to content ourselves with the simpler language of religious symbolism, and speak of the Spirit being given from " on high ", rather than to talk mysteriously about God as a further " dimension of being ".

What is more, in the end Heim tells us that no intramundane relations of transcendence can explain the relation of the world to God. This relation is entirely *sui generis*, wholly other than any form of intramundane relation. In this case, we are left rather wondering what the elaborate discussion of " dimensions " has in fact achieved. Possibly the conclusion that whatever the relation of God to the world, it is *not* to be described in terms of a relation between dimensions. We could wish that those who refer in tones of deep acknowledgment to Heim's book recognized that this was its upshot. Instead, the book has led to an influence of the term " dimension " on theological literature which has increased, is increasing, and ought to be diminished (which conviction may be offered as an excuse for this digression).

But if *no* intramundane relation throws any light upon the relation of God to the world, then if we are to know anything about it at all, we are thrown back on some revelation *ab extra* which is entirely unrelated to our ordinary modes of apprehension. This is of course the conclusion which Heim gladly draws; but if it must be drawn, then, as we have seen, there can be no relevant relation between theology and the metaphysical analogies drawn by philosophers from experience. Revealed theology and metaphysical philosophy must then go their separate ways. But metaphysical philosophy need not for that reason simply be a subjective exposition of the forms of the human mind. It might be a reflection, for instance, upon moments of awareness such as Buber has described in terms of his " I-Thou " relation. In such moments, the subject is aware that he is in *rapport* with another being, and not only egoistically dominating it by his own interpretative activity. Interpretative activity is so generally dominant that the times when we are able to be receptively aware of another, when some real communication passes between us, are rare and of brief duration. But they may come, as by grace, in the relation between one person and another when the tragic veil of subjectivity is momentarily lifted. Such a moment is recorded by Julia de Beausobre in her book *The Woman who could not Die* (the record of her imprisonment in the inner prison of the G.P.U.; a book in which an artist's rare integrity of perception has been able to transmute horror and squalor into strange beauty). The Governor of the prison comes to see her, " There is only a corner of the table between us. We look at each other. And we see each other. In that moment's hush that follows we are both present at the eternal miracle, the lightning-quick nativity of human understanding. I see that it is not only Party discipline that keeps this old and saddened communist from giving up the distasteful work to which he has been appointed. I see that in the unavowed depths of his heart, in the subconscious luminous clarity of it, he knows that it is good and right for him to be Governor of the Palace of Torture, instead of the awful freaks who might be, if he were not. I see him realize with wonder and relief that I am not hostile to him or to any one, or anything. The barrier of cruel superficialities has fallen away, and we both know that all things in all eternity will be good and clear between us. If only — *we do not forget.*

" And because miracles are sacred and must be veiled, he repeats: ' Any requests.' And I say:

" ' I forgot to take my sponge with me when I was brought here. Might I have a sponge? ' "

Because such moments of communication can occur between persons, it is sometimes suggested that they are found exclusively in personal relations. But the possibility of communication should not be narrowed down, as I cannot help feeling that it is narrowed in a good deal that is said and written about the all-importance of " personal relations ". I do not believe that Buber intends to confine his primary " I-Thou " relation to the exclusively personal.

He describes how one might so enter into relation with a tree that one is conscious of it as a whole in its own life and being. "The tree will have a consciousness, then, similar to his own? Of that I have no experience. . . . I encounter no soul or dryad of the tree, but the tree itself."[1] I should go further and say that such moments of *rapport* may arise in any context. They are the conditions of creative work. They can be known by the person being aware of whatever is the matter of his concern not just as subject-matter to be mastered or manipulated, but as there transcending him with its own nature. And he is conscious of an outgoing affection, not for its specific qualities, good, bad or indifferent, but for its individual being. This affection is recognizably distinct from merely personal or erotic attachment. Such power of creative awareness we may perhaps be allowed to call *spirit*. Like the wind, we cannot tell whence it comes or whither it goes; it seems to come of grace; it creates the moment of relationship, of communication, of wholeness; it is thus the bond of unity; and it comes with the promise that it will lead us into truth. But articulated truth is cast in symbolic form; it is the attempt to interpret a moment of awareness by drawing likenesses and distinctions, and thus seeks to describe it analogically in terms of something else. Yet the appropriateness of form and analogy may be controlled by the basic experience of awareness. We have suggested that religious analogies take their rise from such moments of awareness. But they may also sometimes be the hidden sources of the judgments of "importance" from which *metaphysical* analogies spring. The metaphysician throws out such feelers as he has through his powers of responsive awareness. The intellectual excitement of some awareness of relationship may suggest the possibility of achieving a wider co-ordination of experience in terms of it. In this case, its conceptual expression may provide an analogue in terms of which he may seek to achieve this wider co-ordination. How far he can go will depend partly on the power

[1] *I and Thou*, p. 8.

and relevance of the initial experience, partly on his ability to see relations in what seems diverse and disconnected. He is never completely successful, for it is not likely that there is any one clue which can co-ordinate the diversities of experience. Possibly in the end the point at which we can say with most confidence that positive ground has been gained is in our better understanding, through its articulation, of the initial experience from which the analogy has been drawn.

CHAPTER X

THE CONTEMPORARY PROSPECT

There are, then, as we have maintained, two ways in which metaphysical theories may be analogies. As analogies of *being*, they seek to say something about " reality " transcending experience, in terms of relations found within experience. As co-ordinating analogies, they seek to relate diverse types of experience by extension of a key idea derived from some predominant intellectual or spiritual relation. Such ideas share something of the character of scientific models. But whereas scientific models suggest possible patterns for the co-ordination of data of a homogeneous type, the metaphysical model has to suggest a possible pattern of co-ordination between data of different types. A metaphysician has therefore to be sensitive to the diversities within experience, and also to possible modes of relationship. Moreover, whereas in the case of the scientific model the data to be co-ordinated are whatever relevant conclusions from observation may be available at the time in the work of the science in question, for the metaphysical " model " the data themselves must be extracted out of the whole manifold of experience by means of discriminatory judgments of what is important. We saw that some such selection is involved in making judgments about historical events. But in the case of metaphysical " models " it becomes a still more dominant factor. For these are " compositions " which attempt to co-ordinate a wide range of diverse types of experience in terms of certain key ideas. If the judgment from which such an idea derives has been happy in achieving some intuitive grasp of what is really significant in the thought of the time, the metaphysical " model " will commend itself to civilized thought as self-evident.[1] " *Of course*," we say, when it is pointed out.

[1] Cf. *supra*, p. 196.

Moreover, it will be an idea which exercises a creative influence over the intellectual imagination of the age. But we have to recognize that the ideas which make sense in one age, in illuminating and co-ordinating its intellectual experience, do not necessarily make sense in the same way in another. Therefore there is likely to be a shift in the philosophical analogies which will commend themselves as self-evident in different periods of thought. A philosophical system is not disproved; but it is abandoned when it ceases to be relevant.

Possibly a reason why metaphysics in the grand style is out of favour at present is not only due to the preoccupation of philosophers with problems of method and analysis, but is also due to the lack of relating ideas in terms of which some co-ordination of thought and experience might be achieved. This may be due to a lack of philosophers with sufficient breadth of intellectual vision and intuitive penetration. It may also be due to the actual situation both of our intellectual world and of our historical circumstances. In the remaining pages I shall ask whether it is possible to detect any such relating idea or analogy for our time.

Such a question I can only answer tentatively and with extreme diffidence. I am very conscious of the danger of looking for a key idea in what may be a mere intellectual fashion. Also it is very difficult to see the wood for the trees when we are in the middle of the wood. Hence a generalization is likely to be made from judgments based on the highly selective evidence of oneself and one's friends, and of such ranges of experience beyond these as one is capable of appreciating; and these may well miss what are in fact the most significant elements. I am well aware of all this; and I ask the reader to remember our analogy of the Fougasse cartoon.[1] The most a philosophical theory may do is to express a few features, in a selective and probably distorted composition, yet in a way which may bring out some significant characteristic.

Can we point, then, to any key idea or ideas which may

[1] Cf. *supra*, p. 204.

provide a metaphysical analogy in our time? There are plenty of voices being raised to demand one. We are told that we should have an agreed metaphysical, or theological, or scientific outlook; and we are witnessing a resurgence of various dogmatisms, each demanding that the world be seen in terms of its dominant pattern. But the more one tries to penetrate behind all this exhortation, and seek such significant ideas as may really serve to illuminate our intellectual and historical experience, the more elusive these appear to be. I shall try to indicate some reasons for this, and what appear to me to be their implications.

There is an initial suspicion of the instrument. Psychologists have put us on our guard against instances of "rationalization" — that is, arguments which purport to be objective, but are really advanced to support some non-rational and perhaps unacknowledged desire. But whereas "rationalization" may be to some extent detected and corrected, there is the more deep-seated suspicion that the epistemological problem of the objectivity of knowledge is not capable of any satisfactory answer. Perhaps the world is not a world of substances with more or less permanent characteristics which can be intuited and formulated in thought, but is a maze of interrelated processes which can only be seen through the medium of minds which are themselves immersed in the process. So Joyce attempts to express the kaleidoscope of experience, seen through the medium of minds whose processes are not those of "thinking substances", but meander in a welter of stray associations and even physiological sensations. And Mr. Edmund Wilson writes[1] of the novel of Proust: "Proust has created in this respect a sort of equivalent in fiction for the metaphysics which certain philosophers have based on the new physical theory. . . . All that is perceived in any moment of human experience is relative to the person who perceives it, and to the surroundings, the moment, the mood. The world becomes thus fourth-dimensional — with Time as the fourth dimension. The

[1] In *Axel's Castle*, pp. 157-158.

relativist, in locating a point, not only finds its co-ordinates in space, but also takes the time; and the ultimate units of his reality are ' events ', each of which is unique and can never occur again — in the flux of the universe they can only form similar patterns. And in Proust's world, just as the alleys of the Bois de Boulogne which the hero had seen in his youth under the influence of the beauty of Odette have now changed into something quite different and are as irrecoverable as the moments of time in which they had their only existence — just as his people, in spite of the logic of the processes by which they change, are always changing and will finally fade away, disintegrated by illness or old age; so love, of which we hope so much, changes and fails us, and so society, which at first seems so stable, in a few years has recombined its groups and merged and transformed its classes. And, as in the universe of Whitehead, the ' events ', which may be taken arbitrarily as infinitely small or infinitely comprehensive, make up an organic structure, in which all are interdependent, each involving each other and the whole; so Proust's book is a gigantic dense mass of complicated relations; cross-references between different groups of characters and a multiplication of metaphors and similes connecting the phenomena of infinitely varied fields — biological, zoological, physical, aesthetic, social, political and financial. These similes seem far-fetched and silly to the first readers of Proust's novel — but Proust insisted that one of his principal concerns was to discover the real resemblances between things which superficially appear different." Proust's picture is a depressing one; it might be possible to see a world of interrelated processes, as Bergson does, as affording possibilities of growth, as well as leading by a kind of entropy to a state of degradation of psychological energy. But that is not the question which now concerns us.

We are concerned rather with the possibility of finding relations between diverse kinds of experience such that it may be possible to co-ordinate them into some pattern which makes sense. If experience is reflected through the medium of different minds, themselves part of a shifting process of change, is it possible to find such co-ordinating ideas as will be more than metaphors expressing private associations? Hence we are faced in a searching form by the question of the conditions of objective thinking; which is but part of the wider question of the conditions of significant communication. And there is the further doubt whether the different kinds of experience are capable of being co-ordinated with one another in any coherent pattern. Our elders were (and some of them still are) full of hopes and ambitions of achieving a "synthesis" of knowledge; science, religion, art, the practice of personal and political life were to become an orderly pattern, dominated by an agreed philosophical outlook. But it looks as if we were becoming increasingly conscious of diversities and discontinuities in our worlds of thought and experience. People may grumblingly lay the blame on "over-specialization", and with some degree of justification, but this does not go to the root of the matter. Even if we were to turn ourselves into jacks of all trades, or run "orientation courses" in synthetic philosophy in connection with every university department, the real problem would only be covered up. The real problem is that our diverse worlds of thought do not make sense as a coherent unity, and probably cannot and will not do so for some time to come. For the basic suppositions underlying them are in process of a drastic reconstruction of which it is not yet possible to see the outcome. We cannot yet determine clearly what are in fact the main ideas behind the new physics, let alone their relevance or irrelevance for a wider outlook. Nor has the real scope and contribution of psycho-analysis yet been determined; nor that of the new border-line sciences of life, such as biochemistry and biophysics; and nor is it clear what are the dominant ideas which are to express man's life in society. When we have reached a stage when Einstein, Freud, Marx, Barth, Wittgenstein are not names for partisans to conjure with, but the contributions which these may have made to our understanding of the nature of the human mind and its relation to its world, have been clarified, sifted and assimilated, then we may begin to look towards a new synthesis of knowledge. And it may well be that by then we shall have learnt that the old style synthesis in the grand manner is impossible. Meanwhile, as long as different departments of thought are primarily concerned with rethinking their distinctive methods and presuppositions, they are likely to grow apart rather than grow together. Some may concentrate on asserting their own methods and presuppositions in such a way that relevant communication with other types of thought and experience becomes virtually impossible. This might be said of some of the analytical schools in contemporary philosophy, and of certain of the movements of the resurgent neo-Protestantism.

But while basic presuppositions are being overhauled, it is surely important to try to keep open lines of communication between different kinds of thinking and experience and establish some kind of *modus vivendi* between them. Writing this in 1943, it is tempting to see a resemblance to the problem of the settlement of the international situation. How many people who are aware of the deep-seated differences to be reconciled can seriously believe that these are likely to be smoothed out by conferences into some higher synthesis, so that the whole world will settle down to a harmonious era of brotherly concord? Rather, we are likely to see a period in which the legacy of hatred and suspicion will raise all sorts of barriers to communication, let alone co-operation, between people. The immediate task will be one not of settling the affairs of a new heaven and a new earth, but of establishing some *modus vivendi* which can afford people subsistence, essential liberties and a sense of security, until passions can cool, healing sanity be renewed, and such constructive forces as may be present can have had a chance to grow. Moreover, it is from the growth of such forces that the significant ideas may emerge. New possibilities of significant communication may come out of the experience of people who are facing the challenge of reconstruction in different ways but with moral conviction. And this possibility may have its analogue in our intellectual world.

I do not mean that the divisions of the intellectual world ought to be painted in such lurid colours as those of the political; though the divisions of these two worlds may not be wholly unconnected with each other. My suggestion is that both at present exemplify a deep-seated characteristic of our age. We no longer live in a common civilization which speaks a common intellectual language. Hence we are beset by the problem of communication. How are those who start from different presuppositions and different ideologies to hold any vital communication with one another? The preoccupation of contemporary philosophy with problems of language and symbolism may not be entirely an evasion of larger issues. It may be, in part at any rate, due to a consciousness that the media of communication can no longer be taken for granted. Along with this goes a distrust of every kind of *Schwärmerei*, and an almost brutal honesty in the analysis of experience.

This is characteristic of the younger generation of writers and poets. Here again it is hard to generalize. But my own impression is that we are being given a number of short descriptions of experience; these are recorded as nearly as possible in directly conversational form; and the net is cast widely for different types of experience drawn from a wide variety of social settings. But along with these straightforward records goes a sense of frustration, a failure to see how these experiences can be related or make sense in any wider frame of reference. This is not cynicism; the younger writers have grown up with too few illusions to be disillusioned. It is an honest inability to see any larger pattern within which their experience is significant. Some, starting from a romantic zeal for social justice, have tried to find a larger pattern by devoting themselves to the Communist party line; but the best of these have seen through the wishful thinking and casuistries in which this involves them. (Such a story of disenchantment is told by

Arthur Koestler in *Darkness at Noon*.)

Another note, which cannot fail to strike anyone reading the poems of young men and women who are immersed in the war, is their sense of the significance and preciousness of personal relations. Many write poems to their wives; there is a straightforward joy in such relationship which breathes a completely different air from the stale atmosphere of Aldous Huxley. But the incongruity between these tiny circles of light and friendship and the outer darkness is felt the more keenly.

We have drawn attention to these trends as symptomatic of a situation which makes it difficult to point to a key idea which might serve as an analogy expressing our intellectual experience. We should need an analogy which could exhibit discontinuities and incongruities as well as relationship.

There are of course many who would dispute our hesitation. They have their model, their master key which is to unlock all doors. It is the notion of " Evolution " as pointing inevitably to the Planned Society. There is little doubt that in many quarters " Evolution " is not a word used with the strict meaning which attaches to it in natural science; it has become a " blessed word ", as I should say an analogical word, which is to answer all our problems. Above all, it is to lead us into planned perfection. When listening to some of our planners, I have been reminded of the story of an American visitor who found himself watching a circus in the company of a very charming little Russian girl, while visiting Russia in the early 1930's. He remarked (I am afraid) that they had far bigger and better circuses than that in America. " Ah," she said, " perhaps you do have bigger and better circuses in America, but all the same you have no PLAN."

I do not want to burn my fingers by entering into the economic debates of the planners and the anti-planners. I am only concerned to ask whether the idea of the Evolutionary Plan does provide the key idea of our age. It has certain merits as a candidate. It expresses the widespread aspiration after a better world, thought of as a world of greater equality in which the common man can feel secure in his niche. But are there other and perhaps more significant elements in our intellectual experience which this idea does not express, or even suggest?

With great diffidence I shall indicate some of these. First, there is the distrust of Utopian idealism; the conviction that whatever perfection may be, it cannot be achieved by an external organization of the affairs of this world. Perfection may be shown us momentarily in some rare achievement of art, or act of courage or devotion; but human life as a whole is blended of good, bad and indifferent, and grows out of inner struggle and out of the possibility of making mistakes, and is likely to remain so as long as man remains man and not an angel or a conditioned automaton.

Along with this goes a rediscovery of moral obligation, going hand in hand, paradoxically enough, with a breakdown in moral codes.[1] The shock of the impact of evil in a glaring form has brought home the moral duty to resist. We know that we have a duty, but duty drives us to do or acquiesce in the doing of terrible things. Hence there is a renewal of the sense of the transcendent, of an absolute indicated by, but not contained in, the experiences of this ambiguous world. It is perhaps no accident that two writers, Kafka and Bernanos, who can express most powerfully the sense of a supernatural world (though they are very different, and their supernatural worlds are very different) are both haunted by the impossibility of reconciling its claims with those of our human existence.

In another way, the renewed consciousness of a break between the transcendent and the finite reinforces our consciousness of being at the end of a period of thought. The organic analogies of the older metaphysics are a vein

[1] We can perhaps see an explanation for this seeming " paradox ". The upheavals of war have swept people out of the stable and familiar conditions within which their moral habits were formed. But those who have faced the demands, whether of war or of underground resistance, may have discovered something of what, behind code and custom, morality is really about.

which has been worked out, and the shape of a new analogy is not apparent. Some cannot suffer the sense of metaphysical frustration, and turn from it to religious or political dogmatism, or to an anti-metaphysical positivism. But to those who can wait, there may be a note of expectancy as well as of frustration. They may have little to say, no banner to flourish. But they may know moments of communication with those living in different worlds of experience, from which the possibility of relationship may grow. For them, perhaps Eliot's last poems [1] speak best to their condition.

I do not want to exploit what should be an experience of poetry in the interests of philosophical interpretation. But these poems convey to us the feeling of waiting between two worlds. Eliot's supernatural world is not a doctrinal scheme which he can take for granted; it can only be indicated by indirect allusion. And there is also the indication of moments of awareness, of completion, of simplicity; such might be those moments as we suggested in the last chapter could be called the moments of " spirit ". Out of such in due time a new analogue may be born.

To say more would be to enforce a unity which would be premature. Meanwhile, although we may not be able to see wholeness in our world, we may be able to achieve a certain wholeness in our own attitude towards it. We may learn to face its tensions, imperfections, discontinuities positively and with a singleness of mind which itself has something of the quality of faith.

Possibly, however, we may grasp something of the character of our present intellectual experience by reflecting not on any form of words, but on the symbol of the " word " itself. The " word " is the means of communication between beings distinct in their own natures. Yet a purely subjective being would have no words; words are only possible where there is conscious relationship. Whereas when speaking of our relation to the objects of sense perception we gener-

[1] I refer to the *Burnt Norton* series.

ally use the language of vision, in our intellectual intuitive relations to that which transcends us we most naturally use auditory images. I have spoken of the rediscovery of duty, where the sense of an absolute meets us as a "call", a "demand", but not as a clear perception of the pattern in which we should act. We can best express our experience not in the visual symbolism of sight, but in the auditory symbolism of hearing.

The word discloses, yet at the same time it never discloses fully. Through it we seek communication across barriers; but the barriers may be such that words have no shared meaning, and nothing is left for us but to fight. Moreover, words are beset with every kind of ambiguity; they can make confusion worse confounded, as the writer of a book like this knows only too well.

> "Words strain,
> Crack and sometimes break, under the burden,
> Under the tension, slip, slide, perish,
> Decay with imprecision, will not stay in place,
> Will not stay still. Shrieking voices
> Scolding, mocking, or merely chattering,
> Always assail them. The Word in the desert
> Is most attacked by voices of temptation. . . ." [1]

Yet words can also express a shared experience, a moment of communication. They are not magic substitutes for things, nor are they merely practical instruments, or ostensive signs. They are the means by which beings transcending each other in their intrinsic natures may establish relationship. Their function is not primarily to be substitutes for visual perceptions. "They have very much more important work to do. So far from verbal language being a 'compromise for a language of intuition' [2] — a thin, but better-than-nothing, substitute for real experience — language, well used, is a *completion* and does what the intuitions of sensation by themselves cannot do. Words are the meeting points at which regions of experience which can never combine in sensation or intuition come

[1] Eliot, *Burnt Norton*.

[2] *I.e.* sensuous perception.

together. They are the occasion and the means of that growth which is the mind's endless endeavour to order itself. That is why we have language. It is no mere signalling system. It is the instrument of all our distinctively human development, of everything in which we go beyond the other animals."[1]

It is perhaps no accident that the Christian symbol which is being born again in poetry and religious thought and is recovering a hold on men's imagination is the symbol of the Word. The Word is not a reflection of the essence of being (though to many Christians it has meant this); it stands for the possibility of relationship and communication. We must see the " word " not as a " merely verbal " sign, but as the medium of communication between beings who are subjects transcending one another in their intrinsic natures.

But meanwhile we are more conscious of the break-down of relationships and of the confusion of tongues. The remedy in neither the intellectual nor the political world is to smooth over real diversities by idealistic pronouncements. In both the world is looking for a creative mind who can show us a way of relationship. But if neither the master statesman nor the master philosopher comes — and they may well not come, and may better not come, rather than that the world should be deluded again by false prophets — we can only go on working in such a way as can make possible the renewal and discovery of relationship. And perhaps, as we suggested earlier, it is from facing responsibly together the tensions of our time, rather than from seeking abstractly with our present mental and spiritual resources for " agreed formulae ", that significant thinking may come.

To enlarge the possibilities of communication and relationship between diverse worlds of experience has always been a primary function of philosophy. But to-day its professional preoccupations threaten to narrow and even

[1] I. A. Richards, *The Philosophy of Rhetoric*, pp. 130-131 (New York, 1936).

foreclose possibilities of communication, while the " word " degenerates into the " merely verbal ". It may well be that words needed to be stripped of the last vestiges of their imaginary properties as duplicates of reality. But to do this should not be to leave them as the mere instruments of a barren logomachy. We need to rediscover the power of words as the medium, however abstract, indirect and incomplete, of communication, expressing discoveries of relationship amid the diversities of the world. But perhaps we are not yet ready for the " word " which will express the " metaphysical analogy " relevant to our time. Perhaps we need first to be living fully in a responsive and responsible relatedness to its demands with sensitive alertness to new points of growth. The word can give shape and expression to a relationship. It cannot be its substitute.

A metaphysical thinker may try to see life steadily; he cannot see it as a whole. He can only express what he grasps in the perspective of his experience. But the right word, giving articulation to the living relations out of which this perspective is constituted, can enlarge and not straiten further possibilities of responsive awareness. The word gives form to experience; it does not copy the structure of the real. But experience so informed itself arises out of interrelationships. To indicate the possibilities of such relationships and to bring them into conscious articulation is a distinctive task of metaphysical thinking.

APPENDIX

WHITEHEAD'S DOCTRINE OF PREHENSIONS [1]

WHITEHEAD's theory of perception in his epistemological theory is developed out of a view of nature in which " perception " is given a much wider significance. In fact he is concerned to show that perception in the epistemological sense is a particular instance of a much wider relationship which he describes under the general term of " prehension ". " Prehension " is the general word used of any reaction of an organic entity to its environment whereby the environment is organized into a perspective related to that entity. The subject-object relation of experience is fundamental, Whitehead holds, not in the specialized epistemological sense, but in the sense suggested by the Quaker word " concern ". Each entity is an experiencing centre whose nature is constituted out of the selective responses it makes to other entities of the environment, and at the same time the multiplicity of other events is organized into a new unity, as the universe from that perspective. It might sound as though this was putting the cart before the horse; it might seem more natural to say that the selective responses an entity makes depend on its own constitution, rather than that its constitution is, as Whitehead says, " self-formed " out of the responses which it makes. But Whitehead is able to put it in this way because he does not think of a prehension as the reaction of one self-subsistent entity to another self-subsistent entity. Both entities are thought of as fluid processes, and a " prehension " is of the nature of a transaction, or interchange, whereby energy is transmitted from the prehended object into the prehending subject, where it is transmuted into a new unity which Whitehead calls a " concrescence ". But transmissions of energy, while they may be quantitatively measurable (which is the aspect considered in abstraction by physical science), are also qualitative transitions from one event to another. This is perhaps the hardest part of Whitehead's theory to accept; it is the part of it which leads him to describe all physical relationships in terms of " feelings ". [2] But it is basic to his whole theory. As he puts it summarily, " The key notion . . . is that the energetic activity considered in physics is the emotional

[1] In this attempt to state Whitehead's view, I have been greatly helped by discussion with Mr. W. Mays.

[2] Cf. *Process and Reality*, *passim*, particularly Part III.

intensity entertained in life." [1] A transmission of energy is therefore also a conveying of emotional intensity from event to event, and this appropriation of emotional intensity is called a "feeling". A "physical feeling" is the re-enactment in the prehending subject of the emotional intensity in the prehended object; in other words, there is a flow of energy from one event to another without alteration of the qualitative intensity. Whitehead defines causation in terms of this transmission of physical feelings. "A simple physical feeling has the dual character of being the cause's feeling re-enacted for the effect as subject." [2] This is called the "objectification" of one entity in another, and follows from what Whitehead calls the "vector" character of the flow of energy which "transfers the cause into the effect".

The transmissions of energy from event to event which are described as "simple physical feelings" thus produce repetitions of pattern and also repetitions of the emotional tone which is said to be an integral accompaniment of any energetic activity. In what are described as "low-grade organisms", there is mere repetition of pattern. Thus "The low-grade organism is merely the summation of the forms of energy which flow in upon it in all its multiplicity of detail. It receives and it transmits; but it fails to simplify into intelligible system. The physical theory of the structural flow of energy has to do with the transmission of simple physical feelings from individual actuality to individual actuality." [3]

But actual entities are described as bipolar. Besides the "physical pole" (which conforms to the energy pattern of the environment) there is the "mental pole", which shows itself where there is some element of emphasis or diminution of qualitative intensity originating in the actual entity. This is called a "conceptual feeling". "If in the conceptual feelings there is valuation upward, then the physical feelings are transmuted to the new concrescence with enhanced intensity in its subjective form. This is 'adversion'. But if in the conceptual feelings there is valuation downward, then the physical feelings are (in the later concrescence) either eliminated, or are transmitted to it with attenuated intensity. This is 'aversion'. . . . It is evident that adversion and aversion . . . only have importance in the case of high-grade organisms. They constitute the first step towards intellectual mentality, though in themselves they do not amount to consciousness." [4] These "conceptual feelings" of emphasis and elimination of multiplicity of detail are the first step

[1] *Modes of Thought*, p. 231 (Cambridge, 1938).
[2] *Process and Reality*, p. 336 (Cambridge, 1929).
[3] *Ibid.* p. 360.
[4] *Ibid.* p. 359.

towards abstraction. Through these, the prehending subject is not merely receptive of a pattern of energy which it repeats, but it transmutes this into a simplified pattern. This selective power of emphasis and elimination is described by Whitehead elsewhere[1] under the general notion of " Importance ". It means that an organism is a " composition " of a particular structure which arises out of the positive and negative responses it makes to the congeries of countless events in its environmental field. This notion of " importance " is generalized to extend to the elective affinities of chemical sensitivity at the bottom of the scale and to judgments of significance at the top of the scale.

Now sense perception is described as a particular case of the general process of the integration of " physical " with " conceptual feelings ". It involves the integration of two modes, one termed " causal efficacy ", and one termed " presentational immediacy ". " Causal efficacy " is a particular case of the flow of energy from one actuality to another which we have described above, the prehending actuality in this case being the physiological organism. It is thus the transmission of energy into the physiological organism along the events making up its nerve routes, and as " physical feeling " it produces a repetition of pattern and affective tone. Whitehead describes this as the " primitive " (in the sense of basic) state of sense experience. " The perception of conformation to realities in the environment is the primitive element in our external experience. . . . Those periods of our lives — when the perception of the pressure from a world of things with characters in their own right, characters mysteriously moulding our own natures, becomes strongest — those periods are the product of a reversion to some primitive state. Such a reversion occurs when either some primitive functioning of the human organism is unusually heightened, or some considerable part of our habitual sense perception is unusually enfeebled." [2]

But conscious sense perception occurs in organisms in which the " mental pole " of conceptual evaluation by emphasis and elimination is an important factor. Here the " physical feelings " are transmuted into a simplified " conceptual feeling ", with a generalized affective tone. Whitehead describes this under what he calls the " Category of Transmutation ". According to this, the diversities of feeling tone coming through the prehension of a large number of entities in the environing regions are transmuted into a single conceptual feeling then referred as its average character to the nexus of events in that region as a whole, so that we say, *e.g.*, "The tree is *green*". "Green",

[1] Cf. *Modes of Thought*, ch. i.

[2] *Symbolism*, pp. 51-52 (Cambridge, 1928).

which would generally be called a sensum, is called by Whitehead an "eternal object". That is to say, it is not an actual entity; it is an abstractive element which can characterize actual entities.

This abstractive element "green" is then entertained as a qualification of the subject's physical experience, and projected through this on to a region of the contemporary world. Whitehead calls this "perception in the mode of presentational immediacy". The contemporary world is defined as a cross-section of Nature looked on as a congeries of processes in unison of becoming. "Unison of becoming" is defined as causal independence, since it is only a completed event which can be objectified in other events ("Objectification", we saw, was the interpretation Whitehead gives to causal interaction). Hence the contemporary world cannot be prehended in the mode of causal efficacy. It is prehended as the locus of the events to which the subject refers sense objects derived by abstraction from its physiological experience of the immediate past in the mode of causal efficacy. Such sense objects are colours and shapes. If we abstract from these everything but their potentiality for being co-ordinated in a perspective related to the percipient, Whitehead holds that we arrive at an abstract field of relations which he calls the Extensive Continuum. The sensa are projected as qualifying regions of the Extensive Continuum, but the regions of the Extensive Continuum, being contemporary, are not directly intuitable. The sensa are derived from the experience of the immediate past in the mode of causal efficacy, and then used as symbols referring to regions of the contemporary field.[1]

[1] As the logical structure of an abstract field of functional relations, the Extensive Continuum underlies, but is not to be identified with, the homaloidal space of measurement. In this, perceptual entities are considered as having certain geometrical relations to one another in a flat space. The relationships which comprise the Extensive Continuum are those of whole and part, overlapping and contact, which are the general functional relationships which make possible any world of interrelated entities. This makes possible, but is not to be identified with, the perceptual space of measurement ("In its full generality beyond the present epoch, it does not involve shapes, dimensions and measurability; these are additional determinations of real potentiality arising from our cosmic epoch", *Process and Reality*, p. 92). This homaloidal view of space has been criticized by Professor Northrop in his paper "Whitehead's View of Physical Science" in the volume on *The Philosophy of A. N. Whitehead*, in the *Library of Living Philosophers* (edited by P.A. Schilpp, North-western University, 1941). He reports that it has also been criticized by Einstein in conversation, on the grounds of the General Theory of Relativity. But we would point out that Whitehead's Extensive Continuum is not the space of measurement, and still less is it the spatio-temporal character of the actual passage of events in nature, which on his view might

Sensa are symbols; that is, they are abstractive elements derived by the "conceptual" activity of simplification and transmutation from a complex of physical feelings, and then referred to regions which they are considered as qualifying. If they are in fact to convey veridical information about the contemporary world, Whitehead holds that this can only be because some conformity both of energy pattern and of the emotional tone (which he holds, it would seem on speculative grounds, to be a universal accompaniment of physical energy) is preserved throughout the process. For we must reiterate that the sensum is derived not from direct intuition of the external world but from the subject's own physical feelings, and can therefore, he holds, only be veridical if these physical feelings are themselves conformal to the events of the external world.

This, he holds, can only happen if there is a continual transmission not only of structural but also of qualitative character along the whole succession of events which make up the route from the energetic activities in the external world up to the neural activities in the higher centres of the brain. Even on his own showing considerable transformations must take place, as described by his "Categories of Transmutation" and "Conceptual Reversion", and by "conceptual[1] evaluation", so that (to put it crudely) what goes in at one end as a vibration of energy comes out at the other as a sense datum. But he holds that some partial identity of pattern and of affective tone is nevertheless preserved, so that perceptual experience can give veridical information about the structure and character of events in the environment. This is possible, he holds, because the sensa which are "projected" on to the environment by the percipient have a two-way symbolism: they symbolize his physical feelings, and through these the physical events of the environment. The latter have themselves been "objectified" in the former, *i.e.* there has been a flow of energy maintaining a certain constant structure and qualitative character. Whitehead holds that for anything to be used validly as a symbol it must have some structural similarity with what is symbolized. If, therefore, the sensa derived from physical feelings are to be valid symbols of characters of external events, they must exhibit some

well be non-homaloidal (*i.e.* warped according to the physical peculiarities of events), as suggested by the General Theory of Relativity. Does the General Theory of Relativity necessitate that the abstract geometrical space in which perceived intervals are measured by judgments of congruence should be non-homaloidal? I do not venture to express an opinion on this.

[1] We remind the reader that "conceptual" for Whitehead does not imply "mind", as distinct from "brain". It is used of the "mental pole", *i.e.* the power of emphasis or elimination, possessed by every "actual entity", including those we describe as neural events.

identity of structure with those events. "There cannot be symbolic reference between percepts derived from one mode" (*i.e.* causal efficacy) "and percepts from the other mode" (*i.e.* presentational immediacy) "unless in some way the percepts intersect. By this 'intersection' I mean that a pair of such percepts must have elements of structure in common, whereby they are marked out for the action of symbolic reference. . . . The sense data must therefore play a double rôle in perception. In the mode of presentational immediacy they are projected to exhibit the contemporary world in its spatial relations. In the mode of causal efficacy they exhibit the almost instantaneously precedent bodily organs imposing their character on the experience in question".[1] "Truth", therefore, consists in the relation of similarity of pattern and affective tone between a nexus of events physically prehended (*i.e.* objectified in the physical feelings which constitute what we call the percipient's bodily organs), and the nexus conceptually prehended (*i.e.* a construction from sense data projected on to the contemporary world). This of course presupposes that "physical feelings" are conformal to the external events prehended; otherwise judgments of perception would merely be "true" of our own physical states, and not of external events. And we are certainly not conscious of our own neural and cerebral, and seldom of our visceral, adjustments (or if we are, our bodily processes are probably out of order and the sensory information derived through them more likely to be hallucinatory).

But how are we to understand this conception of physiological events as exhibiting identity of pattern with (*a*) external physical events and (*b*) objects perceived in presentational immediacy? We have considered some of the difficulties in this in our Chapter III. At least two major difficulties arise in connection with Whitehead's special view, viz.:

1. What exactly is meant, if physiological events are described as "feelings", by ascribing form or pattern to feelings? Are we misled by an ambiguity in the word "form", which can mean both qualitative character and spatialized structure?

2. Is there a wider gap than Whitehead allows between the physiological conditions of sensation and the conscious perceptions in which sensa are elements? He aims in his theory of prehensions at avoiding a "bifurcation" of nature into physical and mental events. But he is only able to do this by allowing a bifurcation between physical feelings and the sensa as physiologically conditioned. We may ask whether this does justice to the difference introduced by consciousness, the significance of which Whitehead minimizes. He

[1] Cf. *Symbolism*, pp. 58-59.

is only able to slur over the difference introduced by consciousness by speaking, as we have seen, of " transmutation " and " novelty " as effected by feelings of aversion and adversion, this being the function of the " mental pole ". But we have reason to believe that a break in kind occurs when physiological response becomes perceptual awareness, and still more when it becomes a deliberately directed judgment of meaning. Nevertheless, with this essential qualification, there is much in Whitehead's doctrine of prehensions which we gratefully acknowledge to be congenial to the view we are trying to put forward in this book. He shows us experience as arising out of a vast nexus of inter-relationships. Certain of these are brought into emphasis, and only so is significant living possible, since a growing actuality is a " concrescence of prehensions ", seeking to hold together the contrasted elements of its experience in a unity informed by a dominant mode of feeling.

The generic character Whitehead sees as underlying both the selective responses of an organism and the conscious judgments of mentality is the imposition of a perspective upon the vast multiplicity of mere matter of fact. This starts from selective interest aroused by physiological need; it ends in discriminatory judgments as to what is " important " and what can be dismissed into the varying shades of irrelevance, in the frames of reference which make possible the characteristically human activities (art, science, history, morality, philosophy). The notion of " Importance ", as we suggest, needs further elucidation.[1] In particular we should ask how subjective interest, determined by vital needs, may grow into an objectively appropriate discrimination of values. But one merit of Whitehead's theory of prehensions is to have shown how deeply the notion enters, not only into the formation of intellectual theories, but also into the possibility of experience.

[1] See *supra*, p. 195.

INDEX

THE END

PRINTED BY R. & R. CLARK, LTD., EDINBURGH